9307

T0116853

9307

RACISM'S BROAD REACH

Steve Nix

iUniverse, Inc.
Bloomington

9307
RACISM'S BROAD REACH

Copyright © 2010, 2011 by Steve Nix.

All rights reserved. No part of this book may be used or reproduced by any means, graphic, electronic, or mechanical, including photocopying, recording, taping or by any information storage retrieval system without the written permission of the publisher except in the case of brief quotations embodied in critical articles and reviews.

The views expressed in this work are solely those of the author and do not necessarily reflect the views of the publisher, and the publisher hereby disclaims any responsibility for them.

iUniverse books may be ordered through booksellers or by contacting:

iUniverse
1663 Liberty Drive
Bloomington, IN 47403
www.iuniverse.com
1-800-Authors (1-800-288-4677)

Because of the dynamic nature of the Internet, any web addresses or links contained in this book may have changed since publication and may no longer be valid. The views expressed in this work are solely those of the author and do not necessarily reflect the views of the publisher, and the publisher hereby disclaims any responsibility for them.

Any people depicted in stock imagery provided by Thinkstock are models, and such images are being used for illustrative purposes only.
Certain stock imagery © Thinkstock.

ISBN: 978-1-4502-9087-6 (sc)
ISBN: 978-1-4502-9088-3 (ebk)

Printed in the United States of America

iUniverse rev. date: 10/20/2011

In federal prison, a conscientious objector is told who will kill Martin Luther King Jr. six and a half months before the assassination. Learn about these coconspirators.

Contents

Introduction

Six and a half months prior to Martin Luther King Jr's assassination, a workmate stated to me, "My oldest brother Jimmy hates n_ _ _ _ _s so bad, he's gonna kill Martin Luther King! I ain't shittin' ya, you just wait and see—he's gonna kill Martin Luther King!" This and more is said to me by Jodi Ray, as we discuss racism during extremely unusual circumstances in the Medical Center for Federal Prisoners, Springfield, Missouri.

Born and raised in L.A. as a "religious conscientious objector," I'd known since I was about ten years old that one day I'd probably go to federal prison. Further mentored and influenced by two WWII veterans of major Pacific battles, I refuse military induction in 1965.

Starting a thirty-month sentence in June 1966, I do time in nine prisons and jails in five states. Hollywood would eventually make a movie about my first two cell mates' cross-country crime spree. In the L.A. Old County Jail, I spend a weird two days as a cell mate with Timothy Leary.

Doing the last eleven months of my sentence in Springfield, it was then touted as America's most maximum-security prison. Here I was informed that I'd forfeited all my civil rights, not even having the right to my name, that I'm now nothing more than a number: 9307. Then I'm placed into a freezing solitary confinement cell for eight days.

In this prison I have encounters with some of America's most notorious gangsters and criminals of a bygone era, several who have been portrayed in a number of Hollywood movies or profiled in History or Discovery Channel TV programs. I become friends with America's oldest prisoner, a ninety-seven year old stagecoach-robbing killer, then in for sixty-seven years. An inmate, who J. Edgar Hoover had branded as America's most dangerous federal prisoner, saves me from an attack by another con I managed to enrage. The list goes on.

As a hobby I appeal my conviction, becoming a jailhouse lawyer. Meeting with others to research, one relates how he participated in the infamous "escape from Alcatraz" in 1962. Pulling off an outrageous scam on the guards, which was crucial to the escapees' success, it's so embarrassing to prison authorities that they've never acknowledged it yet. When I do, it could become the new gold standard for stupidity.

Taking Jodi Ray's talk about his oldest brother Jimmy at the time, as just another wishful boast of a racist southerner, this changes with James Earl Ray's arrest. By then out on parole, I immediately call the FBI with information about co-conspirators. Reportedly their largest investigation in the bureau's history, their thirty-second triage response to my call then and again ten years later, is shameful!

Moving to Hawaii in 1968, then to Ponape in the Western Pacific in 1970, I live the majority of the next forty years on this historically unique yet remote island. Transitioning from a US territory to the capital of a new independent island nation, law and order begins breaking down. I become a business partner with a young German. He's just become the single largest landowner in Micronesia. A large new local conspiracy to take land back away from white European landowners by adverse possession, had me acting as his lawyer for two years. Eventually hiring real ones, we brought civil actions against hundreds. Repeatedly threatened, attacked by natives with knives, machetes, rocks, and so forth, I survive several life-and-death attacks. Two employees murdered, myself stabbed and stoned, I'm the only one who was consistently arrested and jailed. In one I'm prosecuted, railroaded by corrupt police who are also squatters on our land, and saddled with another felony conviction.

My experiences with what some labeled "reverse racism," filled me with empathy for what many black Americans must have suffered through in the South's past. Haunted by my connection to Martin Luther King and now appreciating his unique contributions to American society, I call the Tennessee attorney general's office in 1995. Although they're interested in everything I have to say, their investigation hits a surprising stone wall. In my last conversation with them four years ago, knowing there are unidentified co-conspirators, they tell me who they believe some may be and why, which harmonizes with what I know.

Whether Martin Luther King ever gets complete justice remains to be seen. These co-conspirators that I can identify are in their late sixties to about eighty, so the clock is ticking. Busy dealing with racism for over twenty-five years in the islands, my nonfiction book that bears my prison name, 9307, will at least bring some of those who knew ahead of time what James Earl Ray was intending to do to Dr. King, . . . to the public eye.

Chapter 1

Early Influences

In 1952 during Easter vacation when I was seven years old, my mother, two sisters and I began a late night road trip riding in a car with another family who were members of the same religion we were. Our destination was a weeklong camping trip to Borrego Springs, California.

We left El Segundo, California, traveling east on Imperial Highway, which borders the south side of Los Angeles International Airport. Five miles east before crossing Crenshaw Boulevard, our car's driver detoured to the right two blocks and stopped at a house. Out came a young family I had never seen before, with three kids. The youngest was a girl, and then there were two boys, the oldest about my age—his name was John.

What caught my attention was his father, whose name I later learned was Denny Gormley. He was badly injured and scarred in the face and parts of his upper body. We then all continued on to Borrego Springs in two cars that now included our new friends, the Gormley Family.

During this camping trip I asked my mother, "What happened to that man? How did he get injured so badly?" The answer was that he'd been injured in World War II. A hand grenade had hit him on the upper back and blown off his jaw. Not too long after this camping trip, Denny Gormley and his family moved to El Segundo, three blocks northwest of our house.

Despite his injuries, Denny was a tall, strong, tanned, somewhat handsome man. At the time, he was in excellent shape due to his job of unloading boxcars of sheet rock. Later, he became a carpenter and eventually a rough-framing contractor.

In 1961, when I was sixteen, Denny would initiate me into the construction trade. First I was a laborer, carrying lumber for his carpenters working on apartment houses, and then he broke me in as a carpenter.

A couple of years before this, when John Gormley and I were both fourteen, we were riding with his father in his 1958 Ford truck to a religious convention held at the Long Beach Rainbow Pier Municipal Auditorium. The truck had a camper shell top with a padded crawl-through opening to the truck cab, and there was a mattress on a shelf that was even with the opening.

As we traveled south down either the Harbor or Long Beach Freeway, while lying in the camper and looking out the front window of the truck, I for the first and only time, asked Denny what happened to him in the war, wanting to know how he was injured so badly.

He started out by stating that he'd grown up in Kansas City, and then he began talking about his experiences as a marine during WWII. He related how he was in the second wave of the amphibious assault on the beaches of Tarawa in the Gilbert Islands. It was the marines' first major landing craft assault in the Pacific. When their landing craft door opened, Denny's best friend was the first one out, just ahead of him and he was immediately killed as he ran off the ramp. He told us how later on the island, he was sometimes fighting and firing at Japanese only fifty feet or less from him.

He and three others spent that first night in a foxhole that was slightly raised from the normal low-lying atoll. When flares went up, Denny would line up his BAR (Browning automatic rifle) on any figure ducking down from the light. He related that the "Japs" were moving around a lot at night. After the flares died out, he would wait five or ten seconds and then spray the area with a burst of automatic fire. Sometimes the next flare would reveal newly dead Japanese in the area.

His group, when trying to catch some sleep, took turns having one man stay awake on guard duty. When it was Denny's turn, another marine whom he called "Red," knew that Denny couldn't stay awake, so Red stayed up also. Denny fell asleep as expected, and in the morning when he awoke, a dead Japanese soldier with a .45-caliber handgun wound in the head lay within arm's reach of him. Red had shot him when he saw him crawling up to their foxhole with just a knife.

After Tarawa, Denny fought in Guam. This was only after the main battles had been fought and the island was thought to be secure. The squad he was in was assigned to mopping up patrols in the mountains, looking for Japanese stragglers.

His small squad of seven or eight soldiers had just passed a small hill. Denny was in the rear with the BAR . . . Suddenly, shouting erupted from behind them: "Banzi! Banzi!" About fifteen Japanese soldiers came screaming down the hill, stripped down, some wearing only their underwear and white headbands. They were waving their rifles and samurai swords above their heads. The marines all turned, and Denny opened up with his BAR, the others with their rifles. Some Japanese fired their rifles wildly in the air, but not at the Americans. The Americans dropped all the charging Japanese, one landing at Denny's feet. He stood there shaking, shocked at what had just happened, wondering why the Japanese hadn't ambushed them from behind. They could've killed their whole squad; instead, they basically committed suicide.

He continued to relate that his next campaign was Iwo Jima. Denny said that his division was held in reserve, but because of the fierceness of the battle, he and some of his division began to be called ashore beginning on the fourth day. Without going into much detail, he skipped to the eighth day of the battle, telling us that his unit began approaching or entering the small area later nicknamed by marines as the "Meat Grinder." He related that the battle for this small area and another adjacent area nicknamed "Turkey Knob," would end up lasting three weeks and be the most costly per acre in US Marine Corps history.

He told us that the Japanese had the area dialed in, and when he and his unit entered it, they walked into an ambush. That was when the Japanese opened up. Mortars began landing in a checkerboard pattern all around them, leaving no place to find cover. His fellow soldiers were dropping all around, and he didn't know if it was a mortar or a hand grenade that hit him just behind his shoulder, but it blew his jaw off, leaving it dangling by bits of tissue.

Denny stopped talking here and there was a period of silence, but being excited and not wanting the story to stop here, I asked him if others had to carry him off the battlefield. He hesitated some more and then replied, "No." He said that he was able to struggle back up on his feet, while others couldn't, cup what was left of his face in both hands, and stumble to the rear.

He told us all this in a matter-of-fact way, not embellishing his role or touting his actions. I wouldn't really begin to fully appreciate what he had just told us until about seven years later, when I would observe from a distance, a chance encounter between him and another Iwo Jima veteran. In addition, reading a book about this battle years later, as well as viewing several TV documentaries, would help me further understand the uniqueness of what he had been through.

Denny Gormely receives his Purple Heart in a military hospital, after getting his jaw blown off during the battle of Iwo Jima in the "Meat Grinder."

Denny concluded with words to the effect that war was awful, never glorious, and that he was relieved that John and I would never be going to war. He never again discussed with us his experiences in the war.

Shortly thereafter, we arrived at the Long Beach Municipal Auditorium for the first day of a three-day circuit assembly of Jehovah's Witnesses. Jehovah's Witnesses are the only religion that I know of that is completely neutral all over the world when it comes to the wars of the nations. Denny knew that as long as John and I were Witnesses, we would never have to experience what he had on a battlefield.

Another man whose war stories were instrumental in reinforcing my commitment never to be involved in the wars of the nations was Mr. Daniel Cummings. When I was about five years old, Mr. Cummings moved into our neighborhood in El Segundo. He lived four houses east, on Walnut Street, from where I grew up on the southeastern corner of Main and Walnut Street. He had three young daughters; his oldest was about four years old. Plus his wife was pregnant and would have another girl.

Two of my best little neighborhood friends lived next door and across the street from him, so we were always playing close by. Six or seven years later, Mr. Cummings would buy a house about two and a half blocks west from ours on Walnut Street. He would have another one of my neighborhood friend's contractor father, Sam Gilbert, add a second story to that house for his still-growing family. He had many kids.

I would continue to see Mr. Cummings almost every day as he walked to and from work. He would pass by our house on his way to El Segundo High School, where he was a history teacher. During the years I was growing up, we would many times greet each other as he passed by.

In 1963, when I was in the eleventh grade, second semester, Mr. Cummings was my history teacher. The class had just finished a chapter of the history book we were using. It was on a subject I can't remember, but the next chapter was about World War II.

As Mr. Cummings started to introduce this next chapter, he commented that he had had some personal experiences with this subject. With his eyes somewhat fixated straight ahead, and in an almost somber, saddened way, he began to relate in detail some of those experiences.

He told the class how early in the war he had been stationed as a pilot on Midway Island; I can't remember the branch of service. They got word that a massive Japanese naval fleet was approaching, intending to invade and occupy.

He continued to say that at the time, no one on Midway knew that US Naval Intelligence had deciphered the Japanese naval code about the attack, and that three US aircraft carriers were almost in position to spring a trap from about two hundred miles northeast of the island.

But hours before these US carrier planes would be launched, the few Midway pilots were ordered to attack, feeling all alone in the world. Mr. Cummings told us that as those few planes took off, against the biggest naval invasion fleet in mankind's history up to that point in time; their crews were all scared, feeling they would not be returning, that this was a one-way flight.

As they reached the fleet of Japanese ships, they just wanted to drop their bombs and get out of there as quickly as possible. So without flying through the fleet and searching for the Japanese aircraft carriers, they needed to start their dive-bombing attacks on the first decent-size Japanese ships they saw. The reason being that they would soon encounter the full might of this massive fleet's air cover, that the Japanese Zeroes would be on them at any time, and they needed to quickly attempt a bombing run with their outdated two seat dive bombers, before being blasted out of the sky.

His squadron passed a couple of small picket ships before diving on a medium-sized one at the direction of his flight leader. Surviving the antiaircraft fire, he released his bombs, but they missed. Pulling out of the dive, a blast of machine gun fire ripped through his plane, killing his tail gunner. Neither had seen the Zeroes coming, and his tail gunner had never even gotten a shot off before being killed.

Mr. Cummings spent the next fifteen minutes wave-hopping, jerking the stick right, left, up, and down, trying to dodge three Japanese Zeroes chasing him. They were constantly taking turns peppering his plane with machine gun fire as he kept coming into the sights of one after the other. Finally shot up so bad, his plane crashed in the ocean. Uninjured, Mr. Cummings hopped out on the wing and had just seconds to confirm that his tail gunner was dead. Then the plane immediately sunk out from under him because of all the holes, with his partner still strapped in.

With his eyes long since filled with tears, he related floating in the ocean long past the Zeroes leaving, before inflating his small life raft and climbing in. Later that day or the next, a PBY floatplane picked him up.

He sadly continued, saying that of all the few planes from Midway that were first to meet the Japanese fleet that morning, none hit a ship with its bombs, and only one shot-up plane made it back to Midway. All the rest were shot down, and only a few survivors were plucked out of the sea, he being one of them. With tears still in his eyes, he became very self-deprecating and critical of himself that day, particularly of his bombing run—that he hadn't taken more time and care, using all the skills and training he'd been taught, to have quelled his fears so he could have improved his chances of at least scouring a hit with a bomb, to have at least made the death of his gunner to not have been in vain.

The death of his rear gunner was obviously affecting Mr. Cummings even then, over twenty years later. He told us that he couldn't even bring himself to mention his name to the class, because it was still too painful for him even up to then. He was now openly crying uncontrollably and apologizing to the class for all of this.

Taking several minutes he recomposed himself, he then continued relating other experiences later on in the war, in other Western Pacific battles against the Japanese. I recall his telling us that on one mission an antiaircraft shell blew a hole right through his wing. The hole was so big that he could crawl through it after he landed. He said he had a picture of himself standing on a ladder in the middle of it.

Finally, he told us how on one occasion he bombed a Japanese position, perhaps an airfield, in support of ground troops. I'm not sure after all this time. But after this position was taken, he landed there and began taking watches, rings, and other souvenirs off the dead Japanese he had personally killed a short time before with his bombs.

By then he was crying again uncontrollably, saying he was so sorry and ashamed of himself for this looting of the dead and that he didn't know what came over him, that war makes you do crazy things. He then begged all in the class to please forgive him, saying that he could only hope that none of us ever had to experience war, saying that it was horrible and all the while sobbing uncontrollably.

That was the most powerful, interesting fifteen or twenty minutes I had ever experienced in school. Through the years, whenever I happened to run into people who went to El Segundo High School, I'd ask them if they ever had Mr. Cummings as a history teacher. A number responded yes. I'd then ask them if he ever related his World War II experiences to their class. So far, the answer has always been no.

I believe that Mr. Cummings's revelations that day was an unusual occurrence for him to discuss with a class. But losing control of their emotions is a common occurrence for those who have experienced the horrors of war, when they dare to reminisce about them. I think that's why many keep these experiences bottled up..

Denny Gormley and Daniel Cummings are two men I have always held in the highest regard. Both had voiced their desire that none of us would ever have to experience what they had in war.

For religious reasons, I was determined never to be involved in the wars of the nations. But that would have me ending up in the most maximum-security prison in the United States at the time, where I would meet some of our country's biggest name gangsters and criminals in 1967. One had been incarcerated since 1900, the beginning of the twentieth century. Also, two months before my release from this prison, I'd be told crucial details of the upcoming biggest racist murder case in United States history, which would occur just over six months later, plus much more.

In 1970, I would move to a little-known remote Western Pacific island that was still so primitive that women regularly went around topless many times. I would innocently get involved in a new racist land dispute that was about to turn deadly. I would almost become one of its victims several times. On this large land in dispute was a former camouflaged World War II battlefield. The Japanese army built it to lure American marines into its killing zones, where hundreds, if not thousands, could have been brought down. Ironically, I would be the only American to ever fight for his life there.

This assassination I was to learn about six and a half months in advance in federal prison, not to mention the land dispute in the islands, would have me dealing with serious racial issues prevalent across the United States, then over to the Micronesian Islands, and beyond to Europe. This would continue over the next forty-plus years. I would end up contacting a succession of attorney generals numerous times in the western pacific islands, plus one in Tennessee.

Please read on to find out more about these still-pending cases and issues—what led up to them, and what I know about their present-day status.

Chapter 2

Going to Prison

Despite Denny's and Mr. Cummings's stories, I had known probably from the time I was nine or ten years old that one day I would most likely go to jail for refusing military induction.

I had already learned from the Bible that Jesus commanded his followers to "keep separate from the world," "to return evil for evil to no one," even "to love your enemies" and to "pray for those persecuting you." So I grew up believing that these and other similar words found in the scriptures were to be taken literally by Christians, that it wasn't optional.

The day for me to report to jail came on June 6, 1966, when I was twenty years old. Approximately fourteen months previously, I had been ordered to report to the Military Injunction Center in downtown Los Angeles.

I had already informed the selective service board that I was a religious conscientious objector. They still classified me 1-A for military service. Even if I had been classified as a conscientious objector, I would have still been subject to military service, but in a noncombatant position.

Jehovah's Witnesses individually, according to their Christian consciences, still refuse to be any part of any military force in any capacity, anywhere in the world. In this, they differ from most other Christian religions that claim to be against killing in war. Many of their members still perform their military service, but only in noncombatant roles.

I passed my physical at the injunction center, but just before the group injunction process, I informed a nearby officer that I was a religious conscientious objector and would be refusing induction.

Without making a scene, he asked me to take a seat in an adjoining room. Soon afterward, he escorted me to another room, where a superior officer of his had me take a seat in a chair in front of his desk. Politely, he said he had to have me officially refuse the induction process, so he asked me to stand and take a step forward. I told him I would not do this for religious reasons. He made the necessary notations in his paperwork and told me I was free to go but added that I would be hearing from the authorities later.

About six months later, I married a Witness girl from a nearby area. Then, in May of 1966, I was ordered to report to the US Federal District Court on Monday, May 22, 1966, to appear before Judge Irving Hill for arraignment.

Waiting outside the courtroom door, I began reading the arraignment schedule posted for that courtroom for that day. I noticed that two other people were being arraigned for selective service violations also. Maybe ten or twelve people were to appear before the judge that morning.

Looking around, I saw another young clean-cut guy. I approached him and asked if he was there for a selective service-related offense. He said he was. He was also a Jehovah's Witness, named Dave Brown, and he was from the Ontario area, east of Los Angeles. He then introduced me to another Witness, an African American brother whose wife accompanied him. I know their last name was Pierce, but I don't recall their first names or what L.A. area they were from. I don't even know the outcome of their case, because I never saw them after that day in court. Dave Brown and I had a similar result before the judge and would eventually end up in the same federal prison camp.

An arraignment is the preliminary court hearing where the criminal charges are read before you, and then you have the opportunity to plead either innocent or guilty. A trial or sentencing hearing is usually then scheduled, depending on how you plead. A guilty plea is normally followed by a probation report and hearing, which usually precedes sentencing, as the federal system in those years was stressing rehabilitation. Even if you weren't granted probation, you weren't sent to a prison. You were sent to a correctional facility, the polite new name for prisons then.

Dave and I both realized that ever since the Second World War, the Jehovah's Witnesses had been routinely sent to prison for refusing induction into the military. It was pointless to plead innocent, unless procedural errors had been committed, such as in the case of Muhammad Ali. But that would still take a lot of money to fight.

Despite the fact that the United States Constitution guaranteed religious freedom, it didn't apply to those who, for religious reasons, wished to abide by Jesus's command not to use the sword, not to return evil for evil, to love your enemy, work good to all, and so on. These issues had been already argued countless times through the legal system, and the selective service law had consistently prevailed over the US Constitution and Bill of Rights.

Dave and I didn't want to waste our time by pleading innocent, and we didn't want to concede to the rightness of the government's policy by pleading guilty either. Thus we took the middle ground and pled no contest, a third pleading option. Pierce pled innocent.

Judge Hill wanted us to have the advice of counsel before he would accept our pleas, so he assigned us a court-appointed lawyer to consult with for about an hour; then we were to appear before him again.

The young lawyer's name was something like Herschel or Henchel. He seemed totally unfamiliar with these types of cases, as most people are. He was surprised to learn that religious conscientious objectors had been routinely going to jail. He wanted us to change our pleas to innocent. He wanted us to litigate this because it didn't seem right to him. We agreed, but we both knew it was futile. We explained the situation to him, that we had no procedural errors in our cases, which would be necessary to beat these charges, given the history of so many similar cases.

He grudgingly consented to our wishes and continued to represent us later, when we went back before the judge. When the judge accepted our pleas, he stated that he was going to pass sentence right then. This seemed to shock our new lawyer. He objected, suggesting that a sentencing hearing be scheduled later so that a probation investigation and report could be prepared, to be considered at sentencing.

The judge, Irvin Hill, said, "No, these types of cases are very routine. A probation report will not be necessary, as these defendants are not to be considered for probation, but sent to prison. Not to be rehabilitated . . . but to be punished!" Words to this effect were to be restated to me many times later by guards and prison officials.

He then sentenced Dave and me to thirty months in federal prison. Dave was single, and the judge gave him one week to be released on his own recognizance, to get his affairs in order and then turn himself into the marshal's office in the same building we were in, before 2:00 p.m. the following Monday. Since I was married, I was given two weeks to get my affairs in order before reporting to the marshal's office.

I had been living the last few months in my mother-in-law's vacant house in Joshua Tree, California. I returned to store away my tools and block up my old 1942 Ford Jeep; then I returned to Los Angeles to work, trying to leave my family as much money as I could before turning myself in.

On Monday June 6, 1966, I reported to the marshal's office at the Federal Building in downtown Los Angeles. After "processing in," getting photographed and fingerprinted, I was put in a holding cell with two other young men.

Upon entering the marshal's office holding cell, the two young occupants already in it had smiling, welcoming looks, as if they couldn't wait to talk to me. Previously, I had been coached by a former witness prisoner to mind my own business, not to stare, and not to talk unless spoken to. It wasn't long before these guys enthusiastically asked me what I was in for. I replied, "I'm a religious conscientious objector. I refused to join the army."

They enthusiastically gave their approval, stating, "That's cool!" Then they proudly began to tell me what they were in for. They related how they'd robbed a small Kansas country store/gas station, and then one of them blew the storekeeper's arm off with a shotgun. They then fled across the country to Los Angeles and went on some sort of crime spree in the Beverly Hills/Santa Monica area. As they finished their story, they sort of motioned with their hands as if to say, "What do you think?" Of course, they had big smiles on their faces, so pleased with themselves.

I hesitated for a moment and asked, "Don't you feel bad about the storekeeper?"

They looked at each other, still smiling, and then answered cheerfully together, "No!"

They sure were friendly guys, even when later we were all handcuffed, chained, and shackled together, then transferred to the Los Angeles New County Jail. I would find out a decade or so later that Hollywood would make a movie about these two guys and their crime spree.

The New County Jail's holding cell was quite large. Waiting to be processed in, I sat down on a bench. On his hands and knees, a filthy, dirty, disgusting drunk was sick and vomiting in a dirty toilet about thirty feet away. He got up, turned, and looked straight at me, despite the other fifty guys in the large cell. He stumbled straight to me, sticking his face about a foot from mine, and initiated the most disgusting, smelliest conversation I've ever had.

I finally got to a private cell in the early morning hours. I spent eight days there. At mealtimes, our whole cellblock marched single file, no talking, to the cafeteria. We sat down by rows and got up by rows, everyone together, at the order of the guard, no talking. I was a slow eater. I could only eat about half a meal before the guard ordered the row up to turn in their trays. That was the hungriest eight days I've ever spent. But while marching single file to or from the cafeteria, I passed Dave Brown a couple of times. He said hi, and another prisoner behind him said it with his eyes, but I had no idea who he was.

The cellblock guards knew if we were state or federal prisoners. Sometimes they'd ask with curiosity what I was in for, knowing I was a federal prisoner. When I answered this question for one guard, his reply was that if it were up to him, he would line me up against the wall and shoot me right there. Replies like this were to occur many more times. I'd never hear of a guard giving a reply like this to a regular prisoner in response to his crimes. I was to come to believe that in many guards' minds, refusing military induction was the worst crime a prisoner could be guilty of. In all the federal prisons I came to be in, we Witnesses were routinely denied some of the few basic privileges most other prisoners took for granted; then we were reminded that we were in jail to be punished, not rehabilitated.

Chapter 3

L.A. Old County Jail

After eight days, they transferred me to the Old County Jail across the street from the Los Angeles City Hall. I was to spend three weeks there in a cellblock on the thirteenth floor, northwest corner of the building. This cellblock had thirteen cells in it, with two bunks per cell, but it was overcrowded, with most cells having three prisoners each. The third one slept on a thin mattress on the floor.

About the only interaction with the guards was when they would open and close the doors remotely and do the count several times a day. Two prisoner trustees ran the cellblock from inside it, issuing cell assignments, making sure everyone was at "attention" when it was time for a guard's count. Their names were Shepard and Carr, African American inmates. They issued my cell assignment, where I slept on the floor for about two or three days.

Then one of the trustees, Shepard, came to me and said one guy just moved out of the cellblock, leaving an empty bunk. Shepard said he let the remaining prisoner choose his new cell mate and he chose me, when he found out what I was in for. Shepard said the prisoner, after learning I refused to join the army, said, "Yeah. Put that guy in my cell!" He went on to tell me that this man was the most famous prisoner in this whole prison, that he was a Harvard College professor who was in jail for turning his students on to LSD.

It was late in the day when I entered my new cell assignment with my bedroll. The occupant welcomed me and told me his name was Timothy Leary. I'd never heard of him before. He appeared to be in his early to mid forties.

I said to him, "I heard you've been teaching at Harvard." He replied that he'd actually been teaching at Berkley. I didn't pay

16

much attention to this discrepancy at the time. We engaged briefly in some small talk, which I don't recall much about, but within a short time, he began to enthusiastically preach to me the virtues of LSD. He told me that when on it, everything you see is in slow motion, but that you can still think and react at regular speed—that you can easily dodge punches but counter at regular speed. While he was talking, the cell doors closed for the day. He continued, claiming that you can almost dodge bullets while on LSD—and a bunch of other nonsense. He spoke for maybe fifteen or twenty minutes; I patiently and politely listened to all his crazy talk. Finally, he finished and gestured with his palms up, as if to say, "What do you think?"

I would find out later that this man coined the phrase "Tune in, turn on, and drop out" . . . or something similar. He was obviously a reality "dropout" that day. I felt that if he had his way, he'd turn me into one of his spaced-out groupies. I didn't appreciate the drug promotion tactics this man was trying to use on me. I then figured it was my turn to talk, so I tactlessly replied to his gestured invitation for me to respond, saying, "Man, you're nuts! That's just all a hallucination!" Then I began to tell him why I was in prison . . . and about our neutrality.

He was polite and listened at first, but he obviously had absolutely no interest in anything religious. Pretty soon he was up on his feet and pacing back and forth the short distance of the cell. He was still looking at me but had obviously failed to "tune in." As he came to the bars, he touched them softly at first, but then he began to grab them harder with each successive visit, as if to test them to see if he was really locked in with me.

I had patiently listened to him for quite a while, and he briefly attempted to return the courtesy. But after about two minutes of my talking, I had him far past his spiritual saturation point, which apparently wasn't very high. He was now trying to force the locked cell door open. I think he would have escaped right then if he could have. I shut up then. We never had any lengthy conversations after that. We obviously didn't hit if off!

The next morning when the cell doors opened, I went out mingling with other prisoners, preferring not to spend any more time than I had to with this screwball cell mate. At the end of the day, when I came back into the cell just before lockdown, Timothy gave me a hateful look, the only one I would receive from another inmate during my entire prison experience. The second morning, the trustee came to me and said, "What the heck did you say to that guy? He asked me to get you the hell out of his cell!" So I was kicked out of Timothy Leary's cell. At the time, I never really appreciated the notoriety of this cell mate.

It would be more than fifteen years later, while relating some of my prison experiences to a lawyer I was working with on Ponape, my longtime home in the Western Pacific Micronesian Islands, that he suggested it must be Timothy Leary. I had forgotten about him over the years. It wouldn't be until 1995 that in a bookstore in Kailua, Hawaii, I ordered a book by Timothy Leary, about his time in jail and later escape from the Men's Colony in San Luis Obispo, California. The book only dealt with his time in prison after his conviction and as he was beginning to serve his sentence at the Men's Colony, starting in late 1966 or early 1967.

Timothy apparently had his good days and bad days. The book seemed well written, logical, and coherent. At least, that's how I remember it. It's been well over fifteen years since I last read it. I found it interesting reading, as it documented his escape in 1967 from the Men's Colony in San Luis Obispo, with some help of the Black Panthers. He told how he then fled to Europe and then later to Libya and was eventually given asylum by Omar Gadalfi. All the while, he was at the top of the FBI's "Ten Most Wanted" list as the most wanted American fugitive at the time, or so he claims in his book.

His picture in the book was similar to how I remembered him, but I was confused by the trustee's statement that he was a Harvard College professor, because he had told me that he'd been teaching at Berkley. The book cleared up this discrepancy by stating he had been a professor at Harvard but was on sabbatical and had been teaching at Berkley at the time before his arrest.

While I was starting to write this book in late 2006, I procured a second book by Timothy Leary. It was also about his prison experiences. It dealt only with his time in jail in the early 1970s, after he got bored in Libya with Gadalfi and surrendered to US authorities. The book did not talk at all about how he was able to finally surrender after his escape and end up only doing a relatively short additional sentence before his release from US Federal and California custody.

I would find out later the apparent reason for his silence on this issue. It was because he became a government informant, "snitch" in prison jargon, against those who helped him during his escape. Apparently, our government at the time was more concerned about a potential race war in the United States, spearheaded by the Black Panthers, who had helped Timothy immediately after his escape from the Men's Colony in San Luis Opispo.

What I did find in the book, though, I found unreadable, obviously written by a spaced-out druggy. This was the Timothy Leary I was a cell mate with, not the sophisticated college professor or successful author.

I can only imagine that when he had an empty bunk in his cell and discussed with the trustee who to fill it with. That upon hearing there was a "draft dodger" in the cellblock; he probably thought I was his counterculture type of guy, telling the trustee, "Put him in my cell!"

I obviously wasn't—but most likely a religious nerd in Timothy's estimation. I would end up coming in contact with hundreds of selective service violators, and most were guys similar to me. I don't think I ever ran into an outspoken counterculture draft dodger in federal prison that Timothy Leary might approve of. They probably all successfully dodged the draft or fled to Canada, then got government amnesty afterward. To my knowledge, none I was in with ever burned a draft card or flag.

I then moved to another cell, which I shared with an African American prisoner. I got along just fine with this man. The first Sunday in this cellblock, I walked up by the entrance door of the cellblock, where five or six other prisoners were gathered. A man had just arrived with a Bible in his hand to preach at our cellblock. He introduced himself and told everyone he was a Presbyterian minister who had come every Sunday for the past fifteen years to preach at every cellblock in this jail, saying that he had never missed one Sunday in all that time.

He began to console the inmates, saying that although they were in jail, all hope wasn't lost—that they could still turn things around, and that God could forgive them. He said that even the apostle Paul admitted he had problems doing what was right, that he too sinned many times. Then he began to read Paul's admission of this from Romans 7:18-25, which reads in part, "For I know that in me, that is, in my flesh, there dwells nothing good; . . . for the good that I wish, I do not do, but the bad that I do not wish is what I practice . . . So, then, with (my) mind I myself am a slave to God's law. But with (my) flesh to sin's law."

The minister then admitted, "We too all sin, and like Paul, we don't always do what's right." In his attempt to console these lawbreakers, he stated that he was sure none of us were in jail for doing God's will—that we had all sinned, having done something against God's and man's laws—but all hope wasn't lost. The prisoners were standing in a row in front of the cellblock door, me at one end. The minister then addressed the young man at the other end of the row with words to this effect: "Son, you're not in jail for doing God's will . . . are you?"

The inmate lowered his head and answered humbly, "No, Reverend."

The minister continued going down the row, essentially asking each individual the same question. They all answered in a similar subdued, humble fashion. As he was going down the row, some of the inmates who knew what I was in for were glancing at me with looks of anticipation, as if they were curious about what was going to happen when he got to me. When he did, I answered, "Well, yes, I am!"

He, along with the prisoners, broke out in uncontrollable laughter. When everyone calmed down, he stated that that was the first time he'd ever gotten that answer. Then he said, "Really, tell me what you are in for, son."

I answered, "Well, I'm one of Jehovah's Witnesses, and we're neutral all over the world. We don't join the army of any nation. I'm in for refusing military induction!"

The minister seemed at a loss for words briefly, and then he looked at his watch and said, "Well, I've got to go now." And off he went.

There wasn't much to do during the day. I read some books and talked with other inmates; I also tried to sleep during the day to pass time. For the first and only time in my life, I was actually able to sleep for fifteen hours a day for several days.

A day or two after that first Sunday in the Old County Jail, I was walking along the corridor in front of the thirteen cells. At the time, there weren't any other prisoners in the southern area of the corridor. As I passed one cell, a lone small African American prisoner motioned for me to come into his cell, saying, "Do you want to know what's going to happen to you when you get to federal prison?" I walked in. He moved to the back corner of the cell, behind the bunks, saying, "Come closer. I'll tell you." As I moved closer, still a couple of feet from him, four big African American prisoners whom I hadn't seen coming pushed me into the corner, up against the little guy, who now had a razor blade against my throat. My hands were pinned down against my side. He said, "What's it going to be, blood on the razor, or shit on the dick?"

It happened so fast that I didn't have time to be alarmed, but after several seconds, I answered, "Blood on the razor!" A few moments later, they released me and left the cell. I left the cell puzzled, thinking, *Were they serious*? They obviously had planned ahead of time what they had just done.

The next day, a white prisoner approached me and told me he had heard what had happened to me the previous day. He went on to say that some of those same prisoners had also tried that two weeks before on another prisoner, who got scared—and they then raped him. I believe the reason they didn't force themselves on me was because they wanted someone who, out of fear, would submit and not make a commotion, to avoid attracting the guards.

In this jail, I had seen the guards take a prisoner out of a nearby cellblock and bring him back a few hours later, all beat up, black and blue, with his head swelled up. I was to see this only in this prison, not in any of the other prisons I was yet to experience. These prisoners obviously did not want to adversely attract these guards' attention.

Later I would remember that just prior to this gang rape attempt, I saw Timothy Leary talking to our two trustees. From the looks on their faces as they all looked at me, I was suspicious that they were cooking up something that involved me. Timothy Leary was the only prisoner who gave me a hateful look during my entire experience in nine prisons and jails. Our two trustees, Shepard and Carr, were among the five participants during this rape attempt.

I now believe that this incident was orchestrated by Timothy Leary in retaliation for my telling him he was nuts. I also believe it would take someone of Timothy's caliber to influence Shepard and Carr to participate. Not as rapists but to help Timothy organize this event to teach a young upstart a lesson. Do I believe he could stoop so low? Yes! Reading his second book about his prison experiences in the early 1970s made it obvious to me that he could fit right in with prison lowlifes.

The prisoner who'd told me about the incident two weeks previously introduced himself as Jack P. Caddy. He was twenty-seven years old, but most of his teeth were already rotted out from many years of heroin use. Over the next two weeks, Jack and I were to become friends, talking during the day, my sharing the kingdom message with him, playing checkers, just "doing time." My heart went out to this man as he related his wasted life story to me as he was sitting in prison: a youth spent in reform schools, later in and out of jail, a drug dealer and an addict, not to mention a Hell's Angel.

He related about leaving his girlfriend's house one day and walking to his motorcycle. Still on the walkway leading to the front door, he passed her dad, who was returning home from work. An off-duty policeman, he was so disgusted by the sight of Jack that he shot him in the back of the neck with his .357 Magnum service revolver, right then and there. He survived, and I found that Jack had a good side, as most do, a potential for good still untapped. He also had a willingness to listen to God's word, which could be a tremendous influence in helping him turn his life around.

The next Sunday rolled around, and I was curious as to whether the minister was going to show up. Some of the guys were hanging around the cellblock door about the time he usually showed up. I went up to the entrance and could hear his voice at a cellblock around the corner to the east. I waited inside the first cell, just out of sight; I didn't want to scare him off if I was a problem for him. When he arrived, he went to the cellblock to the south, across the hall, but he was looking into our cellblock as if looking for someone. He was even craning his neck as he looked. He made this examination several times. I was watching this from the first cell. The bars were at a right angle from the other cellblock, so I could peek between the bars, but from the other cellblock the space looked like an eighth of an inch from a distance, not enough to recognize me if that's what he was looking for. This time the minister had a companion, a young Filipino. After examining our cellblock again, he sent his companion over to preach to our cellblock, while he took the other one.

In short order, it was obvious that the Filipino was a rookie apprentice minister, which the prisoners immediately started capitalizing on. They began having fun with him, leaving him tongue-tied and flustered in no time. The older minister grew concerned and realized he needed to rescue his protégé and get control of the situation. After again craning his neck and examining our cellblock, he came over and took over the conversation. By this time, I'd moved farther back in the first cell, against the wall, so he couldn't see me, even though he was now standing at our cellblock door. I wanted to see if I was really his object of concern.

The minister had now reestablished control. The inmates were settled down and listening. He was right in midsentence, making a point, when I stepped out into his view. He saw me, stopped talking, and looked at his watch, saying, "Well, we have to go now!"

During the next week, late in the afternoon or early evening, just before lockdown, I was having a conversation about the Bible with a prisoner in his late forties. He was a Catholic, and we were discussing "the rock." Catholics view it as referring to Peter, Jehovah's Witnesses as to Jesus Christ being the foundation of the new Christian congregation. This man started getting excited, even confused, and he began agreeing with me, but also getting mad and shouting, making a scene.

I turned my head away toward the corridor, thinking to myself, *Oh, brother. Great. We're going to attract the guards.* I then saw Jack with fire in his eyes, fixated on a guy yelling at me, with a prison knife in his hand. He was angrily walking toward us, now twenty-five to thirty feet away. I immediately excused myself and intercepted Jack, putting myself between the knife and his objective, gently grabbing him and saying, "Oh, no, Jack! That's not necessary. Don't worry about that guy. It's nothing; it happens all the time!" Jack calmed down, but I was surprised how protective he had become toward me.

I was wondering if maybe Jack was developing homosexual feelings toward me, although he hadn't yet said or done anything to make me think that might be the case. I wanted to believe that the kingdom message from the Bible, which can exert a powerful, positive influence on good-hearted people, was at work on Jack, despite his misguided, protective behavior.

The next Sunday was to be my last one in the Old County Jail. Inmates who waited for the minister were to wait in vain. He, for the first time in fifteen years, missed preaching to the nearby cellblocks and ours too.

The following Tuesday, about midmorning, a commissary cart came through our cellblock. I, for the first time since I arrived there, spent some money and bought a piece of pie and a pint of milk. This would be the only jail I was in where inmates could have money on their person and spend it. I'd had about one bite of pie and a swallow of milk when the guard at the cellblock gate yelled out my name, saying I had two minutes to get my mattress, bedroll, and personal effects up to the door to be transferred out. I had to rush. You didn't want to keep those guards waiting. I had to give my pie and milk away to the nearest inmate so my hands were free to roll up my mattress and bedding.

On passing Jack's cell, I saw him sitting next to the rear of the bunk with a hurt, sad look on his face. I stopped to say a quick good-bye. He motioned for me to come into his cell, so I did to shake his hand. Then he motioned for me to come closer, as if he wanted to whisper something in my ear. As I bent down to hear what he had to say, he kissed me on the forehead. I recoiled in surprise, taking one step back. As I looked at this hardened criminal, I noticed that his eyes were full of tears, which then began running down his face. I didn't have time to contemplate what had just happened and why, but I told him, "Jack, when you get out, find the Witnesses and study the Bible with them." He nodded, and that was the last I ever saw or heard of him.

As time passed, I would be more and more haunted by the memory of Jack. I would hope that he had been able to follow my final request, and that I might run into him at a large summer assembly of Jehovah's Witnesses somewhere. But by 1968, that would be more and more unlikely, as I had moved to Hawaii by then; and in 1970, I moved to the remote Western Pacific island of Ponape. But still, hardly a week or month has gone by that I have not thought about Jack and wondered what became of him.

Chapter 4

To Arizona

That tuesday, they transferred me back to the Los Angeles New County Jail for one night. On Wednesday morning, I went to the "processing out" area. Waiting there were five others. Two of them were twin brothers, Ron and Don Nelson, and both were Jehovah's Witnesses; they were from northern California. One was a Mennonite conscientious objector named Mike Senai, also from northern California. Mike had a full beard. I had never heard of the Mennonites before, but based on his appearance, I assumed they were old-fashioned like the Amish.

Four US marshals showed up, and the two Nelsons and Mike Senai were put in the backseat of one car, handcuffed to a chain around their waists. The two other prisoners and I were placed in the other car, also handcuffed to a chain around our waists, with two marshals in the front seat, driving and escorting us. It would be one of the few times I couldn't bite my fingernails for a day.

I was in the backseat in the middle, on the hard hump of the seat. We were to drive about five or six hundred miles that day to Arizona, and because of the seat, it was to be the most uncomfortable ride of my life—also because my nerves were acting up, and I couldn't relax to urinate when we stopped for meal breaks, especially with a marshal standing behind me, watching. This was something that would plague me during most of my prison experience.

As we left Los Angeles, going east out of town on the San Bernardino Freeway, which is now the I-10, the marshals detoured south, down the 605 Freeway, to one of the marshal ex-wife's house for some personal errand, and then we went back to the I-10. The marshals couldn't stop talking about how much they were going to make that day, including their mileage allowance for delivering us. They used foul language and couldn't wait to drop us off in Arizona so they could drive across the Mexican border to some brothels.

In furtherance of these goals, the marshal driving was doing ninety-five miles per hour as we passed Indian Avenue, which leads into Palm Springs. A car was signaling to take the next off-ramp to the right, but it swerved to the left, as that off-ramp was to the left, across the center divider. The marshal lost control for a moment, serving twice to miss this vehicle barely. That was the closest I'd ever come to being in a high-speed accident. In 2003, I was by that area, and the off-ramp no longer exists. It used to lead to the western communities of Desert Hot Springs.

We stopped in Indio for a meal, and it was a bit embarrassing to be watched by civilians as we walked in handcuffs and chains into the restaurant. The marshals uncuffed one of each of our hands so we could eat.

In the afternoon, we arrived at a small prison camp in Florence, Arizona, where the marshals dropped us off. I felt we should've been dropping them off, as they seemed the most depraved of our car group.

As I waited in the lobby to be processed in, I was disappointed. I'd thought I'd be going to a federal prison camp in the mountains outside of Tucson, Arizona. That's where all the Witnesses I'd heard of had been going. This prison camp seemed to have only illegal immigrants in it, from what I was seeing out the windows.

After about thirty to forty minutes, the US marshals returned with some paperwork, informing me that they'd made a mistake, and that they'd take me to another place. They then dropped me off at a federal detention center, also in Florence, Arizona, after again passing by the Arizona State Prison.

After processing in, fingerprinting and mug shots, I met up with Mike Senai, the Mennonite. In that federal jail, he's been forced to be clean-shaven. We were there for two weeks, and we passed most of the time playing chess together. He won the first game, but after he taught me how to play, I won every game. I sort of felt bad for him about that.

For two weeks, that jail consistently had the best food I was to enjoy during my jail/prison experiences. I put back on the weight

I'd lost in the Los Angeles County jails. Mike and I were then transferred by marshals to the Mt. Lemmon Federal Prison Camp, at an elevation of about 3,400 feet, just northeast of Tucson, Arizona.

It was a prison camp for minimum-security prisoners in their teens and twenties, nobody any older. There were no fences and no armed guards. There was only one firebreak around the perimeter of the camp, and prisoners were not supposed to cross it. The camp had been opened since the Second World War and had imprisoned many Witnesses regularly since then.

The camp had three military-style wood barracks that housed maybe 150 to 180 inmates. Many of the prisoners were young American Indians from various tribes, who had committed a crime on an Indian reservation. They were usually drunk at the time, and any crime on a reservation was a federal crime.

After processing in, I was assigned to my barracks and told to just look around the barracks and pass the rest of the afternoon there until the end of the workday, when all the other inmates would return from their work assignments.

A prisoner in the barracks told me that I was allowed to have on my locker one eight-by-eleven-inch picture frame with various pictures of family, friends, girlfriends, wives, and so forth, whatever would fit in that frame. Also, as a way to familiarize myself with the camp barracks, he suggested I check out the barracks and see how prisoners were filling their picture frames.

So there I was, six hundred miles from home, in a federal prison with criminals I didn't know, some who might be potentially dangerous. I didn't want to invade someone's space by walking in between bunks for a close-up look at a stranger's personal pictures on a locker by the head of his bed. So I stayed in the main corridor between the two rows of bunks, looking from a distance of maybe eight feet away at different inmates' collections of personal pictures. I soon realized that you pretty much could tell what race the absent inmates were by their pictures, whether white, black, Indian, or Mexican.

I came to one inmate's pictures, and it was obvious he must be African American, but one picture among the others was of a white girl with blond hair, and from a distance, it reminded me of my wife.

I was thinking that given the racial realities as of 1966, it might be risky for the man to flaunt such a picture.

Twenty minutes later, prisoners would return from their work assignments. One from Manhattan Beach, which was next to El Segundo, knew my wife and me. He informed me that the white girl in the picture was my wife! I hurried back to the barracks where I'd seen the picture from a distance, but it had been removed by then.

Despite this bizarre occurrence, there ended up being an innocent explanation for this. My wife was from a racially mixed congregation of Jehovah's Witnesses. Her longtime best friend there was African American. Previously, she had visited with her friend at the home of her relatives, who were also Witnesses, in Watts. This prisoner, whom I didn't know yet, was her best friend's cousin and got the photo from pictures taken at the family gathering. He put the picture in his frame to impress other black Witnesses, not knowing the girl was now married. I'd come to find out that this guy was our camp clown; that was just one example of his outrageous behavior.

I soon find out that there were about fifty-five Witnesses in the camp, mostly from the West Coast but a few from Colorado, Oklahoma, and Texas. There were also about five conscientious objectors who were not Witnesses. Two were from other religions; three were nonreligious objectors, intellectual types who had varying principles that motivated them. Considering this prison camp and other federal prisons I was later to be in, this ratio for conscientious objectors continued to stay about the same. About 90 percent were Jehovah's Witnesses; 5 percent were objectors from other religions such as Mennonites, Amish, and so forth; and 5 percent were intellectual objectors who didn't make it to Canada, but they weren't the radical type.

I also learned about the federal government's inconsistencies in prosecution of conscientious objectors. Most people think that if you have religious objections to war, you don't have to go. I came to realize that whether or not one is prosecuted starts with the many local draft boards and its members' personal feelings toward those who claim conscientious objection to war. Some board members respect those feelings and do not subject conscientious objectors to military call-up or even noncombatant military service. Others vary all the way up to and going out of their way to classify all conscientious objectors as 1-A, fit for full military service.

It's up to the draft board to press charges if a violation occurs. Once prosecution is pursued, it's then up to the federal district judge in that locality. The judge has discretion to issue a sentence anywhere from probation up to but not exceeding five years in prison.

Thus I was to learn that no Witnesses from Hawaii ever went to jail or were prosecuted. In California, starting with San Diego, Witnesses were being prosecuted but were only receiving four-month suspended sentences. We never saw any brothers from San Diego in the camps. A brother is the term we Witnesses use to refer to each other.

From Los Angeles, brothers were receiving sentences of two and a half to three years. I was one of those. Federal courts in San Francisco handed down nine-month sentences. Brothers came in from Oregon and Washington with eighteen-month sentences. Texas and Oklahoma gave out five-year sentences. One brother somehow managed to come in from Oklahoma with a six-year sentence, even though the law stipulated a five-year maximum. Colorado gave two year sentences.

As of 1966, the country still appeared to be pro-Vietnam War; from what we could see, the antiwar war movement hadn't yet materialized. Our being in jail had nothing to do with how the general public viewed the war or the antiwar movement.

That first day in Mt. Lemmon camp, I met up with Dave Brown and the brother behind him in the chow line in the L.A. New County Jail, Bob Clark from Palm Springs. The Nelsons twins were there, as was the brother I knew from the Manhattan Beach area, John Luchuk. There were about fifty other brothers I would begin getting acquainted with as well.

I also talked and visited with some of the more than one hundred regular prisoners, all of whom were young, minimum security, supposedly not dangerous prisoners. One friendly guy who was about twenty-six years old slept near me in our barracks. The rest of that first week I was confined to the barracks area, so I passed a lot of time talking to him. Before the end of the week, he was released. I shook his hand and wished him well, seeing him off as he left the barracks, now a free man.

A guard drove him down to the bus station in Tucson and dropped him off with just his clothes he had on, a small amount of money, and a bus ticket to wherever he was from. He had an hour or two before his bus left, so he walked across the street to look around at a used-car lot, just killing time. He saw a nice little sports car that struck his fancy. The salesperson suggested they take it for a test drive, having no idea of his customer's circumstances. The newly released inmate liked the car and had to have it. So on this test drive, he killed the salesman and took off with the car. He was captured three or four days later; I can't remember where.

In the barracks shortly after getting the news of this event, I was talking with a friendly Mexican inmate in his late twenties about the need for caution because some of the prisoners could be capable of murder. He sort of chuckled and proceeded to tell me that he was in the camp because he got caught smuggling parrots into the United States—that previously he used to smuggle Mexicans into the States. He claimed that on one occasion, he was flying a surplus military boxcar cargo plane, the kind on which the back fuselage flips up. It had no seats, just open space for cargo. He was bringing twenty-some illegal's up the Gulf of California and nearing the US border when a border patrol plane attempted to intercept him. He flew into a cloud, opened the cargo door, and made a steep climb, spilling all the human cargo into the waters of the Gulf. When the border patrol plane directed him to land for inspection, he was cleared, as no evidence was found.

Well that's just great, I thought disappointedly. Here I was in this new prison camp, and of the first two non-Witness inmates I had gotten close to, one was to shortly become a murderer and the other was a professed mass murderer!

Not long after this, I was assigned to the road-building crew for two weeks. The guard in charge was Mr. Gott, a well-liked guard by all the inmates, especially the Witnesses. Most of that time, I was swinging a pick and shovel in the hot Arizona sun. Sitting in jail cells for the last month and a half, I had gotten out of shape for work. Ironically, I found it humorous that I would have to be imprisoned to handle dynamite for the one and only time in my life. It gave me a horrible headache, literally.

This road ran from the back of the prison camp, west over a hill, and then down to a dam and reservoir that provided water for the camp, about two miles away.

Next I was assigned to the carpenter shop, which was to be my permanent job in that prison camp. Mr. Burns was our guard and supervised the shop. His first assignment for me was to take a lesson on table saw safety from another Witness, Norm Blackburn, who, like me, was a carpenter from the Los Angeles area.

I mildly protested that that wouldn't be necessary, since I was a carpenter and experienced with table saws. Mr. Burns insisted I take a safety lesson from Blackburn, so over to the table saw we went. I was disinterested and easily distracted.

Where I was standing to observe the proper way to use a table saw, there was a window at my back. I turned around and looked out the window as Blackburn started ripping a piece of wood that was three or four feet long. I was fascinated; the shop's wood floor straddled a small river that ran right under the building where I stood. At the edges of the stream were some huge centipedes. As I briefly took all this in, I heard the saw switched off. A couple of seconds later, I turned around and saw that the saw blade was coasting to a stop, but Blackburn was nowhere to be seen. Puzzled, I moved closer to the saw blade and the wood that had just been ripped. Then I noticed a drop of red stuff on the floor in front of the saw. As I looked more closely, I noticed another red drop, and then another, which led away from the saw and toward the exit of the shop. I followed the drops out of the shop and then toward the camp, weaving around some buildings I wasn't yet familiar with. With my head down, tracking the trail of drops, I came to a door. I looked up and read a sign above the door: DISPENSARY. I opened the door and entered. Sitting in a chair there, Blackburn was squeezing his thumb to stop the bleeding. The cut wasn't too serious—it just bled a lot—but I never let him forget his "safety" demonstration. For the next four and a half months, Blackburn was my regular workmate.

I learned that all inmates in the prison camp were given work assignments and paid five to fifteen cents per hour, except recently interned Witnesses. We worked for free. The other brothers and I were told that pay for work is a privilege, and that Jehovah's Witnesses don't qualify for these privileges; they need to be punished instead, which is the reason we're in prison. This government policy toward us during the Vietnam War was obviously a reflection of the pro-Vietnam War mindset of the majority of those in the government. This didn't surprise us at all. Many of the guards were former or retired military and hated us. Soon things were to get even worse for us, as official government policy from the top, the Federal Bureau of Prisons, was about to change.

The scriptures warn us that things like this will occur because of our neutrality. Jesus stated that this hatred toward his followers would result from their "being no part of the world." The scriptures call Christians "ambassadors substituting for Christ," and as such, we stay neutral from the politics and wars of the countries we're in, just as modern-day ambassadors do in their host countries.

A number of historical books show that the early Christians understood Jesus's commands and the scriptures the same way modern-day Jehovah's Witnesses do and adopted a similar attitude toward their Roman rulers. The following quotes are examples of this:

A careful review of all the information available goes to show that until the time of Marcus Aurelius (Roman emperor from 161 to 180 CE) no Christian became a soldier; and no soldier, after becoming a Christian, remained in military service.—The Rise of Christianity (London, 1947), E. W. Barnes, 333.

They refused to take any active part in the civil administration or the military defense of the empire . . . . It was impossible that the Christians, without renouncing a more sacred duty, could assume the character of soldiers, of magistrates, or of Princes.—History of Christianity (New York, 1891), Edward Gibbon, 162-63.

Early Christianity was little understood and was regarded with little favor by those who ruled the pagan world . . . . Christians refused to share certain duties of Roman citizens. . . . They would not hold political office."—On the Road to Civilization, a World History (Philadelphia, 1937), A. Heckel and J. Sigman, 237-238.

It was the early Christians refusing to be "no part of the [Roman] world" that led to their being hated and the eventual cruel persecution that they were to experience at the hand of the Roman Empire.

Chapter 5

The Dork

A preview of things worsening for us started about two or three weeks after I arrived in this camp. A new parole officer, Mr. Bird, direct from the Bureau of Federal Prisons in Washington, DC, was replacing a well-liked parole officer named Mr. Anderson. Within a day or two, the brothers who worked in the administration building reported that Mr. Bird was letting others know that he thoroughly disliked the Witnesses and was going to do something about them.

Mr. Burns assigned Blackburn and me to add a closet to an unused office room up in the administration building. The entrance to the hallway and room, including another unused room, was separate from all the other offices and entrances in the administration building. The hallway also bordered the east wall of Mr. Bird's office.

The work to be done should have taken us a day or two, but since we were working for free, we stretched it out to about four weeks. We spent most of our time eavesdropping on Mr. Bird, with our ears to glasses against his wall, trying to find out what he was up to.

I overheard him talking to someone on the phone about the Jehovah's Witnesses, and what a big problem we were because of all the religious literature we had in our lockers. He said that he wanted to have our allotted quota of literature cut in half so it would be more manageable.

We thought this a petty matter to make a big deal over. As it was, we were only allowed to have four religious books. That included a Bible, plus no more than four religious magazines at any one time. We had fun with it, imagining the guards having a problem counting to four twice. Maybe two was more compatible with their mental abilities. Joking aside, there was no limit to the amount of nonreligious books and magazines a prisoner could have in his locker. It was obvious to us that this issue was just another manifestation of these officials' intolerance toward us.

A day or two later, I overheard Mr. Bird having a conversation with someone at the Federal Bureau of Prisons, and it appeared that he was informed that to get his new policy approved, it had to be authorized by the head chaplain at the Bureau of Prisons in Washington, DC. From the conversation, it appeared that he knew the man personally and was to call him at a certain time the next day.

The next day at the appointed time, I had my ear to the glass, glass against the wall. I didn't want to miss one word. All the brothers had been informed of what was at stake, and they were concerned about the outcome of this issue. Any reduction in our four books and four magazines would seriously disrupt our small prison congregation's abilities to conduct some of our religious meetings that we were allowed to have, which were patterned after the weekly meetings normally conducted by Jehovah's Witnesses around the world. Several brothers who worked in the administration building were positioned to stand watch and pretend they accidentally tripped the camp buzzer, should any guard approach our position.

I overheard the call from the beginning. After a few pleasantries at the start, Mr. Bird launched into his reason for calling, which was to discuss the problem he was having with the Jehovah's Witnesses, dealing with all our books and magazines. "Well, yes, the wife and kids are fine," he then said, and it was clear he had been interrupted. And off they went, discussing personal matters. Mr. Bird was never able to get back to his original reason for the phone call. The head chaplain obviously didn't want to hear anything about the issue and had changed the subject. It was all I could do to keep from laughing aloud and betraying my position. Although Mr. Bird failed in this attempt, he would eventually play a small part in something that we would all find far worse.

The next project Mr. Burns assigned to us was repairing the phone line from the camp to the pump house. It ran about two miles, over the mountains and to the reservoir that supplied the camp's yellow drinking and shower water.

Most of the line was lying on the ground. Reception was practically nonexistent, and it needed a lot of work. For the next two months, Blackburn and I spent every day driving to different parts of the road, then hiking into the mountains and gullies to reattach the lines to new insulators nailed up in trees. We spliced in new lines where necessary, cutting branches and trees out of the way—whatever it took to improve reception.

During this time, several brothers went before the parole board, which included the involvement of Mr. Bird. Ever since the Second World War ended, the Witnesses had always been granted parole after serving one-third of their sentences. Even before entering prison, all of us had expected to be granted parole, expecting to be going home—in my case, after serving about ten months of my thirty-month sentence. But the news started coming back that paroles were denied. When we came back from our work assignment and learned from the few brothers we'd expected to be leaving any day that their paroles had been denied, it was very sobering. It dawned on all of us that this was going to be a new government policy toward us. It meant, for example that those, who had come into prison with a three-year sentence and expected to only do a year would now have to do more than two years instead, getting out automatically on what was called their "good time" date. The mood was quiet and somber. I remember seeing one married brother pull his blanket over his head and cry.

I chalked it up to the pro-Vietnam War elements in the government were having it their way. Some may have been incensed by the draft card burners and other radicals, the "Hell no, we won't go" guys, many who did go to Canada. Whom did the government take it out on? Us. We were the ones they already had and hated most. Later, those who fled to Canada were given amnesty. Over forty years later, my fellow brothers and I are still convicted felons and treated as such. We were never offered or given amnesty or anything else, except twice as much time to serve now.

Not too long after this, Blackburn and I were discussing with Mr. Burns, our carpenter shop guard, some of these events as well as Mr. Bird's possible involvement. Mr. Burns response surprised us. He went off on Mr. Bird with words to this effect: "Oh, that Mr. Bird. What a dork! Do you know what he proposed at a meeting with the camp administrator [warden]? He actually suggested that he be able to take prisoners on weekend hiking and camping trips into the mountains! Can you imagine that? He must be thinking they're Boy Scouts, not criminals. He's so enamored with everything about the West that he actually requested a transfer from Washington, DC, to this prison camp so he could experience the West firsthand. He thinks there's an Indian behind every bush and gold in every valley!"

I had to remind Mr. Burns that around this camp, there practically was an Indian behind every bush, but Mr. Burns wasn't done yet. He went on to suggest that we pull a prank on Mr. Bird, just to see how gullible he really was. He proposed that since Blackburn and I had been up and down the hills and gullies for almost two months, that we should claim we'd found gold and asked Mr. Burns to ask Mr. Bird if we could keep it.

Of course we agreed to be part of this, and off we went, searching for something that could pass for gold. At the garage, we found some small drops and splatters of melted lead from battery post repairs. Back at our shop in the paint room, we found some fast-drying gold spray paint. In short order, we delivered three or four beautiful little gold nuggets to Mr. Burns. He took out a clean white handkerchief and folded the nuggets neatly up in it, placing it in his wallet, stating that he'd drop by Mr. Bird's office the next day with our request.

Later that afternoon, Blackburn and I were returning the truck to the garage after working on the phone line. As we walked south toward the carpenter shop, we saw Mr. Bird coming out of our shop. As we passed, he cast us a curious look of recognition that made me think, *Aha, he's taken the bait.* As we entered the shop, I could see from a distance that Mr. Burns had a devious, satisfied Cheshire cat look about himself.

He informed us that Mr. Bird had just happened to make an impromptu visit to the shop that day, as he was making rounds of the camp to get familiar with it, since he was still relatively new. And that yes, he had taken advantage of this unexpected visit to present our request about keeping the gold that we had supposedly found. But he went further, telling us that he told Mr. Bird he had already confiscated some gold from us and knew the location of our gold mine and was planning a trip there the next weekend. Mr. Bird excitedly asked if he could go with him to the mine. Mr. Burns, feigning a bad case of gold fever, warned him saying "no, that anybody trying to follow me to my gold mine *might not return!*"

Mr. Bird bought the whole story, stating before he left that he'd present our request to Mr. Mackenzie, our camp administrator. This is the polite new word for "warden," part of the government's new Correctional Institution reform program.

Two days later, Mr. Burns told Blackburn and I that earlier that day he finally went to Mr. Bird's office, stating he'd come to show him something he had taken from Blackburn and Nix. He then took out his wallet and carefully removed and unwrapped the handkerchief, rolling the gold nuggets out onto Mr. Bird's desk like dice. Mr. Bird's eyes grew large, and he excitedly told Mr. Burns that he had presented our requests to Mr. Mackenzie, and that Mr. Mackenzie approved it; we could keep the gold!

Just then, Mr. Mackenzie opened the door and walked into the office. On seeing the nuggets on the desk, his eyes grew big and he exclaimed, "Well, I'll be god dammed. Nix really did find gold!"

Mr. Burns then admitted that he now had a big problem. He couldn't carry this ruse on any longer now that Mr. Mackenzie was directly involved. So he ended it right there, and they all had a good laugh.

In all fairness to Mr. Bird, the denying of our paroles was not all his doing, although he may have approved of it. It apparently was done nationwide and came from the Federal Bureau of Prisons in Washington, as we were to learn more about later.

Chapter 6

Prison Camp Life

Life in a prison camp quickly turns into a boring routine. You just can't wait to get out, but it isn't that bad either. You went to work in the morning, after having our breakfast prepared for us. Then lunch was prepared before we reported back to work again. After work, there was dinner and then an hour or so of recreation: baseball, football, basketball, tennis, weightlifting, cross-country running on the camp perimeter firebreaks, and so on. There was a library and a TV room. You had your laundry done for you, clean clothes and bedding. Most of the Indians were much better off in prison than on a reservation.

During my first week or two in camp, a bolt of lightning struck a tree about ten feet from me. Tucson is apparently one of the world's hot spots for lightning activity.

When I got into the camp, baseball was what everyone was playing, so I joined in. I had played in high school, and I thought I was rather good during my freshman and sophomore years. After that, I got worse. Our high school baseball coach, Mr. Stevenson, in practices and pregame warm-ups always wanted us to throw full speed and chatter nonstop. By the time the game started, my arm and throat were sore, and that would last all season long. I guess I just didn't have what it took. Mr. Stevenson was an excellent high school baseball coach and would eventually be recognized as one of the very best in California, if not in the whole nation.

Now my arm was healed. They put me in left field, where I could play shallow and still range back to catch long fly balls or field line drive base hits and throw the runner out at first base, and I did. Plus I could hit. They immediately drafted me into the camp baseball team, and within a day or two, I found myself with the team in the back of an open five-ton stake bed truck. Down the mountain canyon road into Tucson we went for some sort of league play. I can't remember much about the game, except the ride back up the canyon road to camp just before dark. A world-class Tucson electrical storm broke out all around us, with lightning strikes on the mountains on each side of the canyon road, and I was getting cold and wet from the rain, more scared than I'd ever been in my life.

The next game was to be a tournament in the Arizona State Prison at Florence, Arizona, more than one hundred miles away. I'd been driven by that prison twice with the first two marshals I rode with. We'd have to stay overnight there. I had no interest in going back, especially in the back of the truck, so I said good-bye to the team. I mentioned this baseball episode to set the stage for something that would happen a year or so later in a large federal prison far to the east.

The daily routine started with getting up for breakfast, or you could skip it and stay in bed. Back from breakfast, there was time to lie in bed again for a while. Shortly, everyone had to get up, straighten up his area, make his bed to military specifications, dress for work, and assemble for an inspection and count. Only the kitchen staff on breakfast duty could stay in the barracks and go back to bed.

Monday through Saturday, we wore surplus army greens to work. Of all the clothing in the different prisons I was to wear, I was most comfortable in army greens. As a prank, someone in the shop had sprayed a yellow streak of spray paint down the back of the green jacket that I wore. I liked that thin jacket and wore it the entire time at that camp, not caring if someone thought it was a fitting symbol of what I was in for, a coward with a yellow steak down my back.

The guards at morning count were retired military. They had ranks, such as lieutenant or captain. Before proceeding to our work assignments, we had to stand at attention in orderly rows for count.

After count, these guards then inspected the barracks, and if anything was wrong with your area, they'd give you a gig, apparently a military term I was told. They would then post the inspection results on a bulletin board at the end of each day in the barracks. If you got three gigs in a month, you would then lose the privilege of seeing a movie played every Saturday night for the entire next month at the camp theater.

Every Saturday morning, there was a more thorough inspection. We'd stay by our bunks, and the guards would actually wear white gloves, checking for dust even on the windowsills high above every bunk.

One of the guards was Captain McKinney. He had apparently fought in Burma during WWII, as one of "Merrill's Marauders," and later as a marine on Guadalcanal and Iwo Jima. He was still a tall, strong, good-looking man. He didn't like the Witnesses in camp, and he never got close to any of us, as Mr. Burns and Gott had. He was harsh with us and very military-like.

There were about fifty-five Jehovah's Witnesses in this camp, and we were allowed to have three religious meetings a week. I conducted one of the meetings we called the "book study." We held it at night in a small room attached to the camp garage/workshop.

Sometimes after these meetings ended and we had all departed the building, Captain McKinney was spotted leaving it also, maybe five minutes later. We could only speculate that he was out of sight hiding and eavesdropping, hoping to hear something he could use to get our meetings revoked. We doubted he was there because he was interested in our religious beliefs.

Captain McKinney began to target me. In his inspections, he began to give me gigs, three or more a month, so I was losing Saturday night movie privileges. This was to go on for the next few months. Plus at morning count, he'd snap at me for some supposed infraction. He was obviously trying to bring me down a peg at a time.

Another brother who began to have gig problems was Freddy Satler. Freddy arrived in the camp sometime after me with three other Witnesses, all from either Oregon or Washington. Jim Stevenson, Kuburka, and Howe were the names of the other three or what I remember of their names.

Freddy Satler was a goat herder from somewhere outside Portland. He even resembled a goat a little bit, with a few scruffy chin hairs and a naive country boy simplicity, and although he was in his early twenties, he had the look of an old man about him.

Somebody began to deliberately sabotage Freddy's area after he left for work, but before inspection. This was occurring on a rather regular basis, and Freddy was getting more and more upset. Whoever was doing this was getting extremely creative and planting bizarre items in his area, which the guards considered contraband and which were pretty hard to come by in this prison camp.

It got to the point that after work, many brothers and I would hurry back to the barracks just to check the bulletin board, to see what Freddy got a gig for that day. Some items that I can remember were a bra under his pillow, a dirty Kotex in his locker, and women's panties under his mattress. Freddy was going ballistic!

Most of us thought Jim Stevenson was doing it. He was closest to Freddy, being from Medford, Oregon. Even to this day, I've never learned who was responsible, as Jim always denied it. But for several months, Freddy and I pretty much had the barracks to ourselves, confined there during Saturday evenings at movie time.

One of the prisoners in this camp that I remember reading about and seeing on the television news, was Robinson. At fifteen years of age, Robinson had hijacked an airplane at gunpoint in Texas. I remembered the headlines in the newspaper mentioning "Chris Craft on Board," referring to the man who started mass-producing fiberglass boats. The other passengers on the plane jumped and overpowered Robinson.

Robinson had been in prison for three years. We heard he had had it quite rough, being knocked out and raped numerous times. In this prison, he kept close to the Witnesses, since he felt safe with us. This was something I was to see numerous times with regular prisoners who felt vulnerable or outright afraid in prison; they'd stick close to us. This was a smart move for several reasons. We were the biggest united group in the federal prisons we were in. In those years, there were no gangs yet in any of the prisons I was in. Although we were conscientious objectors, as mentioned before, we weren't pacifists. We would fight in certain situations, especially in protecting ourselves from sexual assault.

The prisons had a rule; we weren't supposed to preach to other prisoners. We broke that rule all the time! Some of the prisoners would eventually become Witnesses themselves. I had preached to Robinson, including another Witness, Joe Sedor. There were probably others.

Joe came into the camp two weeks after me. I had known his wife's family; they lived in Lawndale, five or six miles from El Segundo. They were Mexican Americans. Joe would bunk next to me for the next thirteen or fourteen months in this prison and the next.

Ten years later, I would run into Joe at an assembly held at Hollywood Park racetrack in Inglewood, California. He said, "Remember Robinson?" He went on to state that Robinson was later transferred to a prison in Englewood, Colorado. Two old Witness sisters came to the prison and studied the Bible with him, and he became a Witness himself. Joe mentioned at that time another one who later becomes a Witness, but we wouldn't meet him until the next prison.

Preventing sexual assaults would be a problem at times. Some of our brothers were raised in all-female households and were somewhat effeminate because of this. They attracted a lot of attention from other prisoners.

One time while lying in my bunk, Joe Sedar signaled me to look at the far end of the barracks. There, one of these brothers having just showered, was wearing only his underwear and listening to music with his headphones on and dancing to the tune, completely oblivious to everything around him. As we looked around the barracks, five or six Indians were sitting up, fixated on him with lust in their eyes. They couldn't stop looking.

We had to work with these brothers and encourage them not to do certain things such as just mentioned. We tried to get them to work on their masculinity and keep close to the other brothers for protection as a group.

Still, problems would occur. One involved a young Mexican Witness from Los Angeles. He was the smallest of all the brothers among us, and he wasn't at all effeminate. His name was Albert Martinez. I've forgotten many of the names of those I spent time with, but not Albert's.

Martinez worked in the kitchen, and when on the morning shift, he'd get to go back to the barracks and sleep while others were leaving for their work assignments. An Indian who also worked in the kitchen, and whose bunk was not too far from Martinez's, had been propositioning him for some time. One morning, Martinez again rebuffed the advances, but this time the Indian beat him up. His nose was broken, and he had two black eyes, with his face swollen up all black and blue.

None of us could do anything about it afterwards. The scriptures, of course, prohibit revenge and retaliation. But one of our other Mexican brothers, Louie Arriola, was very upset about what had happened and was telling some of us that he was going to do something about it.

We tried to talk him out of it, and he knew all the reasons from the scriptures why he shouldn't, but he felt too close to Martinez. Also technically, Arriolla wasn't a Jehovah's Witness, because he had not yet been baptized. He may have taken a stand for neutrality, but he hadn't yet made a dedication to Jehovah God, which included a vow to adhere to all Christian principles.

Arriolla spent his recreation time lifting weights and it showed. He bided his time, and when he went to the weight room about three days later, there was the Indian who had beat up Martinez, using a stationary exercise bicycle.

Louie walked up to the Indian and told him to get off the bike. He refused, so Louie again told him to get off the bike. The Indian refused again. Louie then knocked him off the bike, put his head in an arm lock around a leg press post, and started pumping his fist into the Indian's face.

A guard rushed in and broke it up. They were both sent down to the Pima County Jail in Tucson. The Indian had three friends who were apparently members of his tribe. They thought that Martinez had put Arriolla up to the incident in the weight room. A day or two later, the three of them jumped Martinez outside the weight room and began beating him up again. Dave Brown, Mike Sinai, and Joe Sedor were nearby, and each took on an Indian with their fists until guards arrived.

The three Indians also got sent down to the Pima County Jail. Eventually, only one of the four Indians and Arriolla returned to the camp. The others were transferred to other federal prisons.

Fearing reprisals by the Indians versus the Witnesses, for the next couple of nights, guards were posted all night long in every barrack as a preventative measure.

In reality, we got along well with most of the Indians. There were about sixty of them in the camp. They were from numerous tribes throughout the West and were not united. The four Indians involved in the beating of Martinez were from the Digger Indian Tribe in southern Arizona. This tribe was apparently considered low class by the other Indians in camp, and they weren't about to get involved on their behalf. Many of these Indians had classic names; Eagle Feather and Spotted Bird are the only two I remember.

Arriolla may have thought that taking revenge would help his friend, but it instead led to Martinez being beaten up a second time. The authorities were worried that it could have led to some sort of prison riot or brawl.

After a week or two, Martinez recovered, and I was at his end of the barracks one evening. Alfred Salgado, another Mexican brother, from the Corona area, east of L.A., bunked near him. I was close to Salgado and was teasing him about all the big muscles he had developed working out in the weight room. His upper body had become so muscle bound that he had trouble combing the back of his hair. I kidded him that those muscles were good for nothing except lifting the weights that had developed them. He disagreed, so I bet him that he couldn't even beat Martinez in an arm wrestling match. The notion of that seemed ridiculous to him, so he accepted the challenge to prove me wrong.

Next I had to convince Martinez to be part of this. Martinez had no confidence at all that he could prevail, but I talked him into trying it, telling him not to be intimidated by Salgado's muscles and his larger size.

Within a short time, I had them on each side of a three-foot-high locker. A crowd gathered around as our little David and Goliath match started. At first, Martinez was surprised that he wasn't pinned immediately. It seemed the match lasted only a couple of minutes. Toward the end, Salgado got a sheepish look on his face as he began to fade, and then little Martinez pinned him. We sure had fun with that.

During most major holidays, the prison recreation officer would organize various athletic events. Winning first place in a particular event was rewarded by receiving four Cokes, second place was rewarded with three Cokes, and third place got two Cokes.

I had been preparing for two events, the cross-country race and tennis. The cross-country race was up and down hills and gullies on the firebreak trail that circled most of the camp, but not all. From what I could learn, the Indians had won all the cross-country races all the way back to the Second World War.

By Thanksgiving of 1966, I was ready for the big games. The first event for me was the cross-country race. Another Witness, a Mexican brother named Vargas, from Texas, also entered.

When the race started, one Indian took off like a jackrabbit, leaving us in the dust. By the second hill, though, Vargas and I passed him, as he had burned himself out with his fast start. The second to the last hill was up a long, steep grade and then down a long, steep, rutted, eroded downgrade, not a good place to fall. Fortunately, Vargas and I were able to come in first and second, respectively. So I won three Cokes for my second-place finish. We'd been deprived of Cokes in prison. I found it much tastier than our yellow drinking water.

I won first place in the tennis singles and doubles tournament, so I ended up winning eleven Cokes altogether. Just having a Coca-Cola was a real treat, something we normally take for granted. I could retrieve them on request, from the recreation officer, during our "free time" periods. He had a refrigerator in his office.

Chapter 7

Visits and a Preview

Sometime around the Thanksgiving holiday, I was called up to the visiting room for a visit. On Sundays or for visits, we had to wear navy surplus khaki shirts and pants with a blue wool jacket. I was never comfortable in these outfits.

When I got up to the visiting room, there was Denny Gormley and three of my other buddies: Woody Hinkle, Rick Cross, and Dewey Bondurant (Woody's father-in-law). They had driven together all the way from L.A. to Tucson, a road trip of about six hundred miles, or twelve hundred miles round trip. Also there was Captain McKinney, the guard on duty that day in the visiting room, along with two other visitors and an inmate.

Denny was probably about forty-one or forty-two years old then, still tanned and strong. When I worked for Denny, we framed mostly flat-roofed apartment houses in places such as Hawthorne, Inglewood, Watts, West Los Angeles, Hollywood, Torrance, Redondo Beach, El Segundo, and many places in the San Fernando Valley.

I still remember the summer of 1962, working on an apartment house two blocks south of Sunset Boulevard in Hollywood. It was a hot and extremely smoggy L.A. day. By ten in the morning, I couldn't take a deep breath without my lungs hurting from the smog. Plus I was packing the biggest floor joists I'd ever handled. They were two-by-sixteen Douglas fir joists, twenty-six feet long, and we were carrying them about one hundred feet and then pushing them up onto the second floor. We used no forklifts in those early years. It was the most miserable day I've ever had in construction, even up to now, almost fifty years later.

Denny walked by and, borrowing a line from a California City radio commercial from that era, said, "Where else can you have fun in the sun and income too?" Ever since then, whenever I was having a hard day at work, I'd remember that ridiculous statement and chuckle to myself. It helps me get through the day.

Woody Hinkle was about twenty-six years old then, a Witness carpenter with whom I worked on numerous occasions, mostly on custom houses. By 1963, it was with him that I learned how to cut stairs and cut and stack roofs. These are technical construction terms. Later, in the late sixties and early seventies, we would work the Hawaii building boom as piecework partners living in Lanikai, on Oahu.

Rick Cross was about my age and in the same congregation in El Segundo. We'd hang out—going to movies, golfing, camping, and double dating. He was a bit of a geek; I wasn't. I was shy with the girls; he wasn't. A couple of times, I dated Witness girls who had younger sisters. We'd invite Rick to go along to accompany the younger sister. I'd be in the front seat, too shy even to hold my date's hand. Rick would be in the backseat making out with the younger sister, even though they'd just met an hour or two before.

Rick was now a pioneer, a term the Witnesses use for those in the full-time ministry work, done on a volunteer basis with no salary. Thus he was exempt from the draft and had probably tagged along with Denny and Woody to get a look at the prison life that he had missed out on. Just as well. I think we could have had a hard time protecting him from the Indians. I couldn't even protect him from Denny and Woody, who, having paid for the transportation costs and motel room for this trip, were now sending shivers through Rick by suggesting he pay for dinner that night.

I'd known Dewey, Woody's father-in-law, since I was about four years old. When he was young, he played professional baseball. His big story was that he was in the spring training camp the day Dizzy Dean first walked in, carrying only a suitcase.

During the visit, I informed Denny that the guard on duty was also a Marine Corp veteran of the battle of Iwo Jima. He said he'd go talk with him in a little while.

After about thirty minutes Denny excused himself, went to the other side of the room and introduced himself to Captain McKinney.

Although Denny told me later that they were not in the same marine division, he said nothing else of the content of their discussion, nor did I ever ask. I didn't really feel as if I had to. My chair was facing them from about twenty-five to thirty feet away. I watched them while continuing to chat with my three other visitors.

I could see Captain McKinney's heart go out to Denny when he realized he was one of his fellow marines from the battle of Iwo Jima. I wouldn't fully appreciate what I saw that day until years later, when I would not only read a book about the battle but also had viewed several TV documentaries on the subject. These would help me correlate events of the battle, which lasted more than five weeks, with the unembellished story Denny had told his son John and me in 1959, when we were fourteen years old.

Two marine divisions stormed the island first. The division Denny was in was held in reserve. The battle was so fierce and casualties so high that the reserves were called ashore and sent into battle on the fifth day. After Mount Suribachi was taken, the first two divisions were then sent to battle their way up to the island's far end, with one division going up one side and the other division up the other side of the island, with the reserves being sent up the middle.

Starting on the eighth day of the battle and lasting three weeks occurred the worst fighting on Iwo Jima, which produced the highest casualty rates per acre in Marine Corps history. This occurred in just a small area of this overall battle, in the area that the marines nicknamed the Meat Grinder and Turkey Knob, which overlooked the airfield. The Japanese defenders knew that every day or even hour they could hold onto these defensive positions, would afford some additional protection for their home islands from the B-29 bombers. The Americans needed this airfield for its fighter planes to be able to escort the bombers over Japanese homeland targets and as an emergency landing strip for damaged planes.

I didn't know if Captain McKinney was religious or not, but I would have bet everything I had that he held the Marine Corps sacred, as much as anything.

As these two swapped campaign stories, Captain McKinney appeared to finally realize that Denny was among the first to fall at the start of the battle for the Meat Grinder on the eighth day, in that small, deadly, and most hallowed area of all Marine Corps battles.

He would have known that the reserves, the 3rd Marine Division, was so tore up in this initial assault, that they were withdrawn and what was left of them then sent around this area to the west, to continue their advance to the islands northern end. Then the Division to the 3rds right, side shifted over to take over this assault, which Captain McKinney may or may not have been a part of, there was a 50/50 chance. But seeing Denny now standing before him and speaking with his deformed mouth and battle-scarred face was all too much for him. He began to visibly lose control of his emotions, eyes filling with tears. He struggled unsuccessfully to choke them back.

Before parting, Captain McKinney tenderly and warmly shook Denny's hand, eyes still wet and misty. Finally Denny appeared to ask Captain McKinney to "look after my boy Steve over there," or something like that, nodding in my direction. The captain then turned and briefly gave me a wet-eyed, somewhat embarrassed, forlorn look. Then despite rules to the contrary for guards, he had to leave his post for a short while to recompose himself.

Another one of the visiting room rules required guards not to take pictures for visitors, as they could not risk being distracted and having others pass contraband. But when Denny got ready to end our visit, before I could stop him, he bolted over and asked Captain McKinney if he'd snap a picture of all of us outside the visiting room. The captain could not say no to Denny. From that day on Captain McKinney never again picked on me or gave me another gig.

Woody, Denny, Dewey, Steve, and Rick outside the visiting room,
taken by Captain McKinney

Sometime afterward, a prisoner named Sandman returned to the prison camp. He had left the camp six or eight weeks earlier with a finger infection; he was sent somewhere for treatment. When he returned, he told us that he had been sent to a large prison that was also a hospital, in Springfield, Missouri. Others and I gathered around as he related his experiences and told us of some of the famous and infamous prisoners he had seen or met while there, including such men as Vito Genovese, Mickey Cohen, Captain John, and others.

He related about Captain John, the oldest federal prisoner in the federal prison system, a ninety-six-year-old black man imprisoned now for sixty-six years for robbing a stagecoach and killing some passengers around the turn of the century.

Sandman had only pricked his finger, but it had gotten infected. His treatment in Springfield included amputation of the finger. So he returned with one missing finger, but with some interesting stories.

Steve outside the visiting room

Early in December 1966, we began to get word from our brothers that worked in the administration building that this prison camp would be closing. No other details beyond this were available, such as where we might be transferred, which was what concerned most of us.

For many years, this prison had operated a sawmill, but it had burned down in the early sixties. A few large four-foot diameter logs were still adjacent to its burned out ruins during my time there.

The camp's current industry during my stay was for prisoners to go up into the Tonto National Forest and build tourist campsites with rock walls, picnic tables, and so forth. Using routers, brothers also carved Forest Service signs out of redwood, painting the carved lettering white.

The camp still had some bulldozers, two dump trucks, and a truck crane left from the former logging operations. Toward the end of our stay in this camp, Mr. Gott began using this equipment to dredge the cattails out of the reservoir that provided the camp's yellow water supply.

Blackburn was given another part-time job: driving the prisoners down into Tucson for their work-release jobs and then picking them up in the late afternoon. They actually paid him ten or fifteen cents an hour for this, the only one of us to receive any pay. He'd usually join me at the shop when he got back from the morning run.

Some days I was assigned to go with Mr. Gott and the guys dredging out the reservoir behind the dam. Mr. Gott let me operate a bulldozer and a clamshell bucket on the truck crane, which were my first experiences operating heavy equipment, other than forklifts on construction sites. At the time, I never imagined that in less than twenty years, I'd start acquiring heavy equipment and become a heavy equipment contractor.

That November and December, during recreation times after dinner, we mostly played flag football, sometimes in the snow. We'd gotten used to having plenty of time and opportunity for a variety of recreational activities in this prison camp. It was almost more like a summer camp in many ways. Things were about to totally change for most of us.

After this minimum-security facility prison did close, I would always have fond memories of Mt. Lemmon Prison Camp. I was reminded of these times especially after watching episodes of *Hogan's Heroes* on TV. The Witness boys pretty much had the run of this prison over the years, and the next one I was to do time in, and some of their high jinks were truly legendary. I mean, we might as well have some fun because we were already in prison, denied many of the meager privileges that even some of the worst criminals take for granted, such as pay for work, work release programs, half way houses, and now we were automatically being denied paroles as a group. One time the guards even took all the prisoners who wanted to go, to a University of Arizona football game, except us.

Most of these escapades I've forgotten key details of, so I won't attempt to relate them now. I just wish I could have contacted some of the brothers I did time with in order to get some of these stories straight. I will relate one though, that was set in motion just before I was transferred out of that prison camp and wouldn't learn of its conclusion until ten years later.

Just before hearing the camp would be closing, Mr. Burns had Blackburn and I build an exhaust hood over the kitchen's large commercial stove and griddle, the biggest I've ever seen. We were instructed to frame it with 2x lumber, then cover it with masonite and paint it silver. It should have been out of stainless steel, obviously, and there wasn't even an exhaust fan hooked up to it.

Since the kitchen was in use from the early morning until after the evening meal, we could only work at night, through to the start of the breakfast shift. Throughout the night, only two guards were on duty. They mostly stayed in the control room, located in the administration building, which was a little more than 100 yards north of the kitchen. One of the guards would occasionally perform a scheduled count of all the prisoners, including us, and patrol the camp at times. The other guard was always to remain in the control room, monitoring all the communications equipment; it was never to be left unattended.

One of the two guards was a big potbellied chipmunk-looking character with an insatiable sweet tooth. He came back to the kitchen once or twice a night and raided the camp's supply of ice cream. It was always under lock and key, but he used the backup key from the control room.

Blackburn and I couldn't stop talking about how cheesy we thought the hood was. We also wondered out loud about when was "Bucky," our nickname for the guard, going to show up again. On the wall nearby were one of many speakers used for broadcasting messages throughout the camp. It never dawned on us that the speakers were all part of a two-way system. Finally over the speakers came Bucky's stern voice, which rudely woke us up to this fact and concluded by ordering us to "get back to work!"

A short time later, the majority of the prisoners and I would be transferred to other correctional institutions, and only forty or so inmates remained, about half of those Witnesses. With so few left to watch, the two night shift guards both began to go down to the kitchen for ice cream late at night.

One of the brothers who worked in the control room during the day began noticing this. He was our camp clown, the same brother who'd had a picture of my wife in his picture frame when I first arrived. Knowing about how long the guards were spending away from the control room, and that it was never to be left unattended, he began sneaking over to it and manning it until just before the guards' return. While there, he began to make good use of his time by calling family and friends back home in Watts.

A healthy phone bill soon arrived. Busted, the two guards scolded him up one side and down the other, threatening him with serious disciplinary action. All the while, he was taking this with his head hanging. Finally, when the barrage began to subside, he was able to raise his head a bit and in true Colonel Hogan fashion asks, "By the way, how do you intend to explain to your superiors how I was able to do this?" With the camp's final closing near, and the two guards fearing a possible transfer to the Federal Bureau of Prisons equivalent of the Russian front, these two guards were then walked away from . . . left looking at each other.

Chapter 8

Camp Closes, off to the Big House

On Christmas Day of 1966, we were all in the cafeteria having a special holiday meal, when a medium-sized light blue bus pulled up and parked in view of where we were eating. It read US FEDERAL BUREAU OF PRISON on the side.

Sandman, though, said that the bus was from the prison hospital at Springfield, Missouri. He claimed that he had ridden in it at one point on his trip to Springfield. It had a distinctive look and was run down. I thought, *Can't a US government agency afford a better bus than this?* But then again, maybe they didn't think prisoners deserved a nice bus! That made more sense to me.

Later that day, we were informed that thirty-three prisoners would be leaving the next morning; the destination was not revealed. It was obvious that it would most likely be Springfield. Three guards accompanied the bus, and I believe Sandman even recognized two of them.

Of the thirty-three prisoners, thirty were Witnesses, and the other three were non-Witnesses selective service violators. So in the minds of some, we were a whole busload of draft dodgers. The group included all those who had come into the camp, starting with me. Our group was not scheduled to go before the parole board until March of 1967 or later. Those who had already been before the board, or who were scheduled to go before it in January, stayed behind and would later go to some other prison after January's parole board hearings. The cutoff point, then, was between Dave Brown and me. So the one week between when Dave Brown reported to the marshals, then me a week later, turned out to be the difference as to where each group would end up, for the most part. Later, those who stayed behind would eventually go to another minimum-security prison camp in Safford, Arizona. We would go to a major maximum-security prison that we would later learn had two of the most maximum-security sections in the United States at the time, according to the guards that would eventually be my new work supervisors. I was to hear later, from other sources, that Springfield was considered the most maximum-security prison in the United States.

We weren't really supposed to know where we were going until we arrived there, but our brothers who worked in the office were able to confirm what Sandman told us.

The next morning, we turned in our bedding and work clothes, dressing in our khakis and blue jackets as instructed. I wished I could have kept my green jacket with the yellow stripe down the back. I was able to keep the boots that I had well broken in, the only part of the traveling outfit that I was comfortable in. The boots were notched in the heel, so we could be tracked should we escape.

Upon getting on the bus, after saying our farewells to our brothers staying behind, about twenty-two of them, we found the inside of the bus in even worse condition than the outside. Previous prisoners hadn't been very kind to it.

The driver's area had two seats with a wire cage separating the prisoners. About one-third of the way back in the bus, among the prisoners, was another wire cage for the third guard to watch from. About halfway back was a toilet with no walls or doors, totally in view of everyone. The bus seats only extended about two-thirds of the way from front to back. The back of the bus was open to provide room for stretchers. In this back part of the bus, we found a stack of old-fashioned folding wood chairs, thus providing seating for all of us.

Shortly before boarding, our brothers in the office were again able to find out why we were going to a prison so far away. Apparently that prison, having so many maximum-security prisoners, needed more minimum-security workers in key positions where security classification was an issue. Therefore, when they found out that a minimum-security prison camp was to be closed, they specifically requested a busload of us.

As I write this, I feel bad that I can't recall everyone's name or face, and I apologize for this. The names I do remember of those who stayed behind were Norris, Bob Clark, Blackburn, Dave Brown, Mike Brown, the Brown from Watts who had the picture of my wife, Salgado, Martinez, and Boone. There are a dozen or more others that I can't recall right now. I can recall the faces of some, but I don't remember whether they went with us or stayed. Vargas, Maguga, the Nelsons, and Abaer are some I remember, but I don't remember which place they went.

Of the thirty Witnesses who boarded the bus with me, the ones I remember are Joe Sedor, the four brothers from Oregon and Washington, Jim Stevenson, Freddy Satler, Kuburka, Howe, and Mel Littlefield.

As the bus left, Kuburka was waving by twisting his wrist with his trademark hand gesture, fist closed, but with little finger and thumb extended. I wouldn't see others use this gesture until 1978 or 1979 in Hawaii, when it came into widespread use, along with the phrase "Shaka Brother." Just this gesture is still in wide spread use there up to the present time.

We left in the morning, December 26, 1966, driving past the eastern side of Tucson, then past David Mothem Airfield, and then east toward New Mexico. All day, the bus seemed to be driving across New Mexico. Some of us were able to fold some chairs up in the back of the bus and sleep on the floor.

I think it was just after dark that we crossed into Texas and checked into a federal prison in La Tuna, Texas. We stayed there two nights. The large shower room was disgusting. We had to avoid stepping in big globs of semen on the floor.

When leaving La Tuna, we crossed into Oklahoma and the bus drove all day long across the state. We ate lunches prepared for us by the prison we had just left. The bus made stops for the guards to use the restroom so they wouldn't have to use the one among the prisoners. We were all without handcuffs, completely unrestrained inside the bus, which had barred windows of course.

Kuburka, the shortest among us, was roly-poly and always jolly. He was also one of those that the prison camp had a psychiatrist examine. Lying on the floor, he noticed that some previous prisoners had worked loose the metal sidewalls that separated the bus interior from the luggage compartment. A bunch of us sitting in wooden chairs screened him from view of the guards, so he finished the job and went down into the luggage compartment. He brought out an entire box of all our prison files, which were destined for our new home. He then pulled his file and began to read it and the files of others.

He couldn't stop laughing and giggling as he read his and the others' psychiatric evaluations, which were meant only for the eyes of prison officials. He made such a scene that I was afraid he'd tip off the guard and get us all thrown into the nearest county jail for attempted bus escape. I urged him to put the files back, but then I couldn't help myself. I dared him while he was down there to open the luggage door at the next red light, get out, and go up and knock on the main door to see what the guards would do. He wisely opted for just returning the files and sealing up the opening.

After dark, we finally arrived at our next stop, the federal prison in El Reno, Oklahoma. From what we saw, this appeared to be a major prison.

After processing in, they took us to the cafeteria for an excellent meal and then to an old-style empty cellblock, single-man cells three tiers high. I was put in one on the second tier. Across from the tiers was what I believe is called a "gun gallery," a catwalk that's about fifteen feet from but parallel with the tiers, for the guards to patrol from while inspecting the cells. I couldn't tell in the dark if they were armed or not.

The next morning, there was a tasty breakfast. Their milk was the best I've ever had. They apparently had their own dairy, so I have to give El Reno and Florence Detention Center my culinary five bars rating for best food of the nine places I was held. The lowest rating goes to the two Los Angeles county jails.

Best of all in the cafeteria, we were able to visit with a few of our brothers imprisoned in this federal prison. They informed us that there were about forty-five of them. We were only able to visit a short time, as we were being rushed to get on the bus and back on the road again.

Chapter 9

Springfield and a New Name

Finally we arrived at the Springfield, Missouri, Medical Center for Federal Prisoners in the afternoon. The sun was out, but it was cold and there was snow on the ground.

As we processed in, I was given a number and told I would only be a number from then on. I was harshly informed that because we were all convicted criminals, we had lost all our civil rights and didn't even have the right to use our names anymore—that only my number would be called. Then I was rudely reminded again, for the hundredth time, that we were not in this prison to be "rehabilitated," but to be punished instead.

They had us turn in all our clothes we arrived in, which was all we had. They then issued us each one pair of white coveralls and some kind of slippers or tennis shoes and nothing else. There weren't any socks, underwear, or anything else.

They then put us separately in solitary cells, each of which had a solid steel door with a small site glass window, with one blanket and a pillow. These cell door windows were about 3" high by 10" wide, just enough for the guards to make inspections. There were no cells in this prison that had traditional prison bars. Each cell also had a heavy steel paned window, with the glass missing in one pane for ventilation. Trouble was, it was winter, and ventilation was not what we needed. We were naked under our coveralls, with nothing to use to block up the windows. For eight days we stayed in solitary, where it was cold even during the day, much less at night. For people they requested, this was a frosty reception. I think they requested us just to have some draft dodgers to mess with.

They'd let us out for meals to walk to the cafeteria. The other prisoners called us new prisoners "fish." Some would stare at all of us when entering the cafeteria with lust in their eyes.

I noticed that most prisoners wore blue prison clothes, while others wore surplus navy khakis. Guess which ones we'd get to wear. Yes, we were issued khakis, but with surplus green lightweight military jackets. The jacket didn't keep me very warm, and I was never comfortable in it, not like the one I had to leave in Mt. Lemmon.

After the eight days, we were assigned to the camp section of the prison and given our work assignments. Again I was to work in the prison carpenter shop.

The camp section was a large two-story concrete building with a paned window above every bunk. This camp building was also within the gun towers and the double row of chain link perimeter fencing, topped by triple concertina razor wire.

We were to learn later that all federal prisons have a camp section where "minimum-security" prisoners are usually housed. All these other prison camps, which only house minimum-security prisoners, are outside the prison walls.

Springfield's camp was the only one in the federal system that was different, for it was located inside the gun towers. Thus we had not only minimum-security prisoners but "medium-security" and "maximum-security" prisoners sleeping next to or near us, some in for up to forty-five years, for all sorts of crimes. Those prisoners had served most of their time and were relative "short-timers," prison jargon meaning they were to be released shortly. In the case of some with long sentences, they could be in the camp a year or two before release.

The camp had three sections with single bunks, set up military style. Two smaller sections were on the first floor, with the control center or guards' station between them. The second floor was one big room, and it was where most of the bunks were located. All together, there may have been two hundred or more bunks in the camp.

Although we were never officially informed, we assumed that prison officials were taking advantage of this prison's unique camp sections situation by easing their medium—and maximum-security prisoners back into society, by putting them in with us minimum security prisoners shortly before they were released.

After getting moved into the camp, we were to get to know thirty-five Witnesses that were already in this camp. They were mostly from the Midwest and eastern United States. With the thirty of us, that totaled sixty-five. I believe there were about twelve hundred inmates in the entire prison, about two hundred of them in the camp.

The second floor of the camp had four rows of bunks. The first and fourth rows were against the west and east walls. The second and third rows were running down the middle of the building, with a three-foot-high tile wall between them. The heads of the bunks were up against the tile wall. In the middle of the west wall, two sets of stairs came up from each side of the control center/guards' station. Where the two sets of stairs came up, between them were two sets of sinks and toilets and a large shower room.

For me to get to my bunk, I'd enter through one of two entrance doors into the first floor of the camp, proceed to the control center, and walk up one of two sets of stairs to the second floor. I'd proceed east through an opening in the middle of the three-foot tile wall to the corridor between the third and fourth rows of bunks, turn left (or north), and walk about halfway up the corridor to my bunk on the left in the third row.

Again, Joe Sedor bunked next to me on my right side. He was assigned to work in the electric shop, which was in the same building as the carpenter shop, adjacent to the west side of the camp. When I reported to my work assignment in the carpentry shop, I was impressed. There was some nice woodworking machinery there.

We were to have two guard supervisors there, instead of one like in Tucson. And just like in Tucson with Mr. Burns, I would be fortunate to have two more guards that I would hold in high esteem to this day, Mr. Long and Mr. Luxton.

The prisoners that were already in the shop upon my arrival were Gordon Steen, a thin, seedy-looking lowlife career criminal in his mid to late thirties.

Then there was a prisoner in his forties named Connors or Conway, something like that. For purposes of the story, I'll call him Conway. He was somewhat dignified-looking. He claimed he'd been a professional golfer at one time, winning second place in the 1952 Western Open, held in St. Louis, Missouri, that year. He was in jail for being part of a stolen car ring that was exporting them to South America. He'd give me golf lessons in the shop with a stick of wood. He wasn't a highly skilled carpenter but was a very good sheet metal man.

About twenty-six years old, Jodi Ray was another inmate in the shop. He spoke with a Southern accent, and he'd been in a surprising number of different prisons and jails in the South. Everybody liked Jodi. He could simply be described as a young southern "good old boy." In the camp, he bunked in row two, just opposite me, the heads of our beds only separated by the three-foot-high tile wall. We'd also be teamed up on many projects over the next almost eleven months. He was in for interstate auto theft, claiming he was just an innocent passenger.

The first project I was sent on was with Conway and Jodi, outside the prison walls on the east side of the joint, past the old prison barn, and into the old farm fields no longer under cultivation. A new guard's pistol firing range building was almost complete, so we were assigned to finish it.

Mr. Luxton would accompany us through the back gate. He had to stay with any medium-security prisoners outside the prison walls, and that applied to Jodi. Except for Mr. Luxton, we were all searched going out and then coming back in. He would drive us to the project site, and on the way, he'd stop at the barn. Jodi had a couple of groundhog traps out back, and he checked them regularly.

Once at the job site, Mr. Luxton would usually take off and leave Jodi in my custody until it was time to go to lunch, even though he wasn't supposed to.

Because of the cold weather and snow, our free time in the camp wasn't like Tucson at all. The outer recreation area adjacent to and for the exclusive use of the camp prisoners was kept closed. I believe the main prison yard in the center of the prison complex was also closed when snow was on the ground. The only recreation area open to us was the gym, which was located above the cafeteria. During the week, it was open in the evening after dinner. Some of the brothers from Tucson and I decided we'd try it; maybe we could play basketball or volleyball or something.

When we got there, we quickly realized this was a mistake, but we couldn't leave. Coming or going could only happen every half hour, so we had to stay almost another half hour.

The problem was that dangerous-looking maximum-security prisoners dominated the games, and the bleachers where we sat to wait to leave appeared to be a big pickup spot for lovers, with plenty of guys checking us out, romances flourishing all around. The whole place gave us the creeps. When we could leave, we did and never returned.

I then began to think about a hobby, something to do to help pass time. The prison had a hobby shop with some supplies available, and they'd make special orders. I decided to take up oil painting, something I could do right at my bunk.

With some money from my family, mainly my aunt, I was able to purchase some basic supplies. I began to look around for something to paint a picture of. I searched for a suitable subject in a number of magazines available in the camp. Some of the first articles that caught my attention were pictures from the Indian Ocean islands called the Seychelles. As I read, I began to imagine how nice it would be to experience places like that. Most anywhere would be better than where I was living at the time, the most maximum-security prison in the United States . . . Somehow those circumstances combined and were so powerful that even today I have a desire to go there one day and learn more about that place. But at the time, I didn't find a picture that I thought was a suitable subject for me to paint.

I finally found some pictures from the islands of Micronesia, also places I'd never seen or heard of before. I settled on a picture taken on the island of Ponape. It showed a native man throwing a net off the bow of an outrigger canoe, with a beautiful rocky mountain in the background. I lightly sketched the scene on a piece of canvas board. Then I started painting. As I worked, I never imagined that in less than four years, I'd end up going to this island to help build a kingdom hall and end up spending the majority of my life there.

After I'd been in Springfield for a month or two, Conway was released, and he left me his carpenter shop Korean War-era US Air Force bomber jacket that he'd been using. Both Steen and Jodi already had one. There were maybe eight or ten in the entire prison, in possession of shop prisoners who had to work outside. These were by far the best jackets in the place. I was always wondering if some mean con was going to try to take it away from me.

The weather began to let up. The groundhogs began to get active, and Jodi began to catch some in his traps. Jodi would put a groundhog in a toolbox, and when going back into the prison and being searched, Mr. Luxton would take the toolbox through, as he wasn't searched.

I thought because it was so cute, Jodi was going to keep it as a pet in the shop. Later I thought he was brewing up some coffee in an electric coffeepot in our tool room. Instead he was deep-frying the groundhog. I was very disappointed with him.

Sometimes when Mr. Luxton was driving us through the farm fields, a jackrabbit would take off down the road ahead of us. He'd gun the truck, chasing the rabbit until it jumped into the high grass on the side of the road. He'd slide the truck to a stop, and Jodi and I would jump off, chasing the rabbit. It was easy to chase the rabbit down in the three-foot high grass. It had to jump high, and we'd easily overtake it, clubbing it with scrap wood on one of its jumps. I had no problem with the rabbit ending up in the coffeepot.

My whole time in prison, I never saw another prisoner who had a better relationship with the guards than Jodi did. Our guards would do things for him that I couldn't imagine them doing for someone else. An incident in the cafeteria highlights this.

When going through the chow line, main courses such as meat or desserts were always distributed one to each inmate. As for some type of potatoes or vegetable, you could dish up as much as you wanted. A guard was always present to supervise the chow line.

One day ice cream was being served for dessert. Each inmate was apportioned one scoop in a small bowl. Jodi put his ice cream on his tray, but then the guard turned his head, distracted for a moment. Jodi grabbed another ice cream and tried to hide it behind his cup. When he got to the end of the line, the guard said, "Hold it there." Reaching over, he said, "I'll take that," removing the extra ice cream from behind the cup. He went on to say, "And just for that, I'll take the other one too," also taking the first ice cream off the tray.

This was just too much for Jodi. He went off, saying, "Well, goddamn it! You can just have the whole thing!" Then throwing the tray with all the food in the guard's face, he immediately got thrown into the "hole," solitary confinement.

Mr. Long and Mr. Luxton immediately went to bat for Jodi. Going to the offended guard, they smoothed things out with him and got him to drop his complaint. Jodi was released from the hole.

Mr. Long and Mr. Luxton were both Baptist deacons. Like most, they didn't like Witnesses, but they never showed it to us. They were always kind or professional toward us. We could talk to and visit with them. We all bonded with them, everyone in the shop.

They both had the same hobby, bass fishing. In addition, they each had a part-time business tying flies and making other types of fishing lures.

They could talk at length about lures, flies, and fishing with Steen and Jodi. We others would just listen in, feeling like amateurs, not wanting to contribute to the conversation for fear of saying something stupid. But when we asked dumb questions, they'd answer as best they could.

By this time, we had two more Witnesses in the shop, Tom Vodopich from Michigan, and Don from the Springfield area. Another brother came into the shop eventually, shortly before my release. I can't remember his name, only that he was from one of the northern Midwestern states like Michigan, and that he was a big good-looking blond kid.

Later, Don would have the misfortune of being the only Witness I was incarcerated with whose wife would leave him while he was in jail.

On one occasion talking with our guards, I told them that as a kid in 1952, I remembered seeing on television a news report about a prison riot, and I'd thought it occurred here in Springfield.

Mr. Luxton confirmed that yes; there was a big riot in 1952 in Springfield. Then he went on to relate in detail and at length that he was a young prison guard then, part of the group that re-stormed the prison. The rioting prisoners had taken control of a couple of cellblocks, including the one that had all the queens. That was apparently the goal of the takeover, a big sex party with the queens, who played the female roll and needed to be sequestered in their own separate cellblock. I was told by Mr. Luxton that this type of control was necessary to cut down on love triangle stabbings. I was about to personally see and experience some of these related problems shortly, almost costing me my life.

He related that when the group of guards broke in, they began busting the heads of all those they encountered. At first, some prisoners were prepared to fight at the cellblock entrance with brooms and mops. In short order, they were all rendered unconscious. Others continued right up to the last moment with their sex party, until they were beaten bloody and unconscious.

As Mr. Luxton moved through the cellblock, he came across a prisoner he knew and didn't think had had any part in the riot (many didn't) hiding under his bunk in his cell. He stayed with him to prevent other guards from beating him senseless. He told us that three inmates were beaten to death by overzealous guards. He also described in detail many of the sexual scenes he saw, but I will not retell them. The same goes for the many other things of that nature that he observed in his career as a prison guard, which he related at one time or another.

Jodi and Steen had their own prison stories. They had both been in several prison farms in either Alabama or Arkansas, probably both. Two of the prison farms they had both done time in. They began telling me how bad the places were, how prisoners were forced to work long hours in the farm fields, sometimes shackled but supervised by sadistic guards or trustees, some on horseback. They would shoot and kill prisoners for even minor infractions, like slacking off, talking back to guards, or even giving a dirty look. Then they would bury them right on the farm in unmarked graves and inform their next of kin that they'd died from pneumonia or something like that. I forgot the name of one of these farms, but the other was Tucker's Farm.

Steen would then go off on us Witnesses, saying that we had it easy in the federal prisons, that we'd be peeing our pants and crying for our mommies if we ever had to do time in a prison like Tucker's Farm. Steen took great pleasure in telling us all this. Of course, I didn't agree with that, but I didn't want to spoil his fun, so I let him run his mouth. Over time, Steen would brag about some of his criminal exploits, usually ones he got away with. He never did tell us what crime he was in jail for then. I assumed that it may have been such a Mickey Mouse crime that he was embarrassed to tell us. I'm reminded of an inmate I was in with in the old Los Angeles county jail: he got caught stealing a $1.25 chicken and was the laughingstock of the cellblock.

What Steen would confess to us was that he was proud of his stint in the US military at a supply depot, where he had a talent for selling military equipment on the black market.

Another story of Steen's criminal exploits that he relished relating to us was how late one night he was traveling somewhere in Tennessee or Kentucky, and he stopped for gas at an isolated station. His car wouldn't restart because his battery was shot. The station owner had the right one on hand, but he wanted more for it than Steen thought was fair. He had no choice, though. He paid and was able to continue his journey. Several months later, he was going back the same route late one night. The station was closed and deserted, so he drove past it a ways and pulled off the road. He walked back and burned the station down to get even over the high battery cost. Of course, the way he told the story, he was some sort of consumer affairs hero.

But my brothers and I were disappointed with him over this. We had gotten close to him and had bonded with him as a fellow worker. We didn't want to think he was that kind of guy. What we needed to do was pinch ourselves and remember where we were, and that most everyone here was some sort of criminal.

That was hard to do sometimes. Take my experience. While incarcerated, I talked at one time or another with hundreds of convicts, and I can say I never met one I didn't like. They all had good sides and something likeable about them, a potential for good.

One scripture reminded me that many of the early Christians had at one time been people who practiced many of the things that these inmates were in prison for, but they were able to change when becoming Christians. However we had no illusions; we knew the vast majority of mankind would never respond to the Kingdom message, including our fellow inmates.

Many of them would express their surprise that the US Government would actually put people like us in jail with them. They thought that the Constitution guaranteed Freedom of Religion.

Steen and Jodi were helpful in educating me in the do's and don'ts of prison life. They explained to me that prison killings usually occurred for one of the following three reasons: gambling debts, homosexual love triangles, or snitching another prisoner out to the guards.

Jodi would go out of his way to warn me about something he thought might get me in trouble. For example, at one point I had a cheap six-dollar Timex watch. The wristband broke, so I began to leave it in a slide-out drawer that was secured by a combination paddle lock, which every prisoner had on the underside of his bunk. One day it was stolen out of my locked drawer. Figuring it must be the work of a master lock picker, and knowing that Jodi being so connected to all the cons would probably know this person's identity. I thus began pestering him to reveal this person to me so I could try to get my watch back. Up to this point, Jodi had not really admitted one way or the other whether he knew who the person was. But with a resigned look, as if he were dealing with an idiot, he takes a shoelace and said, "Come with me. I want to show you something."

I followed as he led me out of the shop, back into the camp, upstairs, and right back to my bunk. He then with his Southern accent said, "Watch this." He wrapped the shoelace around the lock knob and pulled it like a top. It dropped open instantly.

I knew the combination and I couldn't open it anywhere near that fast. Then he went on to explain that many of these inmates could do this also. It didn't take a safecracker or lock picker.

He'd made his point clear with this demonstration.

Then he asked me what I planned on doing should I find out who took the watch. Had I thought about the trouble that might result if I confronted the person? What was the broken watch worth? Was it worth risking serious trouble over?

He went on to say that he did know who took the watch, but that he wasn't going to tell me, because I'd just end up bringing trouble upon myself—that he was only trying to protect me. He said all this in his colorful Southern way.

I must have not been thinking the situation through thoroughly. He was absolutely right and I had to admit it.

I had taken a similar view in another situation not involving me. In that one, a brother across from my bunk was getting cold at night because the prisoner next to him was opening up the window above his own bunk all the way, even though it was still winter. The brother began asking others, including me, what he should do about the problem. Should he confront the guy and ask him to close the window? Or complain to the guards?

This particular convict who opened his window looked intimidating. Regardless, some of the cons had not much else left in life except their prison dignity. To allow a young prisoner, especially one like us to tell them anything, much less complain about something that they were doing, would be insulting. You didn't do things like that to these people, especially involving the guards in any matter adverse to them.

Instead, I suggested he go to the guards' station and request another one or two blankets or sleep in his clothes or jacket if necessary, but not to confront his neighbor. This was the practical solution when considering that our neighbors were oftentimes potentially dangerous criminals.

A few months later, another more serious situation would develop, and a number of our brothers chose an opposite solution. It involved one of our brothers that came from Tucson with us. This brother was a bit on the effeminate side. To top it off, he began visiting a group of prisoners regularly on the first floor of the camp. Apparently, he was enjoying the attention.

I had no knowledge of any of this until a group of brothers on the second floor asked my opinion as to what they should do about it. They were convinced these prisoners were befriending the brother only for the purpose of sex or rape. They were talking to me, I realized, to ask me to join in with a group of them to go downstairs with a show of force, to tell these convicts to leave this brother alone.

I just couldn't believe what I was hearing. Worst of all, these brothers all looked about as far away from intimidating as is possible. I couldn't imagine any self-respecting convict who would tolerate such an ultimatum from this group. I was sure it was guaranteed trouble.

I politely advised them that under no circumstances should they confront these convicts. Instead, they should have a serious talk with the brother about their concerns, reminding him that he was putting not only his own safety but also the safety of other brothers at risk.

Some may try to come to his aid, as they did during the second attack on Martinez back in Tucson, should worse come to worse. And this brother also needed to be reminded of the scriptural counsel about bad association, which was a touchy balancing act here, given that we had to live with these people.

These reminders should have been enough for any Witness with a head on his shoulders. A night or two later though, this group again assembled near where I was talking with Sedor and Stevenson. They had a couple of additional brothers with them by then.

To make a long story short, they claimed to have talked to this one brother but he didn't respond, so they were now going to talk with the convicts.

We implored them not to do this. We related to them what the guards in Tucson were afraid might break out, as an aftermath of the last incident involving Martinez. We were fortunate there that the Indians weren't united. This group of convicts they were going to confront didn't need to be united. Any one of them could be dangerous.

They had their minds made up and didn't want to listen to us, so off they went downstairs. There were about ten or more of them. After about thirty or forty seconds, the group came scurrying back up the stairs like a pack of dogs with their tails between their legs, obviously shaken.

We asked what happened. They said that as they rounded the corner into the smallest dormitory on the first floor, all the convicts in it were holding knives and chains. They turned around immediately, without saying a word, and left.

The next morning in the shop, I talked with Jodi about the incident. He said the cons had gotten wind of the impending visit and were thus prepared, that it was a good thing none of these brothers said a word and instead left immediately.

I myself would later make the mistake of unnecessarily associating with convicts and barely avoided trouble. I'll relate more about that later in the next chapter.

Chapter 10

Prison Characters, Icons, and Killings

We were forced to live and work with convicts in prison, so we really couldn't avoid them. Some liked us, and we could talk and visit with them at length. A few we could share the Kingdom Good News with. Others, especially longtime cons, liked associating with us in general. I guess that after decades of being locked up with run-of-the-mill convicts, we were a refreshing change of pace for some of them, or something like that.

One of them was a con we only knew as Wolf. When we came into camp, Wolf had been in prison for forty-five years and was now finally a short-timer, residing with us in the camp section. Of all the many cons that befriended us, I think Wolf got closer to more Witnesses than any of the others did.

The word we heard on his crime was that he was one of two guys considered to have started the modern era of bank robbery in the early 1920s, in Oklahoma or Texas. In early 2007, nearly forty years after meeting him, I'd see Wolf profiled on a History Channel TV program dealing with notorious criminals of the 1920s. I caught the last part of his segment and saw his picture, a mug shot from 1922. Forty-five years later in Springfield, he hadn't changed as much as most. He'd aged well in prison, still having most of his black hair, now mixed with gray. I never could remember his real name from that program; I only knew him by his nickname.

I've often wondered if he was the Wolf that was later portrayed in the Hollywood movie, `Escape from Alcatraz'. In it a con known as Wolf, attempts to shank Clint Eastwood's character, Morris, in that prisons Main Yard. He could have been, because after that embarrassing escape and Alcatrazs closing, many of its inmates were now here in Springfield.

Once Wolf got within two or three months of his release date, he progressively became more and more of a nervous wreck. Imagine being incarcerated for nearly half a century, old now, and being released to a vastly changed world. I would think that anxiety would wrack anybody. I asked him if he had any relatives he could go to, and his reply was none that he could go live with.

Back in Tucson, Blackburn had told me about an old con he ran into in county jail, Folsom Phil. He had become institutionalized after being imprisoned for so long. Upon his release and realizing the real world was not for him, he decided to go back to prison. Wanting to upgrade his next prison experience to a federal facility, yet not wanting to hurt anyone, he customized his next crime to guarantee his destination. He poured a bucket of tar into a US postal mailbox, which is a federal crime. Thus Blackburn found himself in L.A. County Jail with Folsom Phil, both waiting for a transfer to a federal prison.

When Wolf's release day arrived, a lot of us, including myself, shook his hand and wished him well. I've always wondered if he made it on the outside or if he came back somehow.

Our guards told us a related story about Captain John and his release. He was America's last stagecoach-robbing killer. Captain John was obviously his nickname also. We never bothered to get nosy and ask the nicknamed inmates their real names. If we asked the guards, they'd probably only know their number.

After he had been in for about sixty years, his release day finally arrived. He'd been in prison since before the invention of the airplane. He had absolutely no family left, nowhere to go. All his friends were here in prison. As the guards were driving him to the bus station to go who knows where, he broke down, pleading with them to take him back to the prison. They did, and he was allowed to live out the rest of his life in Springfield, with all his friends. That showed me that in the Federal Bureau of Prisons, there are people with a heart.

I met Captain John in his sixty-seventh year in prison, talked with him for about five minutes, and shook his hand twice. He was a fragile, kindly, ninety-seven-year-old African American inmate. He was tall and thin. Even to this day, I believe he's the oldest person I've ever had any contact with. I'll talk more about him later, because that was a noteworthy day for me, not just because of Captain John, but because of two other special inmates I'd meet and talk with that day as well.

My work assignments took me to most all parts of this prison at one time or another. One notorious prisoner I saw a number of times while traveling through the tunnels that connected the various buildings was Mickey Cohen. He was a West Coast mobster, vicious killer, and right hand man of Bugsy Segal in the late 1940s, when Bugsy was founding organized crimes involvement with Las Vegas casinos. Growing up in L.A., I'd heard his name on TV newscasts and seen his name and picture in the newspapers many times, so I immediately recognized him in person.

The story I got on him in the joint was that as a big shot prisoner in Atlanta Federal Prison, he was throwing his weight around and telling other prisoners what to do. Then a con got out of a long stay in solitary confinement, with a lot of pent-up rage against the world. In the same cellblock together then, he took offense at something Mickey said and beat him up. Then he threw him off the third tier of a three-story cellblock, almost totally crippling him.

Whenever I'd run across Mickey, he was using a walker and was very slow moving. He was busted up bad and barely able to get around with his walker. He'd also only move through the tunnels during off-hours, when the general prison population was not going to or from work or the cafeteria for meals. But more telling was that a guard always accompanied him. I saw this half a dozen times or more. I was to learn the reason for this. The Mob had a contract out on him, and it was good even here in this prison.

Also present in a hospital ward was Vito Genovese, the former self-proclaimed boss of bosses of the five New York crime families, slowly dying of cancer, I was told. He was to die in Springfield more than a year after my release. One of our brothers that came from Tucson with our group, Mel Littlefield, was Vito's nurse in the hospital ward where he stayed. He'd many times relate to me some of his experiences and conversations he had with him.

On one occasion Mel told me had to take Vito to the visiting room in a wheelchair. When he got there, Mickey Cohen was already in it, visiting with what he described as two absolutely beautiful women—"Mob gun molls," in Mel's own words.

Another prisoner that I saw a number of times in the tunnels up by the hospital section was a prisoner with obvious mental problems. He'd been brought down by three shots from a law enforcement officer, who then stood over him and reloaded his pistol twice more, unloading it into him. The officer shot him fifteen times, with eight of those shots to the head, but he lived. He was obviously missing some brain cells.

Most of the different sections of the prison had basements. The tunnels that connected them all together were at basement level but occasionally had high windows aboveground. You were always walking with your head below ground level, so I've referred to them as tunnels, which is not entirely correct. Only the camp, the shops, and the maximum-security cellblocks did not have basements. At least I never saw any basements below the maximum-security cellblocks.

One day after work, as I was returning to the camp, I noticed a new short, fat young man sitting with some brothers. He had an extremely nervous, scared look on his face. His name was Jerry, and he had just arrived in the camp building.

He was in for selling uppers, pills for keeping truck drivers awake at a truck stop where he worked somewhere in Kentucky or Tennessee. He only had a short sentence, like three or four months, but he was terrified to be in this prison. He'd heard about us Witnesses and stuck like glue to us for security. We all got close to him. It took him a couple of months to relax and get used to prison and widen out and associate with a few non-Witness prisoners.

A few months after his release, we got word about Jerry from the guards. He had taken a job as a truck driver. Driving a load of explosives late one night, he got tired and not wanting to risk jail again by being involved with uppers, he pulled to the side of the road to sleep. A drunk driver plowed into him, causing his rig to explode, which killed him. This news saddened all of us.

I was supposed to go before the parole board by March 1967. Instead, I didn't appear until May, which was one month past the date I would actually qualify for parole. That's not supposed to happen. Because of all the parole denials for Witnesses, I assumed that I was to be next. I would have to wait and see to be sure.

Spring was here and baseball season was in full swing, even here in prison. The sun was out, so I thought I would go check out the main prison yard. I hadn't been there yet.

The prison had a nice softball field. Inmates were beginning to choose up sides for a game. *Hey, just like we used to do on the school playground while I was growing up,* I thought like an idiot. Some of the cons asked if I wanted to play, so I said okay. I would soon find out that there were big differences between this place and grade school recess. A big African American prisoner picked me for his team. He played first base and put me in left field. There weren't enough gloves to go around, but it didn't matter because it was softball. The only thing I felt strange about at the time was that I was the only camp prisoner dressed in khakis on the field. All the others wore prison blues and were maximum-security prisoners.

Another oddity was that instead of left and right field fences, there were left and right field cellblocks or hospital wards. The prison/hospital complex surrounded the entire main yard.

Our team was up to bat when the game started. I didn't bat the first inning, being farther down the lineup. There was only one set of dugout benches along the first base side. As we took the field, the other team occupied the benches we'd just left.

Out in left field with my arm long since healed, I was able to warm up enough before the other teams first batter was up. Our team got their first hitter out and when their second batter came up, I moved up a bit. Sure enough, he hit a line drive base hit right at me. I fielded it and fired the long throw to first base, just in time for the out. The guy seemed dumbfounded and shocked at first, but then he started getting mad, pacing back and forth as he began talking to himself like a crazy person. My big first baseman was just tickled pink by the play, laughing at first and unable to stop smiling as he watched the guy fuming along the sidelines and working himself up.

When the third out came, the two teams started switching places. The batter I threw out was one of the last to leave the benches, still very upset. He didn't even get halfway to the pitcher's mound, on his way to his position in left field, when he turned around and

Steve Nix

hurriedly came back at me, now sitting on a bench. Angrily, he began asking me why I did that. I tried to remind him calmly that this was a baseball game and that is what I was supposed to do. That was the wrong answer! He worked himself into a rage and was now yelling in my face.

I was thinking, *Oh, great! I'm about to be attacked by a psychopath! Well, this is the place to run into them.* Just then, my big first baseman said to the guy in a long-suffering, sarcastic tone of voice, "Get out to left field!" The enraged con gave a nervous glance at him and started heading to his position. When about fifty feet away, he turned again and started coming back at me again even more enraged, screaming now. This time the first baseman just gave him a disgusted look and barked, "HEY," pointing to left field. After another nervous glance at the first baseman, the guy then finally went all the way out to his position. Apparently this play and its aftermath instantly endeared me to my new team captain. He warmly came over and asked where I had played ball before, and what position had I usually played. I told him shortstop in high school. He told me that was good because he wanted me a little bit closer to him, where he could keep a watch over me. He then immediately switched me to that position. I got on base two or three times during that game. Growing up, I played Little League, Babe Ruth, and high school baseball. For the first time when on base, not only did I have to keep my eye on the various infield positions for pickoff plays, but I had to keep track of the left fielder out of the corner of my eye as well. Also, I wouldn't have to worry about getting spiked covering second base in this game; getting shiged would be a concern though.

One of our guys, an older man, got a hit and in his hurry to get to first base, his artificial leg flew off. He hopped the rest of the way to first base. As he was strapping his leg back on, a con next to me on the bench turned to me and said, "That guy's been real handy smuggling stuff past the guards!"

By the time the game was over, my new first baseman and I had bonded. He pleaded with me to be sure to come back again next Saturday for another game—and not to worry about that other guy. I thanked him and we shook hands as we parted. Despite this interesting, enjoyable, and unique game, I realized that it wouldn't be wise to risk encountering the other team's left fielder if he truly

76

was a psycho. So despite getting along great with everyone else, I never returned for another game. In fact, it would turn out to be the last time I ever played baseball.

I kept my eye out for that character, especially in the cafeteria, but also anywhere else I traveled in the prison. I never did see him again, and I later suspected that he could have been transferred somewhere else or released.

As I walked into the shop for work on Monday morning, Mr. Long and Mr. Luxton both had unusually warm smiles for me. They deliberately came out of their office just to sidle up to me where I was sitting on a workbench, which was very unusual for them. They began telling me that they heard what happened to me in the "main yard" on Saturday. I was surprised and asked how they knew that. They said that as they were putting their uniforms on that morning, the guards who had been on duty in the yard on Saturday told them all about it. Apparently the guards had a locker room and that incident was the big topic of conversation there that morning. It wasn't the psychopath or me who aroused the guards' attention so much as it was the big first baseman that had diffused the situation with looks and a few words.

Mr. Luxton then asked me if I knew who the first baseman was. I had no idea and I told him so. He went on to tell me his name, which I forgot almost immediately. He continued, saying that not too many years before "he had been listed by J. Edgar Hoover as the most dangerous prisoner in the whole United States Federal Prison system," and that that was why he was in Springfield. He said he used to have a "five-man order" on him at all times. He explained that it was a prison term meaning his cell door could never be opened unless five big "goon squad" guards were present.

Mr. Luxton then related that one day the five guards showed up at his cell to escort him to the hospital for some reason. The big guy either didn't want to see a doctor that day or was afraid to see him and he wouldn't come out of his cell when ordered to. So into the cell went the first guard to bring him out. He knocked the guard out with one punch. Then into the cell went the second guard, then the third, until four guards were knocked out in the cell. The fifth guard quickly locked the cell door with four of his crew unconscious inside, until he could summon reinforcements.

I will always be thankful for that man's intervention that day on the baseball field. He must have been quite violent when younger for J. Edgar Hoover to brand him the way he did. He was older when I met him, mellowed out, maybe in his early to mid forties, and finally a short-timer. I never saw him again after that day. He was released not too long after that. I admired the way he coolly diffused this situation and I'm sure the guards did also. I can only imagine how their blood must run cold whenever they sense that prisoner violence might break out. I regret not remembering the man's name. He may also be one of the reasons many modern maximum-security prisons now have ten or more guards on their goon squads.

Next in the shop, Mr. Luxton had me make some bulletin boards. Then he started explaining to me where I had to install them. He told me that the two cellblocks where I was to go were the most maximum-security cellblocks in all of the United States. He said that big name federal prisons like Alcatraz, Atlanta, Leavenworth and others were notorious for housing dangerous criminals. But when criminals in those prisons made trouble and became a problem, they were sent to Springfield and locked away in one of these two cellblocks. Thus, the worst of the worst prisoners in the United States were currently in these two small cellblocks. He told me that in the past, some prisoners actually had their cell doors welded shut for years at a time. He told me though, that when I would be in there with my tools for the installation, the inmates would be confined in their cells.

Finally he explained how to get there. I was to go just beyond the solitary confinement section where I had stayed for eight days when I first arrived in this prison. Starting there, I would have to pass through three security checkpoints to make it into the two cellblocks.

Prepared by Mr. Luxton to go to these cellblocks, I rolled out of the shop pushing my cart with most everything I needed. I had to stop at the master tool room, where all the high-security tools were kept for the various shops.

With a paper from Mr. Luxton, they issued this tool to me, which I could only imagine would be every escape artist's dream. I'd never seen one before or even since. Milwaukee Tools made it, and its body was similar to one of their sawzalls. I would describe it as an early sort of hammer drill. They instructed me how to use it. As I went there, I found everything as Mr. Luxton told me. Inside the two different cellblocks on different days, one was single story and the other two stories. There were maybe twelve to twenty cells in each cellblock. Each cell had a solid steel door with a small window, the same as the doors on the solitary cells we were confined in on our arrival in Springfield.

While I was installing the bulletin boards only one inmate was out of his cell. He was the cellblock trustee who was sweeping and cleaning.

From what Mr. Luxton had told me, I guess I expected to see some mean Hollywood-type bad guys staring or glaring out their little door windows at me. As I was working, I didn't notice anyone doing that at all. Only one inmate walked passed his window twice, and he didn't even bother to look at what I was doing. I began thinking that maybe most of the cells were unoccupied. I thought the hammer drill sound of the tool would have certainly attracted more attention. And of course, I always had my eye out for my newest psycho friend from the baseball field.

So I went over to look into the window of the nearest cell. The guard didn't stop me, so I continued around looking in all the cells, which were positioned around an open area in the middle of the cellblock.

Days later I had the same experience in the other small maximum-security cellblock, when I installed the other bulletin board. This one had a second tier of cells, but I only looked in the door windows of the cells on the first floor. Here's what I saw.

Most every cell was occupied, but not by anyone who appeared to me to be the least bit dangerous. Looking into the cells, I can only remember one inmate even making eye contact with me. They all simply appeared to be highly medicated or doped up. None looked robust and healthy, just thin, as if drugs had taken their appetites away. Their faces were pale and blank, just staring off into nowhere. So I guessed that if these guys were dangerous, they weren't anymore, now highly subdued with medication. Apparently our government really knew how to deal with dangerous guys!

The high-security tool room where I got that early model Milwaukee hammer drill was located in the large shop building. There was a carpenter shop, plumbing shop, electric shop, and metal and sheet metal shop, all in this one building. These shops weren't used as prison industries to make products to sell on the open markets, as is generally practiced by many other prisons. These shops were used for prison and hospital maintenance in Springfield only.

We entered the shops in the morning by exiting a door opposite the guards' station in the camp, walking sixty to eighty feet to enter the shops. At lunchtime, all the workers in the various shops would gather by a locked, barred gate next to the high-security tool room, adjacent to the metal shop section.

When the gate electrically opened with a buzz, the group would start walking down a ramp to the tunnels that led to the cafeteria. Three tunnels converged from various directions on the cafeteria, so prisoners from other areas would usually be arriving at about the same time. Some would speed walk to avoid a long wait in line at the cafeteria.

Moving through the basement level tunnels about three hundred feet, just before getting to the cafeteria, we'd first pass what appeared to be a boiler room on the left. A little farther on the left was a small kitchen and dining room for the guards. It also made meals that would be transported to the hospital wards and maximum-security cellblocks, where prisoners were fed in their cells or cellblocks. Thank goodness we didn't have to eat with the criminally insane.

Next we'd arrive at a cross tunnel where we could turn either right or left and take a flight of stairs up to the first floor, where there were actually two cafeterias, with the first-floor kitchen behind them.

A tiled wall that was approximately six and a half feet high separated the two cafeterias. Upon entering either cafeteria, you'd move to this center dividing wall, then move forward to get in line along this tile wall.

Just before reaching the far end where the serving area was, there were tray, silverware, and cup racks. You'd pick out what you wanted. The silverware selection contained only forks and spoons—no knives, of course.

Then you'd slide your tray along the stainless steel serving line. As mentioned previously, main course items and deserts were usually dished out to you by kitchen staff and supervised by guards.

Potatoes and vegetables you could dish out yourself. Coffee and chilled water were usually always available, as much as you wanted. I only drank water. Milk was available for breakfast. I never went to breakfast, preferring to sleep in instead.

There were usually several guards supervising each cafeteria area, especially main courses and desert distribution, as well as silverware returns.

For seating, there were small square tables with four chairs around them. As long as there was an empty chair, you could sit at any table of your choice.

You could take your time eating. The guards wouldn't rush you as they did in the Los Angeles County Jail. I don't ever remember the table and chairs filling up, leaving no place left to sit. There were always several tables with empty chairs available, even at the busiest of times.

There was one guy, though, who always ate by himself. He'd sit alone at a table at the far end of the cafeteria, with three empty chairs around him. I never saw anybody else sit at his table.

The story on this guy was that he was an Eskimo from a remote area of Alaska. During a severe winter, he killed his wife and two kids and ate them to survive. So apparently nobody wanted to eat at the same table with a cannibal.

After finishing a meal, we'd turn in our trays at a tray return cubicle near the door, proceed downstairs, and return to the camp by a different tunnel route than the one we used to get from the shop to the cafeteria.

Back at camp, we could relax and lie in our bunks for fifteen to thirty minutes before having to return to our work assignments. We could listen to our headphones during this time. We had a choice of only two stations, both country music ones. Being from the L.A. area, I didn't even know country stations existed before going to the camp in Tucson.

Anyway, I'm going into some of the cafeteria arrangements to set the stage for a couple of notable events that occurred there.

One happened during lunchtime. I was eating at a table next to the tile wall, the closest table to the tray and silverware racks. Joe Sedor was with me at that table . . . and maybe Steen and Jodi. If Steen and Jodi weren't at the same table with me, then they were at the one next to us along the tile wall. These tables along the wall were about four or five feet away from it because a line of inmates were next to it, moving forward through the chow line. The chow line was the same on the other side of the wall in the other cafeteria, just a reverse layout.

As we were eating, a commotion and clatter of falling trays came from just the other side of the tile block wall, less than seven feet away from me. Trays continued dropping going toward the serving line, and then it sounded as if the silverware and cup racks hit the floor.

Inmates in line on our side began chinning themselves up on the wall to look over and see what was happening. Jodi and I got up also. I sat back down because no more spaces were available on the wall.

The commotion of crashing, falling trays continued back the other way toward the cafeteria entrance door. Then it was silent, but the inmates along the wall continued watching for another fifteen or so seconds, still following some sort of action.

When the guys came down off the wall, they were all somber. Both cafeterias were quiet and a subdued atmosphere seemed to prevail. I knew something significant had taken place. I asked Jodi a couple of times what happened. He just kept his head down, halfheartedly picking at his food, not acknowledging my questions at all. So I shut up and was quiet like most everyone else, but I knew something had gone down and that I would probably find out shortly.

As Joe and I finished eating, five or ten minutes after the commotion, we turned in our trays and walked downstairs. As we reached the bottom, several guards wheeled into view a hospital gurney with a bloody prisoner on it. It had come down a freight elevator from the first-floor kitchen to the basement kitchen and was now heading to the hospital through the basement-level tunnels.

It stopped right in front of us, about three or four feet away, so the guards could open panic bar equipped double doors in order to proceed. The bloody inmate had a bluish color to him. I couldn't tell whether he was still alive, but the guards didn't appear to be in a major rush.

Off they went down the tunnel, turning left at the first intersection that would take them to the hospital a hundred yards or more away. Joe and I followed but went straight at the intersection, which eventually made a right turn to the south, taking us back to the camp.

A picture tells a thousand words. Seeing that inmate on the gurney answered most of the questions I had about the disturbance in the cafeteria. But the reactions of the inmates I saw, their becoming quiet and somber, showed me that even hardened criminals could be moved and sobered up by the death of another.

As others returned to the camp from the cafeteria, we got the whole story of the killing. It didn't take long for it to be breaking news on the local country music radio stations that we got on our headphones. We heard about it on our headphones before we even had to return to the shops after lunch.

It was a homosexual love triangle killing. The killer worked in the kitchen but was off duty. When he saw his competition in line, he walked back to the kitchen and talked one of his on-duty workmates into handing him a kitchen knife. He worked his way back to the dining room, coming up behind his target just as he grabbed a tray. As he sunk the knife into his back, the tray was dropped, and others were knocked off the racks as the victim began running away from his attacker. As he turned at the silverware and cup racks, he slowed down enough to get the knife stuck in him again, also knocking over those racks. Reversing his direction, he ran the other way past the other side of the tray rack and then back along the tiled block wall with his attacker one step behind him. Guys in line were diving out of the way, knocking over food trays of inmates eating at the nearest tables.

As the victim slowed enough to turn when reaching the next corner, he got the knife sunk in his back again. The same thing happened at the next corner, twice, where the two made a circle around the tray return cubicle.

The victim then ran back behind the serving counter, where the guards had been watching all this from. As the victim passed the guards, one of them stepped forward and held his hand out saying, "Give me the knife!" The attacker stopped and handed over the knife, as his mission had been accomplished.

The victim slumped down against the inside of the serving counter. The gurney was sent for from the hospital, but he was already gurgling as his blood began filling up his lungs.

My only criticism of the situation is not that the guards didn't jump in sooner; they would've been foolish to do so, I think. But they should have ordered six or eight inmates to hustle the guy to the hospital immediately, rather than wait for a gurney to arrive.

Chapter 11

Jail House Lawyers, Alcatraz Escape

I finally got the official response to my parole hearing. It was denied, which is what I had been expecting. What I hadn't expected was that it would take them so long to get around to denying it. I should have been informed within ten months, but it took months longer in my case, thirteen and a half, apparently because of the transfer from Tucson.

So I was looking at doing another eight months in prison before getting out on my good time date. "Good time" was a prison policy that rewarded prisoners with time taken off their sentences for not making trouble and taking their punishments, as in my case. For every month of being a good prisoner, eight or nine days are taken off your sentence. Thus in federal prison, you only have to do a little more than two-thirds of your time before you were automatically released, at least in those years.

By then, I was long since bored with the monotony and restrictions of prison life. I needed a break from oil painting, and I'd had plenty of time to read all the small amount of Bible literature we were allowed to have. To get involved in some sporting activity, you'd probably be playing with psychopath sore losers or some other sort of unpredictable, dangerous characters.

I came up with the bright idea to appeal my case, to become a "jailhouse lawyer." That seemed an interesting project to take on. Assessing the feasibility of this undertaking, I talked with a camp inmate that others had recommended. He was more of a con man than lawyer, but he knew enough to get a case filed. And of course, I had an excellent case that should be filed, he advised.

All that was left was to discuss his fee. Since inmates in federal prisons aren't allowed to carry money, the inmates' economy revolved around a system of barter, mostly using cigarettes. Any money an inmate made or had sent to them was held in an account administered by the prison. No more than $15 dollars a month could be spent at the commissary, which was deducted from their account. We settled the fee at ten cartons of cigarettes. I remember trying to carry them all back from the commissary; I felt like an idiot in front of the other Witnesses. Yet they knew what I was using them for and supported the appeal.

Nowadays, no Jehovah's Witness would have anything to do with cigarettes, even in this fashion, because of scriptural admonition and principles against any activity detrimental to our fellow man's health. I was to make this payment not at the beginning, but once the paperwork was done and ready to file.

To start with, my lawyer/con man was supposedly researching pertinent similar cases and others that might have a bearing on these issues. He recommended that we meet with other jailhouse lawyers who were working on their own appeals at the prison library, to pick brains and do some research. Thus on Saturday mornings, the big legal brains from the maximum-security sections usually congregated there, so I was told.

So off we went, the only two leaving the camp for the library at an authorized time when the camp guards would open the gate for that purpose.

The prison library was located in the basement level, under a medical recovery ward in the northeast area of the prison complex. When we arrived, six inmates were already sitting at a table. They appeared to be a sophisticated group of convicts, late forties and older.

My con man lawyer seemed to know them all. We both knew one, a camp prisoner in his late forties or early fifties, who had somehow already arrived at the library. I'd had several conversations in the past with this inmate. He claimed to be a union business agent who was somehow convicted because of the conspiracy investigation that also brought down Jimmy Hoffa. He never would answer specific questions about that when we had talked previously.

He would talk though, a great length about a yacht refinishing and painting business he ran in Florida for a while. It was almost as if he were training me how to do it—to wait for dry weather, low humidity, and so forth. I still almost feel as if I'd be qualified to go out and paint a yacht tomorrow.

Now looking for law books, my con man started telling me who the guys were already sitting at the table. One had been a Thompson submachine gun-killing gangster in the early 1930s and was now in his thirty-fifth year of incarceration. He was small, wiry, and still dangerous-looking. Another was or had been a grand wizard or head of the Klu Klux Klan. He looked creepy. I believe he was the clan leader I saw profiled on a Discovery Channel program in late 2010, convicted in 1957 and sent to federal prison. Another was some kind of mobster, an Italian. He was distinguished and classy-looking, with one glazed-over eye. When I saw him at other times, mostly in the cafeteria, he always seemed to have an entourage with him.

I can't remember the rap on the other two, but one of them, after we sat down with the group and prison stories were swapped, related one of the most memorable stories I was to hear while imprisoned.

Keep in mind that a lot of prisoners resent being incarcerated and in subjection to the guards to varying degrees, some violently so. Most are content just to have a good laugh at the guards' expense, the bigger the better.

He tells us that prior to coming to Springfield, he had been in Alcatraz until it closed in 1963. His work assignment there was in the prison laundry. Then he started detailing his participation in the infamous escape from Alcatraz in 1962, which led to its being closed the following year. He explained that not only did all the shipments of prisoners' clothing come into the laundry, but the guards' clothing as well. He and a few other inmates unpacked it all and distributed it even to the guards, with very little supervision. They would issue the pants and shirts to the guards, including the heavy jackets and raincoats for those who had to work outside during the cold, foggy, or sometimes rainy San Francisco weather.

He went on to relate that for the escape, they provided the used raincoats that were then turned into the floats and rafts. But there was a problem: there weren't enough of them. So to get additional material, they decided to come up with a new fashion statement for the guards, the Alcatraz short-sleeved raincoat made from the latest shipment. If any guards had any questions, they'd play dumb, responding that it must be a new manufacturer's model for those who need more freedom of arm movement, for men of action!

After Morris and the Anglan brothers paddled away from Alcatraz, our storyteller asked us to imagine as the search party at a nearby island found some floats, how stupid guards must have looked if they had on their latest prison issued raincoat.

It took awhile for the guys to compose themselves after almost falling out of their chairs from laughter. Even right after hearing this tale, I felt that if it were really true, prison authorities would probably be too embarrassed to ever acknowledge it, most likely joining a long list of government cover-ups.

One of the guys asked our storyteller if he got in any trouble because of this. Half turning to him he replied, "I didn't think so, but I am in maximum security here in Springfield!" This man and three of the others, I had never seen before this day or afterwards. That told me that they were in a maximum security section, being feed in their cells, having their laundry delivered and only let out occasionally to research their appeals at the library.

During this trip to the library, I didn't get any useable legal tips from these guys, just some illegal ones. I did get a good marketing idea that I've always wanted to try: the Alcatraz short-sleeved raincoat. I think it could be the perfect gift idea for the woman who wants to tell her man of action, that she "still loves him anyway."

Back in the camp, my con man/lawyer eventually got the case ready for typing. He had a few pages of preliminary introductory stuff. The rest was supposed to be typed directly from some other precedent-setting case, which supposedly was similar to my circumstances.

When I read it, I didn't see the connection at all. It didn't even make any sense to me. My lawyer assured me though, that I was as good as out—once I filed it. That's when I was truly suspicious that he was just a con man.

It was only going to cost me thirty dollars of commissary money and would be something to do, sort of a hobby. Plus, it might qualify me to be an official jailhouse lawyer, although possibly a bad one.

I already had one of the brothers lined up to type it, the warden's secretary. I wonder what the warden thought when he saw his secretary so industriously typing right under his nose. If he knew, he might equate it as just another legal escape attempt, as some in the Department of Justice obviously would. I did go ahead and file the appeal and would have to wait awhile for a response, which I didn't expect to be favorable now.

Speaking of escapes, we had one in Springfield while I was there. A minimum-security prisoner from the camp used a dump truck every workday to dump part of the prison trash in a landfill on the west side of the large prison farm fields. The landfill was next to a road with houses across the street. He left the bed of the dump trunk up, jumped the fence, and was gone. He was captured four months later in Oregon.

Chapter 12

Reasons for Neutrality

Housed in the maximum-security section of the prison was another prisoner who wanted to have regular Bible discussions. His name was Mr. Weaver and I would estimate that he was in his mid forties. I can't remember where I met him. It was probably at a cafeteria table or on one of my work assignments.

The only place we could meet regularly was the main prison yard on Saturday afternoon. So back I went to the main yard again. Some of the guys from the ball field tried to get me to play baseball again, but I politely declined. When I asked about my former team captain, they told me he had been released.

Because of the prison's policy of no proselytizing, we couldn't openly use books and Bibles in our discussion. So in my bomber jacket I smuggled two of the only four books I was allowed to have to loan to him. Then he could read a different chapter during the week on a different subject, conveniently in his cell. On Saturdays we would then discuss that week's topic as we strolled around the main yard, as if we were just getting some exercise. This routine lasted for two months, until mid-September of 1967.

The only problem with this was that each of the two books had an authorization stamp with my name inside the cover. Well not actually my name but my number, 9307, which was my name in this prison. It was contraband for anyone else to possess these books and I would find out later, following unusual circumstances involving Mr. Weaver, just how serious an offense this could be.

I also met another young prisoner who had just arrived in the camp. He was an Amish conscientious objector. He had that just-shaved look, same as Mike Sinai did after we got booked into the Florence, Arizona, Federal Detention Center. That's when he was officially in federal custody and thus required to have his full beard shaved off.

His name was Jesse Brumbaugh, from somewhere in Pennsylvania or Indiana. I talked to him that first day and expressed an interest in knowing the scriptural basis that he, as an Amish, relied on as a conscientious objector. He didn't seem to know.

So I offered to show him some of the scriptures from the bible, which Jehovah's Witnesses use to base our neutrality on. He accepted, and we agreed to meet the next day, after I got back to the camp from the shop.

I don't remember the exact scriptures I shared with him on that day. There are so many pertinent ones to choose from. To help some readers further understand our strict position of neutrality, I'll briefly discuss two that could have been used.

Jesus had his apostles prepare for the Passover celebration, during which he was to institute the "new covenant." It was to be the day of his execution as well. Jewish days ran from sundown to sundown back then. As he had some of his apostles gathering items for that meal, which would start his last day, he was continually trying to strengthen them for the trials ahead and reinforce important lessons that they hadn't yet readily grasped.

After that meal, at Luke 22: 38, the apostles apparently reminded him of other items they may have acquired at his request, saying, "Lord, look! Here are two swords." He simply responded, "It is enough." What final lesson would Jesus teach his followers about swords?

After then having gone to the Garden of Gethsemane, Jesus's enemies eventually arrived to arrest him. Peter lashed out with one of these swords, taking the ear off the high priest's slave as this group started to take Jesus into custody. Jesus then, despite the stressful, trying situation, took the time to teach his apostles one last lesson as a group. He told Peter, "Return your sword to its place, for all those who take the sword will perish by the sword" (John 26:52). Imagine that, for this last important group lesson before his death; he had them bring a sword, to impress on them the importance of never using a sword.

Jesus was the greatest man who ever lived, the Son of God, and he didn't even want his followers to fight for him or resort to using violence. This fits right in with everything else he taught. This is what the early Christians practiced, according to historians, as previously quoted.

The scriptures indicate several ways to identify Christians. One of these is recorded at John 13:34-35, where Jesus states in part, "All will know that you are my disciples, if you have love among yourselves." Actions speak louder than words. Jesus taught his followers to love even their enemies. That would certainly preclude killing your Christian brother in another land because some politicians declare war. At least that's how we take it, and we extend it to our enemies. I also remember talking to Jesse about the example of Jehovah's Witnesses in Germany during Hitler's rule.

For those who might want to learn more, a wealth of information can be found at this website: www.watchtower.org. Please click on "neutrality," "Nazi," or any other subject or scripture of interest.

I would like to share one experience I personally learned of, related to the Nazi subject. During 2006 to 2009, I spent a lot of time at my sister's ranch in Templeton, California, helping after the death of her husband, mainly with repairs after an earthquake in nearby Paso Robles. One of the Witnesses there, Matt Hermes, told me about their family vacation they took to Washington, DC. While there, they went to the Holocaust museum. They were surprised and delighted to learn that that day was Jehovah's Witness Day at the Museum. During their guided tour, the guide stated, "If all Germans were like Jehovah's Witnesses, Hitler would have had no power!"

Shortly after our discussion, Jesse Brumbaugh was assigned to work in the electrical shop, where Joe Sedor had already been working. I offered to have regular discussions with Jesse that second day of his in the camp, but he declined at that time. Joe, working with him every day was eventually able to continue these discussions regularly.

One day coming back into the camp from the lunchtime meal, I saw an old-fashioned horse and buggy on the road outside the prison fences and gun towers, headed toward the old prison barn.

When Jesse arrived several minutes later, I told him I thought he was going to have a visit in the afternoon, relating to him what I had seen. Sure enough he did. His relative, or relatives, had come all the way from another state in a horse and buggy to visit him. How many hundreds of miles, I can't remember. Being from Los Angeles and used to those roads, I was thinking that horse must've been a nervous wreck.

About ten years later, I was to meet Joe Sedor at a convention at the Hollywood Park racetrack. That's when he told me about Robinson later becoming a Witness. Now I remember that he also told me that after getting out of Springfield, Jesse also became a Witness.

But then I forgot about Jesse until just about ten years ago, when I was reading an article in a 2001 issue of *Awake!* magazine. It was titled "Dress and Grooming Was My Stumbling Block." In it, an Amish woman said that after studying the Bible with Jehovah's Witnesses, her biggest objection to becoming one herself was that she thought they were sinful because they wore modern clothing and used other modern conveniences, such as automobiles. It showed a picture of her next to a horse and wagon that she was selling vegetables out of, dressed in old-fashioned Amish attire.

She wrote that her husband's brother, Jesse, had become a Witness after first coming in contact with them in a federal prison in the mid 1960s, as an Amish conscientious objector. That he then introduced them to the Witnesses.

When I read that story, I couldn't remember Jesse's first or last name. I wondered if this was the Amish guy I'd talked to when he first came into the prison, and who eventually worked with Joe in the electrical shop. Later, when thinking about it more, I figured that if I could find the last name, it might jog my memory. I felt there was no way of doing that, especially with my living in an isolated part of the world, on a small island like Ponape.

A couple of weeks passed and then, when thinking about the article again, I remembered that those types of stories sometimes list the author's name. As the wife of the prisoner's brother, their last name should be the same. So I looked for that magazine and when I found it, I checked for the name of the articles' author. There it was! The last name was Brumbaugh. When I put the name Jesse, mentioned in the article, with the last name Brumbaugh, saying them together, it all came back to me.

I then remembered that when I first asked him his name and he told me Jesse Brumbaugh, I thought, *What an old-fashioned-sounding name*. I'd never heard that last name before. *Fitting*, I thought at the time, *for an Amish*.

My view of names then may have reflected a little where I was raised, Los Angeles, a place notorious for people who change their names for various reasons. Many want to make themselves sound more modern, sporty, or movie-starish.

Even I never use my first and middle name as it appears on my birth certificate: Stephen Blair. I use it so seldom that whenever I have to, which is rarely, I have to look for my birth certificate to check the spelling.

In the early evening after dinner, the guards would announce over the speakers, "Mail Call!" With many others, I'd go down to the first-floor control center/guards' station to see if I had any mail. There the guard would call out numbers, not names. You'd have to listen for your number, acknowledge it with a "here," and then claim your mail. Many prisoners hardly ever or never got any mail, so a lot of inmates didn't bother to go to mail call. Jodi Ray was one of those. He also told me he had never even had a visit the whole time he'd been in this prison and the others before Springfield.

One day while at mail call, I heard Jodi's number called out. I used to know it; it was his name here also. When I got back to my bunk, I told him over the low tile wall separating us that they'd called his number. He had mail. Afterward he told me the letter was from his oldest or second oldest sister, which one I'm not quite sure of after all this time.

Then a month or two later, late summer of 1967, while in the shop one of our guards got a phone call and then yelled out, "Jodi, you've got a visitor!" After his visit I asked who had come to see him. He told me it was his sister, the one whom he had received the letter from recently. I gathered from what he said that she was the only one among his family that he ever had any contact with, only rarely receiving a letter from her during his numerous incarcerations, but never a visit before this one.

All of our mail was already opened when we got it, censored, certain things blacked out. They had rules about certain things that could not be mentioned, besides the obvious. It seemed that even my mail and other witness's, on the majority of occasions, managed to have something blacked out. It was clear that prison authorities were on the ball, and that the mail was not a medium for cons to mention or attempt to carry on any illegal activity thru.

On another day at mail call, Freddy Satler got a letter early and went to his bunk to read it. I had to pass by him on the way back to my bunk. As I was going by, Freddy looked crushed, tears in his eyes. I thought some family member probably died. Stephenson bunked near Joe and me, so I called him over and directed his attention to Freddy, telling him what I had just observed. Joe and I suggested to Stephenson that since he was closer to Freddy than any of us, he should go down and check on him, find out what happened, and give him some comfort. So off he went, approaching Freddy, who was now openly sobbing, with a look of compassion and concern.

We were watching from a distance as Stephenson sat on the edge of the bunk and appeared to be softly inquiring into the situation. All of a sudden, he practically fell off the bed laughing. We were shocked; we couldn't imagine what had just transpired. Stephenson composed himself, acted compassionate again for a while, and then returned to us. We were waiting expectantly. He reported that he had sympathetically asked a sobbing, sniffling Freddy if he got some bad news from home. He even asked if somebody died. With his voice crackling, Freddy then sniffled and snerted out in a painful, quivering response, "Yes, my dog died."

Well shame on us for also losing our composure too, which took us awhile to regain. Remember that Freddy was a goat herder, and it was probably his longtime herd dog. They were obviously very close.

Stephenson never would fess up to being the one who was spiking Freddy's living area back in Tucson, getting him gigs at inspections. Perhaps he was innocent, but now Freddy had a good reason to get back at Stephenson, and he would.

These four brothers from the Pacific Northwest that came with us from Tucson on the bus, Freddy Satler, Kuburk, Jim Stephenson, and Howe, had all come into Tucson at the same time, with sentences of the same length. They were then all released at the same time, on their "good time" date.

They were given new suits made in Leavenworth Federal Prison, a bus ticket back to their homes, and enough money for the four-day bus trip back to the Pacific Northwest, to buy meals on the way, not much extra. Then they were dropped off at the bus station for the trip.

After they left, we heard from the brothers working at the administration offices that when they got to Denver, they had an overnight layover. They had to sleep in the bus terminal. When they awoke, they discovered they'd been robbed, not only of their money but their bus tickets also, all except Freddy.

We could just imagine Freddy leaving the bus station on schedule, waving good-bye to the others and probably laughing at Stephenson. They ended up being homeless in Denver for a couple of days while police contacted the prison to get them replacement tickets and traveling cash.

Afterward, I got a letter from the Ninth Circuit Court of Appeals. They at least used my name, not my number. That's about all I got; they denied my appeal. I'd expected as much after reading it before filing it through the mail. What I didn't expect was the Legal Opinions' scathing condemnation of it. The writer went on and on about how bad the appeal was, and that it didn't even make any sense. He even complained that he had to waste his time reading it. He further stated that he felt it was the most absurd legal pleadings he'd ever come across in his professional career. Well, at least I had an expert legal opinion of my assessment of my ghost lawyer. The only trouble was that I got the blame! Plus, the Ninth Circuit Court of Appeals probably now considers me the worst jailhouse lawyer in federal prison.

Actually, I did have a good case; I just needed a good lawyer and money. The particular circumstances of my case were much the same as Muhammad Ali's situation and he won. My biggest problem was that I was late properly claiming "conscientious objector" and "ministerial" status when I registered for the draft. So I figured I was in default and had forfeited my legal rights. Doing proper paperwork has always been one of my biggest weaknesses and has cost me a lot over the years. I even find it hard to believe it's me sitting here writing this book.

I actually had a much better case than Ali or any of the other brothers I was in with. When I got out of high school, I went right into the full-time ministry as a regular pioneer, a term Jehovah's Witnesses use for those who devote at least one hundred hours a month in the public ministry. Those who do this are routinely granted a ministerial exemption by the draft boards . . . but not me. I was in the full-time ministry when I registered for the draft, prior to induction. I started doing this work even shortly before graduating from high school in June 1964.

In that month, I had started a Bible study with an interesting man. He and his wife were really down-and-out. I found them in a flophouse motel on Imperial Highway, a half block west of La Cienega Boulevard. This man was big and from Texas, but now was almost totally crippled, using crutches and a wheelchair. He had been one of President Eisenhower's Secret Service bodyguards during his presidency. In this capacity, he fell off a high stage during one of the president's speeches and ruined his back. He was now embroiled in a disability dispute with the government and obviously coming out as the loser.

He and his wife had flown into Los Angeles and settled in the cheapest place close to the airport that they could afford taxi fare to get to. It was an old single-story motel—dirt driveway, white paint weathered off—about one step up from sleeping in a junk car, and they didn't even have one of those.

Last year when in California, I saw a History Channel biography on President Eisenhower. He had been raised as a Jehovah's Witness[1]* also, but obviously had chosen a different course when grown. But in some of his speeches, I recognized my study standing near, protecting and looking after our country's president, something they were not doing for him in his time of need.

We do this work free on a voluntary basis, and I knew I had to go back to construction work soon to take care of my financial needs. Plus, I was, thanks to Denny Gormley, a construction worker and just not cut out to be spending my days in a suit and tie, walking around talking to people all the time.

---

[1] * Jehovah's Witnesses took this name in the early 1930s. Prior to that, they were known as the Bible Students.

Doing this on a part-time basis and working hard on a job seemed to be more suitable for me. Doing too much white-collar-type activity just drove me up a wall. Knowing I'd be back into construction work shortly, I didn't feel I had a right to push the ministerial exemption with the draft board. It was also a waste of time to pursue conscientious objector status as well. They'd still just draft me, but into noncombatant military service, which was still a violation of my Christian neutrality.

Chapter 13

Another Dangerous Neighbor

A more desirable bunk location opened up, just across from mine but one bunk farther up the aisle. It was late summer or fall of 1967, and the weather was still nice. I thought being on the outside wall with a window over the bed that I could control as the weather dictated would be a nice change. Plus, the early morning sun wouldn't be such a nuisance in this location.

My neighbors all pretty much remained the same, but for well over a year in Tucson, and now in Springfield, Joe had bunked on my right. My new neighbor on my right also worked in the electric shop. We'd gotten along fine in the past, never any problem, and I had no reason to think that that wouldn't continue. He was in his early forties, sort of small and wiry, and had that classic look of a dangerous criminal, five o'clock shadow and all. He had been in prison for twenty-two years for a murder while in the military, and while in prison, he'd killed another inmate also.

In those years and before, life was cheap in prison. To kill another inmate might result in just a few years extra added to your sentence. That's what happened to this man I was told, but I was long since used to being around guys like this and didn't give it much of a second thought.

A new prisoner in his late twenties moved into the area just three beds beyond where I used to bunk, almost right across the aisle from my new neighbor to my right. Well, the two of them hit it off immediately. They would lie on a bunk together in the evenings, flirting with each other like young lovers. We tried to ignore things like this. You just didn't stick your nose into other people's affairs in prison.

Late one night I woke up sometime after midnight needing to take a leak. As I stood up, I noticed that right next to me my neighbor was busy making love with his new friend. I was shocked for a moment, like a deer caught in the headlights. His eyes made contact with mine with a glare. I walked to the lavatory and stood in front of the urinal for about fifteen minutes, trying to relax in order to relieve myself. That scene had really creeped me out. As I returned to my bunk, I saw that my neighbor's friend was gone. All was quiet, so I went back to sleep.

The next day I told Jodi and a couple of brothers in the shop what I'd seen, but that was about all. I figured that was the end of it. Two days later my new neighbor's friend's bunk was empty. He'd been transferred out of camp.

When I walked into the shop the next morning, I looked to my left into our guards' office windows. Mr. Long and Mr. Luxton were talking to Jodi with worried, concerned expression on their faces. As they noticed me, the expressions from all three transferred to me; I seemed to be the object of their concern. One of the guards grabbed the phone and started dialing, still looking at me. The other was instructing Jodi to do something but hardly taking his worried eyes off me. It was obvious that something unusual was up, and I seemed to be involved. Out came Jodi saying directly to me, "Come with me." He led me to the back of the shop and into our secure tool room, locking the door from the inside.

I tried to ask him what was going on and why were we locked in the tool room. He wouldn't tell me. He said he couldn't at the time but would later. But for now, we had to wait there awhile.

I was clueless, I had no idea what was going on. But we soon got comfortable and started passing the time talking. There was nothing else to do and we talked about many different things for hours. Lunchtime came around and the guys came back from their various assignments, asking us why were we still locked in the tool room doing nothing. Jodi wouldn't say, and I didn't know, so off they went to lunch. I asked him, "Aren't we going to lunch?" He said again that we had to wait until we heard from Mr. Long or Mr. Luxton.

Shortly afterward, Jodi finally began to explain what was happening. He revealed that my neighbor to my right and his lover had been snitched out. The guards had moved him out of the camp to the cellblock with all the other gays that play the female role. My neighbor was furious and thought I was the one responsible for informing, that he was going to kill me that night, slitting my throat while I slept.

Now I understood why we were locked in the tool room. I could easily see why this killer might think I was the snitch, after spending so much time away that night standing in front of the urinal. He probably thought I went downstairs and informed on him to the guards—that that's what took me so long to return to my bunk.

Jodi explained that our guards were contacting the warden, and that we'd continue waiting for whatever response they deemed appropriate. Of course he didn't use those particular fancy words, not Jodi, but that basic idea.

I was concerned, but I never got afraid. I hadn't yet been afraid in prison, except of the lightning. I thanked Jodi for his help; he'd probably saved my life, kept me from being blindsided. I also expressed to him that he and Steen had been correct about the three reasons that led to most prison killings: gambling disputes, homosexual love triangles, and snitching to the guards. I'd already seen evidence of one, the cafeteria killing. Now I had a guy who thought I broke up his love affair by snitching him out to the guards. So in his mind, I was guilty of two out of three most common reasons inmates are killed. This man was a killer, and his convict pride and self-respect would probably demand he kill again.

I wasn't too upset about all this at this time; I'd wait and see what the prison authorities came up with. Jodi and I continued to pass the time talking about a variety of things. Then thinking of Jodi's Southern accent, I asked him why people from the south hated blacks (actually using a term that would now be considered derogatory but wasn't at the time, colored people). He answered like a racist southerner would at the time, essentially saying that they were stupid, dirty, ignorant, lazy, and so on, relating numerous other unflattering terms used by bigots to denigrate black people.

When he finished, he stated that he didn't hate n_ _ _ _ s . . . that he wasn't a racist. I interjected that I didn't think so either, because of how well he got along with our black carpenter shop worker we had in our shop when I first arrived in Springfield. He agreed with that, but then stated that although he wasn't racist, his oldest brother Jimmy really hated blacks. "In fact, he hates n_ _ _ _ _s so bad, he's gonna kill Martin Luther King! I ain't shitting ya. You just wait and see. He's gonna kill Martin Luther King!"

I thought facetiously to myself, Yeah, sure. He'd probably have to wait in a line with about ten thousand other racist southerners to be able to get a shot off! I, like many other people, thought that many in the South wanted Martin Luther King dead, and many would be more than willing to do that. I took Jodi's statement about his brother as just another wishful boast of a racist southerner. Besides, I had my own killer to worry about then.

Jodi continued talking about his older brother Jimmy and as he continued, I could tell he admired him, was proud of him. Not for the reasons we normally admired an older sibling, but because he was a criminal and had already escaped from prison a couple of times, he bragged to me. In fact, he then boasted that he had "just escaped earlier this year from the prison," while pointing in a somewhat northerly direction from where we were sitting.

The only prison I knew of that I thought was toward the north was Terra Haute, Indiana, from talk of other inmates. So I responded, "Terra Haute?"

Jodi answered, "No, the Missouri State Prison!" He then told me they were from St. Louis, Missouri. He related that he was much younger than his older brother and by the time he was old enough to remember, Jimmy had already moved out on his own. He said that he never had much contact with him as he was growing up, only seeing him around town on occasion. He also mentioned that other older brothers had been in prisons too, which he talked proudly of as well.

I then asked him somewhat incredulously, "Are all of your brothers criminals?"

He thought for a moment, as if trying to figure out how to answer that question. He then replied, "One brother is a businessman." He wouldn't tell me though, what that business was when I asked. Then in furtherance of my question, he added that a younger brother drowned at twelve years of age, inferring that he wasn't a criminal.

I said, "That's terrible losing a brother like that," all the while trying to act compassionate.

He then said he lost one of his younger sisters in a house fire when she was about eleven years of age. He went on to relate that besides living in St. Louis, they sometimes lived on their grandmother's farm somewhere to the north or east, in another state—Indiana, I think. I could tell he enjoyed talking about his childhood experiences there, trapping and hunting with his brother who was about his age, before he drowned.

He went on to tell me his parents had three boys and two girls, then no kids for about ten years. Then they had two boys and two girls.

From what he'd said about the age gap between his parents' older group of five kids and the younger group of four, which Jodi was part of, plus most of his brothers being criminals, I just had to ask the obvious question; I couldn't stop myself: "What, your dad do about a ten-year stretch in the pen?"

I could see this question made him uncomfortable. Shame on me! He struggled a bit, and I could tell that he was about to say no. But then he hesitated and just said outright, "Yeah," a bit deflated. I felt bad then for even asking that question. I had seen how he loved talking about his brothers' criminal past and accomplishments, but it was clear that he didn't want to think about his own father in that way.

Feeling bad for even bringing his father into our discussion in that manner, I decided to change the subject. As I tried to move on to another topic, Jodi interrupted me and again stated, "Remember, I ain't shittin' ya. My brother Jimmy's gonna kill Martin Luther King!"

Moving on, we talked about other things for an hour or so. Then in the mid-afternoon, Mr. Luxton called me out to the office. As I left the tool room, Jodi again reminded me, "Remember, I ain't shittin' ya. You just wait and see. My brother Jimmy's gonna kill Martin Luther King!" We had spent six or seven hours together locked in the tool room talking that day.

Again I chalked these claims of Jodi's to just another wild prison story, which I'd heard a number of. One of the most unlikely stories I was to hear was from one older distinguished con. He claimed he'd been railroaded into prison because of something to do with the Kennedy family selling gold to Russia on the black market, because the price was better. Who knows, maybe one day that may prove true, just as Jodi Ray's story would six and a half months later, when James Earl Ray assassinated Martin Luther King.

I remember the approximate date to within a day or two of my conversation with Jodi, not so much because of his statements about his brother Jimmy, but because of this very real problem I now had to deal with, and the changes in my life that would start taking place within the next half hour.

Mr. Luxton told me to report to the warden's office, gave me a pass, and told me not to worry about the guy in the electric shop, because he was under close supervision by his guard and Mr. Long too. He then sent me on my way. This was approximately between the twenty-second and twenty-fourth day of September 1967.

In the warden's office I was directed to see the assistant warden. He immediately informed me that they had already made arrangements to transfer me to the BOQ, which was outside the prison walls. He cautioned me that I would still have to go to work in the carpenter shop and go to the cafeteria, but to be careful and take precautions. He said my guards, Mr. Long and Mr. Luxton, would talk with me more about this. Also, he cautioned me not to go anywhere I didn't have to go, like the gym, main yard, or library.

He then gave me a pass back to the camp to gather my things, telling me to then report to the main entrance of the prison. At the main entrance the guards were expecting me. They explained the procedures for entering and exiting the prison via the BOQ.

The BOQ was the former bachelor officers' quarters. It was a two-story four unit apartment house, now converted to house twenty-five or so minimum-security prisoners, all short-timers. I would estimate that it was four or five hundred feet from the prison entrance, just outside the northeast corner of the prison's fences.

I was informed that I would be searched coming and going at the main entrance. When we were leaving the main entrance for the BOQ, the guards would call the guard towers; otherwise we'd be shot. When leaving the BOQ for the prison entrance, we had to make a phone call to the main guard tower; otherwise, we'd be shot.

How serious were they about this? Others and I would absentmindedly forget to make that call on occasions. We didn't get shot or even a warning shot, just a big scolding by the guards at the main gate. If we had deviated off a direct route between the BOQ and the main entrance, the tower guard may have taken some action. As it was, any prisoner bent on escaping from the BOQ could easily escape by taking another route after dark. There were no guards stationed at the BOQ; they only came over a few times a day for the "count" and then left. Only short-timers were put there anyway. A prisoner would have to be an idiot to escape. I was only looking at doing another six and a half months until my ` good time' release date.

This was the best place to be doing time. The BOQ had some private rooms, a couple of double occupancy rooms, and some with four beds per room. It had two kitchens with refrigerators on the first floor. Plus there were a couple of living rooms with TVs. There were two other TVs in rooms that appeared to be enclosed porches, with beds and couches. I really don't recall the second floor layout. In the basement, there was a weight room. Outside to the north was a basketball court that also doubled as a tennis court.

Yes, this place was much better than the camp. I found an empty bed in a bedroom that only had two beds in it. I could tell from the items around it that the other occupant was a Witness. I moved in there, my choice. No guard told me where to bunk.

There was no "lights out" time at night like in the camps and jails I'd previously been in. You could stay up as late as you wanted at night, watching TV or doing whatever. I didn't care about that, and late TV would prove to be a liability because of the TV's sound disturbing those who wanted to sleep instead. Growing up in El Segundo, a block south of Los Angeles International airport, noise didn't bother me. I could sleep like a baby through noise.

Back to the first day in the BOQ . . . My new roommate returned from work and of all the brothers in the prison, he just happened to be the one who had a frosty attitude toward me. It stemmed from back in the camp, when I informed him and others that paroles were probably going to start to be denied for the Springfield Witnesses from the eastern United States. He didn't want to hear that and kept insisting that it wasn't going to happen. Sure enough, after our busload arrived in Springfield, all the Witnesses, including me, began being denied parole.

I think I'd just represented to the poor guy the last thing he wanted to hear, that he would end up doing twice the amount of time he'd expected to do when he came to prison. Now together in this room in the BOQ, I learned that he had already gone before the parole board and was waiting to hear back. He acknowledged that paroles were now being denied but insisted that he would be different. That his parole was going to be granted . . . that he'd be leaving soon.

The next morning in the carpenter shop, Mr. Long and Mr. Luxton informed me that I wouldn't be sent out of the shop on rounds for a while. They wanted me in the shop right in front of their office windows, where they could keep an eye on me. Since the entrance to the shop wasn't in their view from their office, I was advised while working not to turn my back to this entrance, to always keep it at least in my peripheral vision.

The biggest problem I faced was going to lunch at the cafeteria. The electric shop killer would be among the group of inmates waiting at the tunnel gate from the shops for lunch. I was told to hang back, to always keep this guy in front of me and in my sight—to keep close enough behind him to see which cafeteria he entered, then go into the other one. Then while waiting in line, I was to keep my back to the wall and use my peripheral vision. As far as eating, I was told to look for a table by the outside wall and only sit in a chair where my back would be against the outside wall there. I was also advised never to make eye contact with this man or go anywhere I didn't have to go.

My bosses kept me in the shop. They had me start making a cabinet for the prison hospital's X-ray room. I was left alone working in the shop for several weeks, while the other workers were sent out on various assignments.

That first day for lunch, I followed the advice and held back at the tunnel gate, kept the guy ahead of me and acted cool, like all was normal. I had to show no fear or weakness, act as if I knew nothing about his threat.

I talked to Joe Sedor about this problem and the one weakness that I saw left to this problem. What if the killer hung back in the shops somewhere out of sight and then after the tunnel gate buzzed open, came up behind me as we walked to the cafeteria? I couldn't be constantly looking over my shoulder, because that would be too obvious. So what we worked out was that if the guy wasn't ahead of me at the gate, Joe would drop behind me about thirty or so feet, and watch my back while I walked through the basement level tunnels to the cafeteria. If the guy came up from behind and passed him, he'd casually call out my last name, saying something like, "Hey, Nix, wait for me!" Using my last name was the signal. I would also always walk next to the right hand wall. If I heard my last name, I was to stop and turn my back against the wall, pretending I was just waiting for a buddy to catch up so we could eat together.

Most prison stabbings are in the back, and I had to avoid presenting that opportunity to him. My hope was that he'd just cool down and forget about me, but I had no way of knowing his intentions, other than the ones he'd already previously made known. If he were to find out that a conscientious objector was playing him like a fiddle, his convict pride would probably push him to come at me straight on. Short of that, most cons would bide their time, looking and waiting for an opportunity. Working in relative close proximity to me, he may have been taking his time and waiting for the right situation, thinking it would eventually present itself.

On two occasions during the next two months, the killer was not anywhere among the inmates waiting by the shop tunnel gate to open for lunch. So Joe dropped back. When it opened, the crowd began moving through the gate and into the tunnels. About a quarter of the way to the cafeteria, I heard Joe call, "Hey Nix, wait up!"

I stopped, turned with my back to the wall. As I looked back at Joe, not making eye contact with the killer, he passed by walking noticeably faster than I had been.

A third occasion was different. Neither the killer nor Joe was at the gate. A few inmates walked fast to lunch, trying to be at the head of the line. I decided to try that, and as the gate buzzed open I began to work my way through the crowd, walking faster than normal. As I did, I heard a voice from behind say, "Wait for me Nix," but it wasn't Joe's voice. I pulled up to wait as the killer walked past, speed walking faster than I was.

I thought only Joe and I were privy to this plan, not wanting to risk others knowing and it possibly leaking to the killer. It wasn't even a Witness who warned me; it was Jesse Brumbaugh, the Amish conscientious objector. He worked in the electric shop and Joe may have asked him to cover for him, knowing he'd be late. Jesse stayed with me through the chow line, but once we got our food trays, we could see there was only one empty chair available against the outside wall. It was at the far end of the building, the last table, and one inmate was already eating there. Jesse excused himself then, preferring to eat at a closer table with some of his other friends.

So I sat with the Eskimo that day, just he and I. I thought it would be cool to be able to say I've dined with a cannibal. This man was shy, always alone and didn't seem used to talking. I tried to engage him in conversation and he did attempt to respond, but I could see he was uncomfortable. So I gave him his privacy as we ate together, and then bid him farewell. He always looked lost to me, so far from home. My heart went out to this poor lonely man who had really messed up his life by eating his wife and two kids.

Chapter 14

Bunny and Others

Mr. Luxton wanted me to make a couple of heavy-duty screen doors for the prison laundry. I was done building the X-ray room cabinet, so I went over to the laundry to take some measurements.

The laundry pretty much had nothing but gays, who played the female roll in those relationships, working in it. We Witness boys got the biggest kick out of their animated behavior and antics. We'd never seen anything like them before. Every Saturday morning we had to take our dirty clothing to the laundry, enter one of the screen doors, and then going along a long counter, dropped off our dirty shirts, pants, underwear, socks, sheets, pillowcases, and towels. Then we'd pick up a clean replacement from a different one of these characters for each item, before exiting the second screen door at the far end of this long narrow room.

Mr. Luxton would sometimes talk a lot about them. Before being assigned as a carpenter shop supervisor, he worked around them a lot as a younger prison guard and had witnessed many of their activities. This was long before homosexuality had come out of the closet and became socially acceptable, as it seems to have become in today's world.

In the laundry was one old one named "Baby Doll," a crippled, short, skinny African American man in his late seventies. Mr. Luxton told us how he'd been injured many years before. On a cold day, he and his partner had made a nice little love nest among the warm freshly dried sheets still in a large commercial dryer. While they were inside, another inmate shut the door and turned the machine on. It crippled Baby Doll and killed the other inmate.

He told us about others and their comical names, which I've now forgotten. He then asked us which Hollywood actor we thought had been one while in Springfield. Of course we had no idea. He replied, "Rory Calhohn!" He claimed that he was a "flaming" one in Springfield.

At some point, he told me I reminded him of Pretty Boy Floyd. He had apparently been in Springfield from what Mr. Luxton said. I did know he had done some time in a federal prison.

Springfield had imprisoned a number of infamous criminals and others, men such as Chuck Berry, John Gotti, Ted Kaczynski (the "Unabomber"), Larry Flynt, Mickey Cohen, Vito Genovese, and many others that I'm sure I don't know about.

Three or four weeks after the beginning of the threat by the electric shop killer, my guards began sending me out again on maintenance and repair projects around the prison and hospital wards.

Before they sent me out, they'd call the electric shop guard and coordinate my whereabouts with the killer's so our paths would never cross during working hours. Mostly he was just kept in the electric shop permanently now, I was told.

Even before the incident with him, and now continuing with my rounds again throughout the prison and wards, it was becoming obvious that I had an admirer. His name was Bunny, one of the full-blown laundry room gays.

His job was to deliver in a laundry cart all the clean laundry to the wards, hospital and cellblocks, for inmates who were unable or not allowed to come to the laundry themselves.

I'd be working somewhere, either alone or with Don, when Bunny would come wheeling by. When seeing me, he'd then put the brakes on his little delivery cart. He would then hang around where I was working twenty or thirty feet away, talking loudly to another inmate so I would notice and stealing glances at me for hours. This would continue until either lunchtime or the end of the workday rolled around. Bunny was sort of a Nathan Lane-looking character, a bit heavy but in his mid to late thirties, I would estimate. I tried to ignore him, never saying a word to encourage him, but on and on it went.

Don figured out what was going on and got the biggest kick out of it. Then I had to put up with some of his choice comments: "Here comes your girlfriend" and "Don't be sneaking off to the gym this evening!" On and on he'd go. After a while, I got tired of coming out on the short end of all the Bunny jokes. I began to think about whether there was some way to turn the tables on Don so I could have a laugh at his expense.

Soon Don and I were sent to install the two new screen doors I had made for the laundry room. Well, we were certainly the star attraction there that day. When we entered, Bunny had the cart full and was just about to leave on his rounds. Upon seeing me, that trip got cancelled and there he stayed not too far beyond the door I was installing, talking loudly to another co-worker. Don, installing the other door had his own crowd down by him, vying for his attention.

There was quite a distance between the two doors. As I was working I had a brainstorm; this was my big opportunity. I'd wait until Don had his back turned, quietly call Bunny over and tell him that the guy down by the other door liked him, saying that he should go over and talk to him. Well, it seemed like a good idea at the time.

So I waited until I thought Don would be turned around awhile, and then I softly said to Bunny "Psst," motioning for him to come.

He looked surprised and turned to look behind him to see if I was trying to contact somebody beyond. Seeing only a wall there, he turned back toward me with his hands motioning toward himself saying "*Me*", with a look of excited anticipation.

"Yeah, yeah, come here," I said softly, also motioning.

So he hustled right over to me very excited. I thought he'd stop, so I could tell him about Don. Instead, he grabbed my left hand, saying, "Yes! Yes! Yes!" I couldn't get a word in edgewise.

I was now intent on peeling his hand off mine. As I did, he'd grab higher up with his other hand. This process continued all the way up to my shoulder and all the while I was moving backward and he was moving forward, still saying nonstop, "Yes! Yes!"

With my left side now immobilized by Bunny and his face only about a foot from mine, I still tried to salvage the situation. Half turning back toward Don, I started pointing at him and saying to Bunny, "See that guy therrr . . . !" There was Don, watching all this with his jaw dropped almost to his chest.

111

Well what could I say, that sure backfired on me.

After finishing the doors, we had two possible routes back to the shop. I suggested we take the one through the camp so I could stop and take a shower. We did but when we got there, with all my stuff now in the BOQ, there was no way Don would let me use his towel. I ended washing up in our carpenter shop lavatory. It had an extremely large picture window facing the shop, which provided no privacy at all. With my shirt off and trying to dry my left side off with paper towels, I then had to suffer through the snickers of all my co-workers as Don revealed what happened.

Back in the shops, Mr. Luxton had finished sharpening some shaper blades to use in the making of hundreds of wooden window screen frames, to replace broken ones throughout the prison. We spent weeks gluing them together, having them painted, stapling the copper screen material to the frames, then the trim pieces, also attaching some hardware clips to secure them to the prison window opening. Yes, I said copper screens . . . nothing but the finest for all the criminals!

The beginning of October, 1967, Mr. Luxton or Mr. Long informed me that I was now going to be paid five cents per hour. Well it was better than nothing. I would be pulling down about eight dollars a month. It also might be signaling that the Bureau of Prison's hawkish policy toward us might be softening.

The reason so many screens were damaged and needed to be replaced had to do with how the guards were checking for escape attempts. In the individual cells, the windows were fixed, heavy steel-paned windows with glass. The panes were small enough that an inmate couldn't crawl through, even if he broke the glass out. In the medical facilities, the ward, and some dormitory sections of the prison, not the camp, double-hung steel widows were used. In these, the bottom part of the window slid up, allowing for ventilation. Outside the windows were the screens, and outside them were the bars.

On a regular basis the guards were supposed to make rounds with a hammer, tapping each bar to determine if it was intact or had been cut. They were supposed to do this from the outside of the building, where the bars were. In the motor pool, the prison had a ladder truck for this purpose.

This however, was just too much work for the guards, positioning the truck for each window, cranking the ladder into position, climbing up the ladder and then down, and dealing with the weather. Moreover, there were thousands of windows in this large prison, some up five floors if counting the basement.

Instead, taking the easy way, they'd simply open the windows from the inside and tap on the bars through the screen. A sharp tap would produce a ring or a thud, telling the guard if the bars were intact or cut. However, tapping the bars with the screen in between would obviously damage the screen.

The first couple of days installing the replacement screens, Mr. Luxton didn't have anything nice to say about the guards causing the need for what we were doing. It was a pain in the rear, climbing up and down that ladder, taking a screen replacement up and the broken one down. And so far, we'd only been doing the first floor above the basement windows.

This would be the last job that I'd work on with Jodi Ray outside the shop. Toward the end of October, 1967, Jodi was transferred out to the BOQ. I was glad to see him out here; it would be a nicer place for him.

Around late October, 1967, a new brother was transferred into the hospital from a prison somewhere on the east coast, Danbury, Connecticut, I think. His first name was Russell, which is all I knew. Because he was very sick, he was never able to come to any of our religious meetings, therefore most of the brothers never had an opportunity to meet him. Russell was having chest pains and was sent to Springfield for diagnosis and medical treatment. We heard all this from brothers working in administration and in the hospital sections.

Chapter 15

Last Good-Bye

We eventually got word that Russell was soon going to be operated on, so we were all concerned about the outcome for him.

As you entered the carpenter shop on the right side, the large spray paint room was first, followed by a built-in rack for lumber storage. Next to it was a flight of concrete stairs leading up to an open platform with a handrail, used for miscellaneous material storage. Next to the stairs was our shop's secure tool room.

The lumber racks were recessed in a bit from the spray booth, tool room wall, and start of the stairs. One day I needed a piece of lumber for whatever I was working on. I went to the lumber rack and stepped up on lumber sticking out a little bit on the lowest rack, right next to the stairs. I was in an awkward position, hanging on with my right hand, using my left to sight lumber for a suitable piece.

Just then Steen, with Jodi following, started walking up the stairs to get something above. Steen stopped to tell me something, his head a foot or two above mine now. As mentioned before, Steen occasionally took great pleasure in running us Witnesses boys down over our neutrality and not fighting for our country. At other times, when talking about Tuckers Farm and other southern prisons that he and Jodi had both experienced, he'd claim we'd never be able to take it. Usually I just let him run his mouth off, feeling it would be a waste of time to respond. This day though, he linked the two subjects, threw in WWII and again claimed that we would be wetting our pants if we ever had to do time in Tuckers Farm—that we'd be crying for our mommies. Steen was very pleased with himself when he finished.

My response would be different that day; I'd had enough of his talk. Despite this awkward position I was in, I replied, "You're a fine one to be talking like a patriot! We've all heard from your own mouth how when you served your country, you stole from it instead, selling military hardware on the black market! I've put up with a lot of this type of talk, but I don't think I should be hearing it from you. And let me tell you something about World War II. Even when Hitler first came to power in the early thirties, he began to imprison every Witness he could get his hands on, men and women! They could be found in every jail and concentration camp the Nazis had. But the young Witnesses like ourselves, who were drafted and refused military service, were usually hung, beheaded, or shot by a firing squad! Any of my brothers here, if we had to, would do the same as our German brothers! Besides, your Tuckers Farm and the others are kiddies camps compared to Hitler's death camps. I don't think you could do time in one without compromising or collaborating! But anyway, in this country, you'll only find Witnesses in jail for one thing, what we're in for, and only in federal prisons. You'll never find any of us in Tuckers Farm or the like. They're state facilities, built for your average common criminals—*like you Steen*!"

I'd been so intent on telling him all this that I hadn't noticed his demeanor changing as I was talking. He was now red, livid, shaking, veins bulging out of his neck and forehead, fist clenched, ready to knock me off my little perch. Jodi had a look of surprised delight, getting a big kick out of the way I'd just talked to Steen. I noticed all this in a fraction of a second and figured I'd better get out of there, Steen's about to go off!

Quickly saying "BYE," I was gone in a flash as Jodi busted out laughing. Steen had built up so much steam that when I glanced back at him from the other side of the shop, he looked deflated, almost exhausted, and hunched over with his head hanging. Jodi was bent over a little, seeming to comfort him, while still chuckling with a big smile on his face. Steen had almost blown his cork.

We got word that Russell had his operation and the news was bad. He had inoperable lung cancer. They just sewed him back up; nothing could be done for him. He was to be released back to his home as soon as he was recovered enough to travel.

About the same time, my roommate heard back about his parole application. It was granted! I was wrong and he was right. I was glad for him that I was wrong. Hopefully, maybe this would be a start to reversing the government's policy of no paroles for us. I said my good-byes to him.

A couple of days later, Don and I were sent to the hospital wards to repair some floor tiles outside one of the elevators, a high-traffic area. A few feet away from where we were replacing tile was the door to Mickey Cohen's cell. Because of organized crimes contract out on his life, he was the only prisoner who was allowed to block his cell door site window out, with a piece of paper on the inside for privacy.

We were making noise as we worked, and Mickey began to call out to us in a quivering, crackling, and fearful voice. "Who . . . who's there? Wha-what are you doing?" He was obviously afraid we were hit men, bent on breaking in to do away with him. It must have been a pathetic last few years for this notorious mobster and killer, if Don and I could terrify him.

This would end up being a memorable day for me. After finishing the tile and getting Mickey calmed down, then bidding him farewell, we went through the recovery ward and were able to visit with Russell. He seemed to be recovering well and he was looking forward to going home, obviously. This was the first and only time I was to see him. He was a nice-looking small young man with red hair. He was taking the realization that he didn't have long to live quite well.

There were many good people working in the federal prison system, from guards up to administration and all the way to the Federal Bureau of Prisons in Washington, DC. I'll always be thankful to them that they acted to get Russell released so he didn't have to die in Springfield, as so many others before him. They didn't have to do this. Springfield was the place that most old federal prisoners were sent for medical attention and to die. I'd see these types of guys, old cons in the wards, obviously on their last legs or bedridden.

Not too long before this visit with Russell, I was to see one old con that I remembered well. I was waiting in a hallway between two wards. Don had gone somewhere to check on something. I was alone waiting by our cart, keeping my eye on our tools with my back against the wall. Then out from one ward came one old inmate. He looked about seventy and was sick and walking slowly as if every step was going to be his last. Slowly moving along the opposite wall, heading toward the other ward, he lost his balance and fell against the wall several times, which kept him from going down. I was expecting him to hit the floor at any step and was prepared to run over and assist him if necessary. But as he was walking toward me, I was trying not to stare. I'd long since learned not to stare at other cons. This guy though, looked about as far away from dangerous as any con I had yet seen. Not until he finally got opposite me, with my back still against the wall and looking straight ahead, did I get a good long look at his profile as he slowly passed six feet away. As he continued until out of site, I was moved by his pathetic situation, slowly dying with no family around.

You can make real friends in prison—true ones, I would learn—but as you get old and sick, confined to a prison hospital bed or ward, even they can't come to visit and comfort you. I was only allowed in those wards with a pass for a specific purpose. So I had reason to appreciate the unique opportunity of freedom extended to Russell, as brief as it would be, to die with his family around. Bless those officials!

Almost forty years later in early 2007, as I was writing this part of this book, I'd call the Medical Center for Federal Prisoners. A helpful official there, Al Quintaro, gave me a Bureau of Prisons website where I could find the information I was seeking. This was necessary I was to find out later, as prisons only keep prisoner records for twenty-five years before forwarding them to a Washington, DC, archive division.

From these websites, I was also able to get mug shots of Vito Genovese. His mug shot looked familiar; especially the profile, but I couldn't place it. Waking up in the middle of the night two days later, it came to me; Vito Genovese was that sick old man struggling to walk past me in the hallway between those two medical wards. I also remembered then that Vito's nurse, Mel Littlefield, had told me he was housed in one of those wards above the prison library. The two-page bio that I got with the mug shot said he continued to run his crime family via visits from his brother, right up to his death in Springfield, on February 14, 1969, from heart failure. Mel had told me that Vito was slowly dying of cancer, colon cancer I thought. But as I think about that day, as sick as he was, he did have a determined look on his face. Plus he was still husky and burly and looked to me like someone who could have really busted some heads in his heyday. Little did I imagine at the time that this guy was still up to no good and was potentially still powerful and dangerous, despite appearances at the time.

Not knowing when Russell would be released, we said our good-byes to him and continued through the ward to another elevator at the opposite end of the building. As we neared it, Captain John came over to us smiling, happy to see us. He liked talking with the young Witnesses, and Don had met him on previous occasions. We visited with him for about five minutes. He was polite and friendly. It's hard to imagine that he was the last stagecoach-robbing killer still alive in the United States. I could only think that he's a completely different person from the one who committed those terrible crimes more than sixty-seven years previously, at the turn of the century. For a shrunken ninety-seven-year-old, he still seemed several inches taller than I am, and I was five feet nine. He was skinny and frail, though. Shaking his hand, we said our good-byes to him as well. This would be my first and last time seeing him. At ninety-seven, every day could be his last.

When we were finally on our way back to the shop, Don commented that we hadn't seen Bunny that day. He wanted to know if we had broken up.

At the end of every workday, we had to clean the shop. On Fridays, we'd do a better job of it, oiling the metal surfaces of our woodworking machinery for the weekend.

Jodi had been complaining to me for several days that he thought Vodopich had been slacking off during cleanup. He advised me that I'd better have a talk with him or he'd be sorry. So I took Vodopich aside and explained the situation. It wasn't that he wasn't doing anything, but Jodi apparently thought he was doing the easy tasks, leaving the harder ones for everyone else, which he was.

Come Friday, while we were cleaning up, Jodi started grumbling about Vodopich again, saying that I'd better quickly talk to him. So I did, but it was already too late. Jodi had gone off. When I got to Vodopich, Jodi was about five seconds behind me, demanding to know why he wasn't doing more. When he didn't get the answer he wanted, he just dropped Vodopich right at my feet. Vodopich covered up as Jodi continued to pound on him, although not really doing any serious damage.

I gently put my hand on Jodi's shoulder and softly said, "Okay. That's enough. He's learned his lesson." Jodi stopped and walked away.

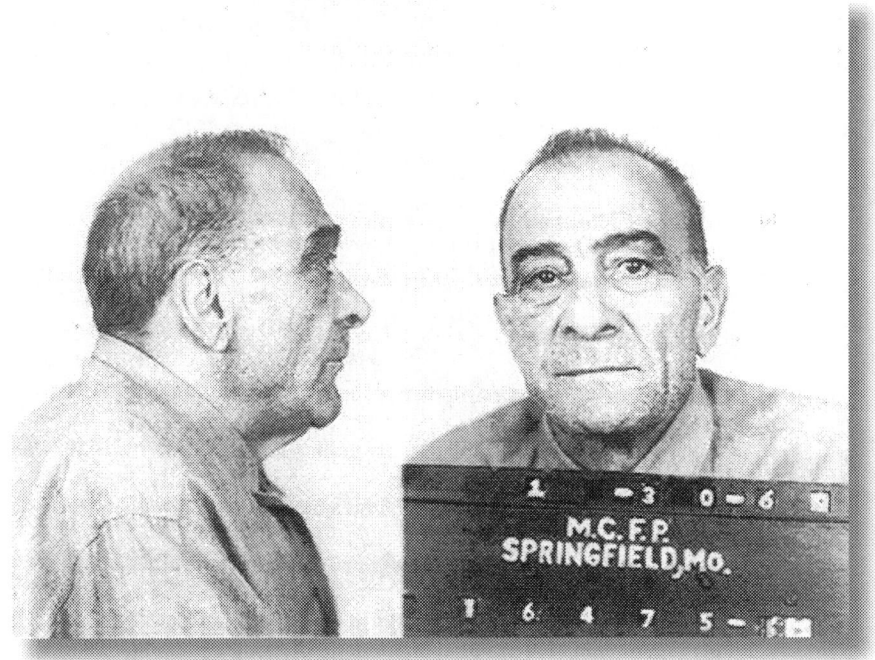

Vito Genovese

When Vodopich got up, I reminded him, "Remember where we're at? I tried to warn you! We're not in some high school wood shop." Jodi had obviously made the point even clearer to him.

I think it was the next Monday, November 20, 1967, that I was finally sent to install the cabinet I'd made for the X-ray room in the hospital. Steen had done a nice job spray-painting it a light green, a common interior color around there.

I put it on a cart and was sent to the X-ray room alone. At least I wouldn't have to put up with Don's Bunny jokes that day. At the hospital, I took an elevator up to the first floor, where the X-ray room was. Inside it I was alone, the only one there.

I put the cabinet in position and was about to secure it to the wall when a guard burst into the room. He was all excited, telling me I had to leave immediately. "Hurry! You've got to go right now!"

For the first and only time while in prison, except for the lightning in Tucson, I had a jolt of fear sweep over me. I immediately had visions that the electric shop killer had slipped out of his shop and was coming to get me, maybe ambushing me somewhere.

I started to move with my cart and tools toward the elevator. The guard said "No, leave them! Take the stairs—this way. Hurry!" He started to accompany me toward the stairs.

"What's happening?" I asked.

"There's been an escape attempt; bars have been cut. They're bringing the guy in now!" Well that was a relief!

The guard escorted me to a door, opened it, and sent me down the stairs. I'd gotten three or four steps when a door flung open down below and in rushed about four guards, giving one inmate the bum's rush as they began coming up the stairs.

As they reached the landing halfway up and turned toward me, I recognized the inmate. It was Mr. Weaver, my bible student. I pressed myself up against the wall so they could all pass me on the stairs. As they did, Mr. Weaver and I made eye contact. His expression never changed; just a hopeless resigned look to whatever consequences were awaiting him for this escape attempt. They were obviously taking him for X-rays to see if he had any hacksaw blades or something hidden up his rectum.

As I was walking back to the shop, I started fearing that I could get involved in this escape attempt investigation that was just starting. Mr. Weaver's cell was going to be gone over with a fine-tooth comb. They'd find the two books he had of mine. Again, they were contraband for anyone other than me to possess and the authorization stamps on the inside covers, issued by the prison's Protestant chaplain had my number, 9307 written on them.

I hadn't seen Mr. Weaver for almost two months, ever since the assistant warden told me not to go to the main prison yard after the electric shop killer threatened me.

Back in the shop, I was still thinking I might get sucked into this investigation—at the very least, scolded for allowing another inmate to have possession of my property.

A call came into the office and Mr. Long and Mr. Luxton called me over and handed me a pass saying, "Go see the Protestant chaplain. He wants to talk to you about something." They had unusual expressions on their faces.

As I was walking to the office of the Protestant chaplain, the one who stamped and signed my books, I was thinking *Oh boy, here it comes!* I was envisioning, at the very least, a scolding by the Protestant chaplain—or I could end up before the warden and have some good time taken away.

It was nearing the end of November, and I was about four and a half months away from my good time release date. I was wondering just how hard they might come down on me and I had to be prepared for the worst.

When I got to his office, it seemed he had me cooling my heels for about ten minutes on a bench. He then invited me to sit in a chair before his desk and started saying words to this effect: "I've never seen this happen before! In all my years doing this job, this is the first time I've seen this. I don't understand why, but you're going home!"

Surprised, I asked "What?" I also briefly wondered if I had somehow committed the magic mistake that gets you kicked out of prison. He went on to explain to me that for some reason, on their own, the parole board in Washington had reconsidered my parole, months after denying it, and decided to now grant it. He said he had never seen them take such action before.

I was still a little dumbfounded. Why was I hearing this from him? Then I noticed a sign high up on the wall to my left; it had his name followed by "Parole Officer." I turned and read the open door behind me, where it read not only "Protestant Chaplain" but "Parole Officer" as well. So he had a dual job there, chaplain and parole officer. A large prison like this apparently had more than one parole officer. When I had gone up for parole, I had dealt with the other one.

He went on to tell me that the parole was granted starting that day. Also, they had already contacted my family in California, who wanted to send me an airplane ticket back home so I wouldn't have to spend four days on a bus. I was then told they would keep me there until the ticket arrived and then release me.

I was next sent to the release area of the prison, the same place I'd entered when arriving from Tucson almost eleven months previously. They fitted me with a new suit of clothing, complete with a heavy wool overcoat, which were all made in Leavenworth Federal Correctional Institution. The clothes were then put away, waiting for my exact release date. I thought to myself as I returned to the BOQ, that I had sure skated on that whole escape situation.

This was Monday, November 20, 1967. It wouldn't be until Thursday, November 23, Thanksgiving Day, that I'd be released, the ticket having arrived late the day before. My family, thinking they were doing me a favor by sparing me a four-day bus ride back to California, instead caused me to spend the better part of four days more in prison. Thanks! I'd much rather have spent that time free, seeing parts of the country I'd never seen before on a bus, rather than looking at this prison for four more days.

On my last day in the shop, Wednesday, I left the nice bomber jacket with Vodopich, since he had seniority in the shop as far as being in line for the next available shop jacket. Of course, I had fun telling Don I'd have given it to him if not for all his Bunny jokes. I was to learn that day that Russell was also to be released on the following day, Thanksgiving Day, 1967.

I said my good-byes to as many of the brothers as I could, also to Gordon Steen, Jodi Ray, Mr. Long, and Mr. Luxton. They had been memorable workmates and bosses, to say the least. I have never forgotten them.

In the morning I had an early departure for the airport, so I had to get up an hour or two before everyone else. The phone rang in the BOQ at the right time, acting as an alarm clock for me only. When ready to leave, I made sure to call the guard tower. I didn't want to risk getting shot my last day.

Chapter 16

Free at Last

Back in the main prison for the last time, I dressed in my Leavenworth prisoner-made suit and overcoat. I was so excited that I didn't realize yet just how bad this outfit was. The prison gives me twenty dollars in traveling money, plus all the money I earned the last two months in the carpenter shop, at five cents per hour.

A guard drove me to a small airport that seemed to be west of Springfield, northwest from the prison. I never got to see the town of Springfield, despite living there for almost eleven months. I asked the guard when Russell was leaving. He said that in perhaps another hour or two, his family was coming to pick him up; they had arrived from somewhere on the East Coast late the day before.

Later I was to wonder many times what happened to Russell. Ten years later I would run into Joe Sedor, and he would tell me that Russell died about two months after my release. He would also tell me about Captain John dying not too long after his release in Springfield. Vito Genovese also passed away in Springfield Medical Center, less than a year after his release. Joe would be released about four months after me, getting out on his good time date.

Now at the Springfield airport, I was excited to be taking my first airplane ride. I was twenty when I'd gone into prison and was twenty-two when I got out, about to fly for the first time, despite growing up right next to LAX.

I got on a small prop plane for a short flight to Kansas City, where I'd board a 707 for Los Angeles. The small plane had about fifteen or so seats. As one of the first ones to board, I was able to get a window seat; I wanted to see the view.

A young eighteen-year-old girl recently out of high school then came and sat next to me. She was more excited than I was and couldn't stop talking. She was from Springfield and on her way to the "big city" for the first time. She had a job lined up, a place to stay with relatives, and her parents' blessing. I heard all about it as she excitedly chattered along nonstop.

She eventually ran out of things to inform me about, so she asked me where I was coming from and going to. I hadn't even spoken a word to her yet. So I then told her I'd just been released from the Medical Center for Federal Prisoners less than an hour earlier and was on my way back to Los Angeles. I think once she heard "Medical Center for Federal Prisoners," she was terrified and didn't hear the part about what I was in for. With a worried look, she eyed an empty seat across the aisle and up one row and then quickly started to move for it. Unfortunately, she had already loosely buckled her seat belt when first sitting down and when reaching its limits, she recoiled herself right back into the seat. Then she was too scared to move.

Well that sure shut her up and totally dampened her demeanor. I didn't hear a peep out of her the rest of the flight. I could only imagine that as a young girl growing up in Springfield, the prison was probably where all the bogeymen were, and that was true to a large extent. To get her parents blessing for this move, she probably heard quite a bit from them. Just leaving them at the gate and then sitting next to me, all in less than thirty seconds, she may have feared that in the short walk from the gate to the plane, she'd moved into her worst childhood and father's nightmare.

After landing in Kansas City, in a flash she was the first one off the plane. The last I saw of her, she was more than one hundred feet ahead, speed walking and casting a nervous look over her shoulder back at me.

I had a six-hour layover in Kansas City, so there was a lot of time to kill. It started feeling hot in the terminal, so I took the overcoat off. I noticed that some people were checking me out. I was thinking, *Maybe I'm looking good in this new suit.* It was still hot, so I took the suit coat off too. I had been sweating in the coat as I had walked around and I was now catching even more looks. When I went into the restroom and looked in the mirror, I couldn't believe what I saw. Where my nice new white dress shirt was wet with sweat down to

Parole Form H-8
(Rev. Jan. 1967)
(Formerly Parole Form 17)

The United States Board of Parole
Washington, D.C. 20537

Certificate of Parole

Know all Men by these Presents:

It having been made to appear to the United States Board of Parole that

STEPHEN BLAIR NIX , Register No. 9307-PCS , a prisoner in

the MEDICAL CENTER FOR FEDERAL PRISONERS, SPRINGFIELD, MISSOURI ,

is eligible to be PAROLED, and that there is a reasonable probability that he WILL REMAIN AT LIBERTY WITHOUT VIOLATING THE LAWS, and it being the opinion of the said United States Board of Parole that the release of this person is not incompatible with the welfare of society, it is ORDERED by the

said United States Board of Parole that he be PAROLED on NOVEMBER 20 19 67 ,

and that he remain within the limits of CENTRAL DISTRICT OF CALIFORNIA until

DECEMBER 5 , 1968 ; or in the event of a committed fine or a committed fine and costs, until the same have been paid or he has been discharged under the provisions of Section 3569, Title 18, U.S. Code, or until other action may be taken by the said United States Board of Parole.

Given under the hands and the seal of the United States Board of Parole

this 20th day of November , nineteen hundred and sixty-seven .

UNITED STATES BOARD OF PAROLE,

By

Parole/Youth Division Executive.

[SEAL]

ADVISER

PROBATION OFFICER Mr. Angus D. McEachen, CUSPO, Los Angeles, California

This CERTIFICATE OF PAROLE will become effective on the date of release shown on the reverse side. If the parolee's continuance on parole becomes incompatible with the welfare of society, or if he fails to comply with any of the conditions listed on the reverse side, he may be retaken on a warrant issued by a Member of the Board of Parole, and reimprisoned pending a hearing to determine if the parole should be revoked.

Steve's certificate of parole from Springfield

my lower rib cage, it had sucked the black dye out of my black wool Leavenworth suit coat. I quick put the coat back on, but that wasn't all. I knew the shoes were bad, but as I looked more closely at this suit, I realized the pant legs were extremely high and not the same length. They were off by almost a couple of inches in length. The length on the suit coat sleeves was about as bad.

No wonder people were staring at me. I should have been alerted when picking it out, upon seeing the "Leavenworth" label. What do prisoners making ten cents per hour, fifteen cents at the most, care about quality? I think they were competing among themselves to see who could make the worst suit and get away with it.

I had several hours in Kansas City to reflect on the experiences I had been through in the last year and a half. At the beginning of this story, I mentioned that by the time I was nine or ten years old, I believed I could possibly go to federal prison one day for refusing to join the army. As I got older and talked to other Witnesses that had preceded me through this experience, I had a preconceived idea of what to expect. But my experiences would be much more intense than others I had spoken with, or heard of, or read about, at least ones from the United States.

The thing that surprised me the most, which I didn't expect, was how I would view all the many hundreds of convicts and criminals I had met. I liked them. I found that they each had a good or friendly side, some redeeming quality. Not one was all bad. Even the psychopath on the baseball field would have probably been the same under different circumstances. Before being threatened by the electric shop killer, I had gotten along with him just fine also.

Another surprise was the prisoners' foul language, which was rather tame by today's standards. I was used to worse on the jobs I had worked on before incarceration. The worst I heard goes to the two US marshals that drove me from L.A. to Florence, Arizona.

Another thing I forgot to mention before: what type of federal crime can you usually tell an inmate is guilty of just by looking at him? Go to the end of this chapter for the answer.

Once back in L.A., I had three or four days to report to my parole officer in the Federal Building in downtown Los Angeles, right across the street from the Los Angeles City Hall. For the first month or two, I had to report to him personally and then afterward just by mail, sending in a form properly filled out at the end of the month. Mr. Angus D. McEachen was his name.

One week after being released, I got a letter from my local draft board. They'd reclassified me 1-A, apparently ready to draft me again. This was a common government tactic during World War II. Some Witnesses were drafted, imprisoned, released, and then the process was repeated repeatedly, so that some of our brothers spent the whole war and more, incarcerated.

After the Second World War, Stalin adopted the same practice toward Jehovah's Witnesses in Eastern Europe, but expanded it to include entire Witness families. All he could capture were sent to the Gulags in Siberia, where many were worked to death.

Many of our East German brothers, starting in 1933, spent as many as twelve years in Hitler's prisons and concentration camps. They were then cycled into the communist system's prisons and Siberians gulags, doing in excess of twenty years altogether in some cases. The fact that these German brothers had refused to kill any Russians during WWII, mattered little to the communists.

Laws had changed in the States. As an ex-convict and felon now, I was prohibited from qualifying to serve in the US military, considered morally deficient because of my criminal record. I couldn't join if I wanted to; the draft board was just messing with my mind. I never heard from them again.

I was to also learn then what had happened to my two little friends I'd grown up playing with in the neighborhood, the ones that had lived next door and across the street from Mr. Cummings. One, Tommy Brennan, was stabbed to death in a Manhattan Beach bars parking lot. The other, Melfy Traber, went to Vietnam and was awarded the Silver Star for his actions in battle.

Going by to visit him after my release from Springfield, I came upon him and his two brothers still running around the neighborhood playing cops and robbers, despite all being in their twenties then. It was probably our childhood war games, always against the japs then, which may have partially prepared him for his heroics in Vietnam. We had always been about the same size and height up to and through high school. But when seeing him on that occasion, he had grown six or seven inches since graduation, and was by then a hugh harley riding biker.

I went back to work as a framing carpenter, sometimes working with Denny Gormley. Denny and I would become closer than ever before. His oldest son John, had estranged himself from his family, and his youngest son Dan, was always a bit of a screwball. At fifteen or sixteen years of age, while I was in federal prison, Dan became the youngest person ever to do time in California's Folsom Prison. He was a big, muscular kid. John was also big and was our high school heavyweight wrestling champion his last two years in school. His last year, 1963, he won the CIF California State Championship, heavyweight AA division. But with Denny's two sons out of control at the time, I was about all he had left for a while. Dan would eventually return, but not John.

At least once a week, Denny and I would take off work and go play golf. Sometimes his business partner Alex Escalante would go with us. Alex always reminded me of Charles Bronson, but much bigger and heavier. We'd usually play Baldwin or Fox Hills, Alondra, Palos Verdes, Western, and once Valentia. Denny loved golf; I'd been playing since I was thirteen.

On occasions, Denny could get feisty on the job. Sometimes he'd get in an argument with another tradesman or the general contractor over some work-related issue. A few times it appeared they might even come to blows. When this looked like it might be about to happen, Alex would become overly protective of him. He loved Denny dearly, and because of his glass jaw and how he got it, he would go wild at the thought of someone hitting Denny. With tears almost starting to come into his eyes, he'd jump in between the two, ready to take the other guy on but also scolding him up one side and down the other for even thinking to hit someone who looked like Denny. This usually ended the matter, for back then most any American would be ashamed to ever hit someone even wearing eyeglasses, much less someone whose face was messed up as bad as Denny's was. Even from behind, Denny had a big crater in the muscle between his neck and shoulder, where the mortar or hand grenade had detonated. Denny nearly always worked with his shirt off.

When I was nineteen, we once entered a small diner out in the San Fernando Valley before work. As we started to sit down at the counter, a man got up to leave and seeing Denny, he gave him a disgusted look as if he were a freak. At seeing this, Alex got right up in the guy's face saying, "What are you looking at! This man got this fighting on Iwo Jima for guys like you. Show a little respect!" The man apologized profusely and left looking embarrassed and ashamed.

During these types of situations, Denny would usually have a long-suffering smile on his face as if to say, "Oh that Alex, isn't he something!"

I witnessed another relatively mild incident involving these two and a building owner. This occurred shortly after my release from Springfield, and I was the cause of it. It occurred on a four-unit apartment house in Culver City, not too far from the MGM Studios. As we finished the framing, the owner asked me to put some wormwood siding on the front of the building. We never even had any scaffolding, so I jeri-rigged some up with 2X4's and 2X6's on the job site, something we normally did in this situation. The owner came back and had a fit over my use of this lumber. Denny got into an argument with him over this. The owner spoke with a heavy German accent; he'd been a former Nazi U-boat commander during WWII. No way was Alex going to let this man even argue with Denny. He barged in between the two saying, "Hey, don't come to this country and talk to a war hero like *that*! Look at him!" Alex told him then that he too had served in the Merchant Marines during the war and stated, "I wish I had ran into you during the war. I'd of sunk your ass to the bottom of the sea!" Denny then told the owner to finish his own siding and off we went over to the nearby Baldwin Hills Golf course and played a round, just he and I.

In late January or February of 1968, a big scandal was exposed in the press and TV news. It was about the murder of inmates, falsification of death certificates, and other abuses committed by sadistic prison guards and authorities at prison camps in Arkansas or Alabama. It was reported to have occurred at Tuckers Farm and the other prison farm that Steen and Jodi had told me all about while we were in Springfield.

Everything they had told me that they had seen and experienced while there was now being exposed publicly in the news media. Still, I gave no thought to what Jodi had told me about his older brother Jimmy killing Martin Luther King.

When Martin Luther King Jr. was shot and killed on April 4, 1968, I had no recollection of ever connecting what Jodi had previously told me about his oldest brother Jimmy's intentions toward Martin Luther King. I, like many others, was not surprised about Mr. King's shooting. It seemed to me, as I've previously stated, that many thousands of racist people in the South wanted to shoot Martin Luther King.

As a person who didn't watch much TV or read the newspapers, I didn't truly appreciate Martin Luther King's contributions to the civil rights movement yet. At that time, I had no idea that over the next forty years I was to have a running off-and-on involvement with this assassination.

It took awhile for the shooter to be apprehended and identified in the media. During this time my wife and I decided we wanted to move to Hawaii. Five or six carpenters that I had previously worked with had already made that move. A building boom was underway there, and I was able to get a commitment from one contractor to hire me if I moved there. Being on parole, however, I needed to get permission from my parole officer before I'd be allowed to go.

While I was going through this process, I was working with Denny and Alex on the nicest custom house I had ever worked on up to that time. It was a large secluded home in Palos Verdes, overlooking the ocean and Catalina Island. About the time we finished this house and started working on a commercial store in Rolling Hills, I got permission from my parole officer to transfer to Hawaii.

It was just about this time when watching the news after work one night, that I saw that the killer of Martin Luther King had finally been captured. They reported him to be James Earl Ray from St. Louis, Missouri. They went on to report that he was a career criminal, and that most of his brothers were as well. As I was watching this, everything was falling right into place with many of the things Jodi had told me about his brother Jimmy; not one thing was inconsistent.

Then they showed a picture of James Earl Ray. I could immediately see the family resemblance. James Earl Ray was Jodi's brother, whom he called Jimmy. I would later see a picture of James Earl Ray's other brothers, but Jodi resembled him more than the other older two did. The real clincher was that James Earl Ray was reported to have escaped in early 1967 from the Missouri State Prison, exactly what Jodi had told me that day in our carpenter shop tool room. I was convinced. How many prisoners with the last name Ray escaped in early 1967 from the Missouri State Prison? Only one, I bet!

Despite my friendship with Jodi and his most likely saving my life, I knew I had a superior obligation to someone else, the same one who led me to be in prison in the first place, our Heavenly Father and Creator, Jehovah God. How could I be any part of covering up the murder of the one man I knew of who tried to solve one of the most serious, longest-running problems in the United States, in a nonviolent and peaceful fashion? I would rather the electric shop killer had slit my throat. I immediately got the phone book and found the number for the FBI office in Los Angeles.

The news report had mentioned how James Earl Ray had eluded capture for more than a month by fleeing to Canada, England and then to a couple of other countries in Europe. I thus figured the FBI had some jurisdiction because of interstate flight to avoid prosecution. The news broadcast had also stated that the FBI was conducting its "biggest" investigation in the history of the bureau, into this assassination. I figured I had to call them; even though Jodi Ray was among those whom I would never want to bring trouble upon, I just couldn't keep quiet.

When I called the FBI, a male answered. I began stating why I was calling, explaining that I was a parolee from the Medical Center for Federal Prisoners at Springfield, Missouri. While there, an inmate whom I believed to be the younger brother of James Earl Ray told me as early as late September 1967, that his brother was going to kill Martin Luther King.

The person I was speaking to interrupted me and said, "Sorry, we are not interested in this type of information. Thanks for calling."

I couldn't believe this response. Before he could hang up, I quickly said, "Well, what do I do with this information?"

He replied, "Put it in your parole report!" That ended the phone call with the FBI. Well, being a Witness I was used to this sort of rejection. But it just didn't seem right. Why did the news report claim that the FBI was conducting the largest investigation in its history and then dismiss my call, when it could have led to possible co-conspirators? Anyway, I did what the FBI told me to do. I reported it in my parole report at the end of May, to my parole officer, Mr. Agnus D. McEachen.

The parole report is a one-page form. In the space available, I briefly informed Mr. McEachen about Jodi Ray's statement concerning his oldest brother and his intention to kill Martin Luther King, stated to me approximately two months before my release from Springfield, which was six and a half months before the assassination of Mr. King.

I was never to hear back from the FBI or the parole officer. Well certainly not from the FBI. They never asked for my address or my name either. I probably wasn't on the phone much more than thirty seconds before they dismissed my call.

Since James Earl Ray pleaded guilty, there was no need for a trial. I heard all this through the media. Still, there were media reports that James Earl Ray didn't act alone, certainly afterward as he fled to Europe before his apprehension. I also believe he had coconspirators, that if not helped after the assassination, they certainly knew about it before and shared some legal culpability.

Answer to previous question: a moonshiner

Chapter 17

Moving to Hawaii and Beyond, to Kingdoms by the Sea

The end of May, 1968, I moved to Hawaii. I stayed with another carpenter, Bob Trivet and his wife Sandy, for two days. They were living in Lanikai on Oahu. I arrived on a Sunday. That first day Bob took me out diving, swimming out from Lanikai beach about three-fourths of a mile to the reef. Despite getting seasick out in the swells coming over the reef, it was the start of my becoming an avid skin diver. By the mid-1970s in Ponape, I would eventually be able to free dive down to ninety feet.

The next day, Monday, was Labor Day, the docks were closed. So I went to work with Bob and his piecework partner, Vic Wrangel, another Los Angeles carpenter I'd worked with occasionally. They were finishing off a nice custom house right across the street from Henry Kaiser's estate, out on Koko Head by Hawaii Kai. Bob and Vic told me that just a week or two before, President Nixon had stayed at the Kaiser Estate. While there, his helicopter had been landing just across the street from this house.

The next day, Tuesday, I was able to pick my truck up at the docks that I'd shipped via Matson to Hawaii. Later that day I found a one-bedroom house that I leased for one year, about a half mile farther into Lanikai. Not knowing Hawaii, I had really slopped out by settling in Lanikai, one of the nicest secluded communities on Oahu. I'd live there the majority of the time over the next twelve years when in Hawaii.

Before long I became a Hawaiianized carpenter, stripped down to working in nothing more than a pair of short shorts and tennis shoes with no socks. I was always as tanned as could be. The only drawback was that when walking on Lanikai Beach, my feet were bright white.

By 1969, my wife found another house closer to the beach. It was the third house back from the ocean, where I kept a small boat either in the water or on a boat trailer in the front yard. This would be our home until late 1974.

Early in 1969, I heard that my former workmate Woody Hinkle was finishing a job in Sitka, Alaska, where he had gone after visiting me in Mt. Lemmon Prison Camp outside Tucson. So I wrote him and got him to come down to Hawaii rather than return to California. Before he arrived, I had finished sheathing most of the roofs on Spinnaker Isles and the first increment of Robert Grant homes on Lunalilo Home Road, in the Hawaii Kai area.

A new tract of duplex condominiums opened up: Kuapa Isles. We were able to get away from sheathing and into cutting and stacking roofs, fascia board, and the decks and patios along the water of each condominium unit. We'd also cut and stack roofs on Pearl Ridge and custom houses here or there.

Occasionally one of two other brothers would work with us. One was George Walker from Waimanalo, a local *hauoli* and former Honolulu police officer. He was relatively new to construction work, having left law enforcement when becoming a Witness. Guy Pierce was the other brother and in the Kailua congregation with me. He had moved to Hawaii shortly after me to work on a large custom house that overlooked Kaneohe Bay, built for the man who owned the Sambo's Pancake House chain of restaurants.

Guy, a northern California carpenter, was about ten years older than I was. To me, that was almost like being from a different planet. The first day Woody and I picked him up for work, I asked him right off if he had just come from a Sears catalog photo shoot for work clothes. Shame on me. The next day we got him into shorts at least, but he still looked more like a Waikiki tourist from the Midwest. Despite Guy being older than both Woody and I, we made it a project to try to make him a piece working Hawaiianized L.A. framer. It would end up taking several years.

I was making far more money than I needed, so I decided I should work part time and my wife and I go into the full-time ministry. So this we did, starting in 1970. I still wasn't anywhere near comfortable going around dressed up so much. So I let the branch office in Honolulu know that I'd be willing to volunteer to travel around and work on Kingdom Hall construction, if that was needed. The Hawaii branch office oversaw the activities of Jehovah's Witnesses not only in the islands of Hawaii but also the Micronesian Islands in the Western Pacific, which are just north of the equator. They also oversaw the work in Nauru, which is four degrees to the south of the equator. The branch servant Brother Kawasaki, asked me not only to help finish the Waimanalo Kingdom Hall, but also to draw a plan for one in Truk Lagoon, in Micronesia. The Truk projects start was being delayed by property title problems, so Brother Kawasaki invited me to go to Lahaina, Maui, to help on a new hall there.

About two blocks behind the Lahaina sugar mill, we stayed in an old plantation house with two other Hawaiian Japanese pioneers. We split the thirty-five-dollar monthly rent three ways. I stayed there about four months. We got the foundation in and the first floor block walls up. For the second floor, we were facing a lengthy delay waiting for materials, so I returned to Oahu for a while.

The branch then asked if I'd be willing to go to Ponape to build a hall there. I accepted and off we went in October of 1970. A Continental 727 jet, called the "Island Hopper," flew from Honolulu, with stops at Midway, Majuro, Kwajalien, Ponape, and Truk, and then to Guam. The route was so long and remote that all flights carried some spare parts and a mechanic onboard.

Ponape has always been known as one of the wettest places on Earth. It gets approximately four hundred inches of rainfall a year on its highest mountain (the mountains are about twenty-six hundred feet high). It decreases to about one hundred and seventy to two hundred inches of rainfall around the seashore yearly, and it is rather evenly distributed. Unlike Hawaii, where every island more or less has a tropical side and a desert side, complete with cactuses, Ponape is 100 percent tropical.

Ponape is only a little over 10 miles by 10 miles, 125 square miles in all, with rivers and waterfalls everywhere. It is probably one of the most luscious tropical rain forest-covered islands on Earth. With the high rainfall, so much topsoil is washed down around the seashore that instead of sandy beaches, there are sixty square miles of mangrove swamps around the seashore. Some of these mangrove swamps on the south and west of the main island are simply magnificent. Every river cuts a channel through the swamps, which have huge trees, some up to one hundred feet tall and five or more feet in diameter—something you might expect to see in a dinosaur movie.

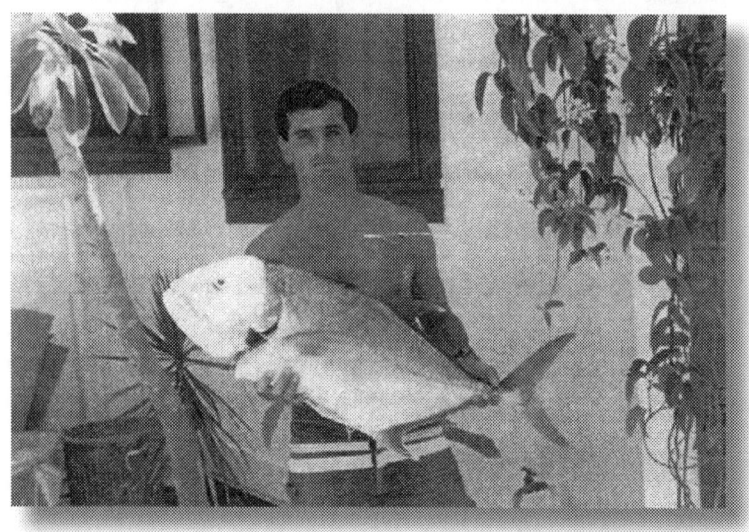

Steve in 1969, with a Hawaiian ulua speared that morning

Steve Nix, 1977

High up in the mountains, above where people have planted local crops, are even more impressive forests. There are also many rocky cliffs on Ponape. Most are so completely covered with vegetation, that it softens its appearance, making it appear not quite so rugged.

About a half mile to the west of the airport is one of the most beautiful rock promontories in the world. It's called Sokehs Rock and is right next to the ocean. It's much more impressive than Diamond Head or the Rock of Gibraltar, in my opinion. To me, best of all was the diving out on the barrier reef, equal to the best anywhere in the world. But even better, I was to learn, was trolling for yellowfin tuna the way poor simple outer islanders do, which is economical and low-tech trolling with hand-lines.

Two Witness brothers originally from the island of Mokil, Carl and Amon Dannis, would be the ones to get me hooked on tuna fishing. With one or the other, we would go out to sea in a small fifteen-foot wood boat; usually one Amon had built, with only a twenty-horsepower Johnson short shaft motor and a paddle. The boats were not much wider than four feet at the bottom, and the transom was fifteen inches high for the motor and not much more than eighteen inches freeboard overall. We used a monofilament line of about two—to three-hundred-pound test, which we'd hold by hand with a leader and lure attached. On many days, if leaving early, preferably before daybreak, a fish could usually be caught by trolling right outside the reef. More productive, though, was to follow the birds around, using them to lead us to small or large schools of bonito or yellow fin tuna.

Carl was the chief sanitation official for the island. Amon was older and in his late thirties, just a humble small boat builder and fisherman. Amon was the one I went out fishing with most of the time, so we became close friends.

I was to learn that Micronesian men hold hands with their friends. When Amon first did that with me, I found it a bit awkward to get used to, but I got over it. Ponape is also an island where many women go around topless, some right in the middle of town, but to show their knees then, was considered improper.

One windy, rainy day, Amon and I went out trolling on the windward side of the island. About twenty miles out, we caught around three hundred pounds of big twenty-pound bonito. They call this size barrel aku in Hawaii. About halfway back to the reef, I heard several big bangs, as if a canon were being shot off somewhere. Amon's English wasn't good enough to explain to me what was going on, but he slowed down and turned south toward the sound. A minute or two later a huge whale surfaced alongside our boat. It was fifteen feet away from us, going in the same direction. His tail slapping the water surface earlier had produced the loud noise.

Shortly after, Amon hooked a big yellow fin, which pulled him back over the transom. He couldn't hold the line but was able to throw out an orange plastic ball, which we each had to keep our lines tied off to. The balls were about a foot in diameter and were pulled underwater by the tuna for a while, before popping to the surface again. It would then take a couple of minutes to pull these fish up hand over hand. When getting them to the side of the boat, we had to be careful not to be on the same side of the boat; otherwise we could capsize or swamp it. Then reaching over the side, Amon would grab the tuna by the gills and pull it into the boat, then knocking it out with a club.

In a short time, we caught five seventy-pound-plus yellow fin this way. I hooked two of them and when they bit, they yanked me right over backward onto the floor of the boat, before I could toss my ball overboard.

We had to tie the large tuna in place so the load couldn't shift, which could sink us because we had the boat to overloaded for rough water. One had its tail tied right under the seat I was sitting on. It regained consciousness enough to slap its tail powerfully on the bottom side of the seat, giving me the worst spanking I'd ever had.

Usually the night before going out trolling, Amon and I sat around rigging up lures. He'd never seen a turkey, so to him all feathers were from a chicken. As he was trying to explain how to tie the turkey feathers to some lure heads in his limited English, he was verbally stumbling for words saying, "Tie chicken leafs to nudes." So "chicken leafs" were turkey feathers, and "nudes" is the Ponapean word for lures.

Carl told me that one time when he traveled on government business to Hawaii for a workshop and training, a fellow worker gave him money, asking him to bring back nudes for him. When he returned and gave the guy his lures, the recipient disappointedly said, "No, no, I mean the magazines!"

Twenty miles to the west, and about thirty miles to the northwest from Kolonia, the main town on Ponape, were two beautiful atolls, Ant and Pakin.

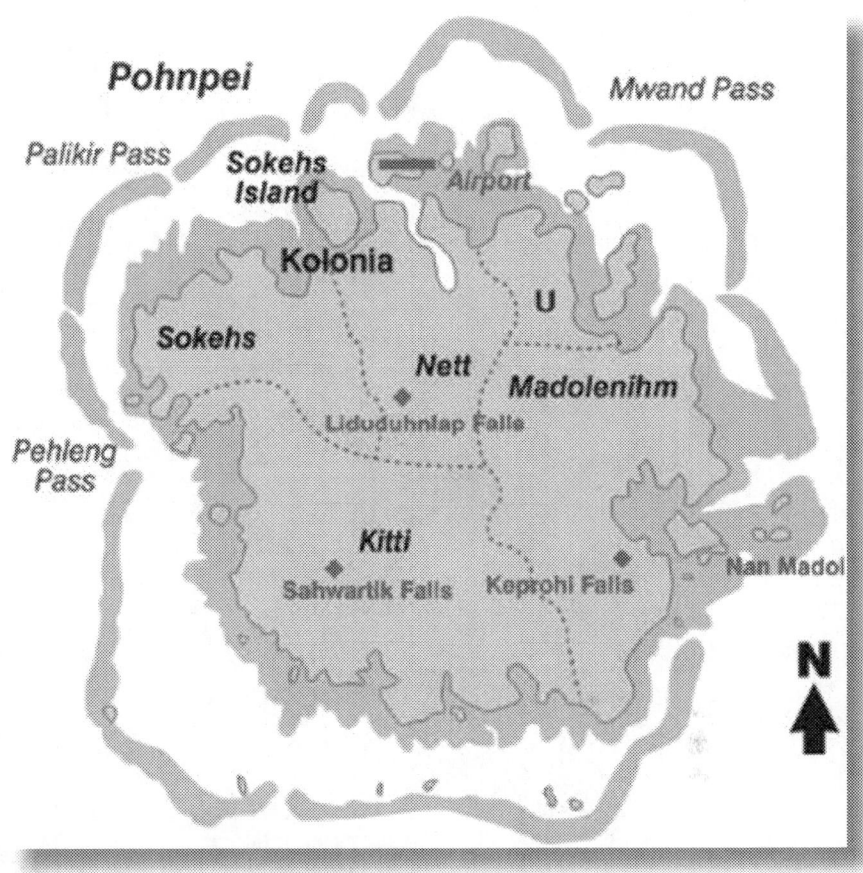

Map of Pohnpei, courtesy of http://www.doi.gov website

Kolonia and Vicinity

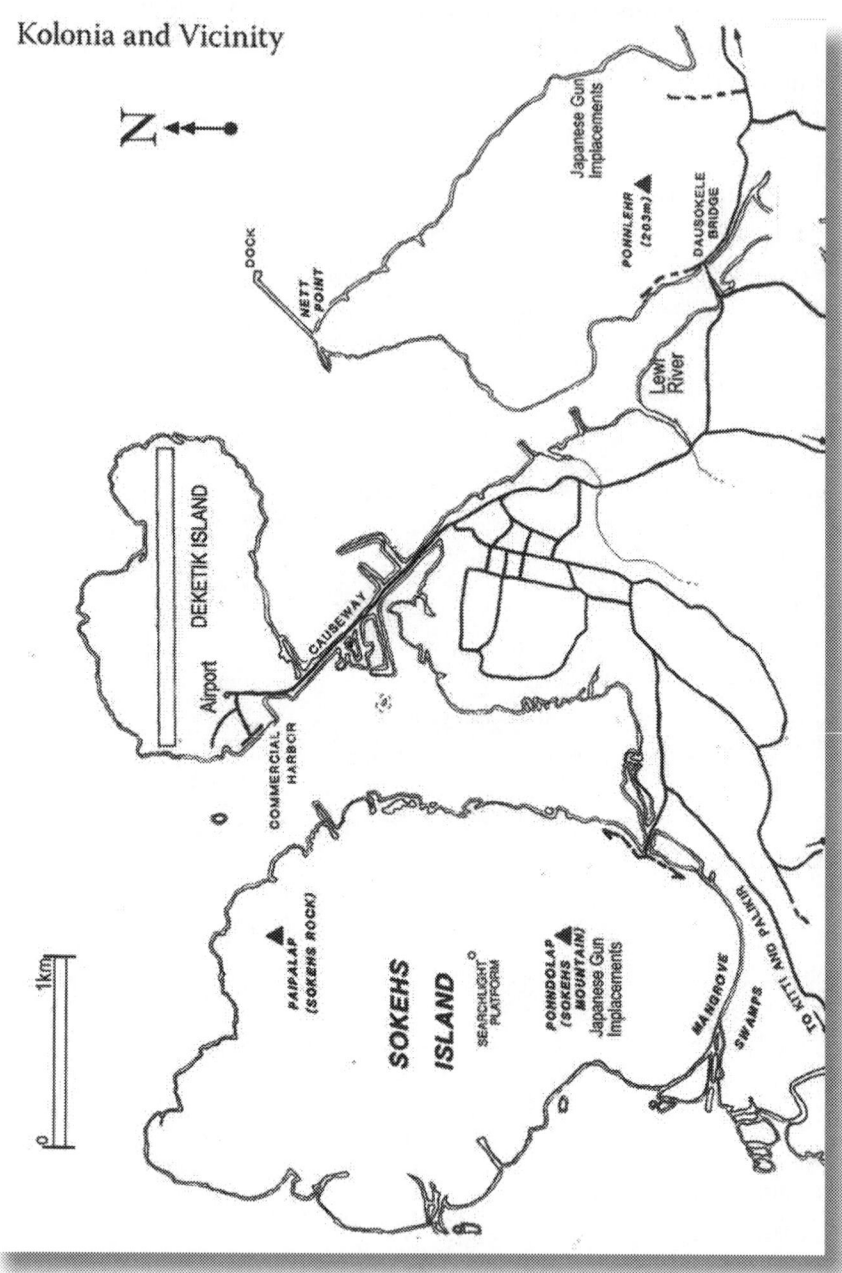

In 1970 when trolling off the south side of Ant Atoll, I learned that the copra price had collapsed just a couple of years before and a number of picturesque thatch houses were now abandoned on the island, less than fifty yards away. It was a beautiful scene, one that must have looked exactly the same hundreds of years before, when white men in their sailing ships first came by these islands.

Every January or February, wahoo migrate through Ponapean waters, and the hottest spot to catch them was off a point of the reef on the east side of Ant Atoll. As Amon and I crossed the channel, a windy rainstorm closed in and for the entire day, we couldn't see more than a few hundred yards at the most. So we stayed close to the eastern reef of Ant and on around to its northwestern tip, where there was a small bird island, an albatross breeding and nesting site. If we didn't, we could easily get lost in the ocean, not having a compass or any means of communication.

It was no problem though; all day long we caught fish no matter where we were trolling. Wahoo, bonito, yellow fin, rock tuna . . . everything bites better in the rain. The raindrops hitting the water's surface excite the fish, as it imitates the look of baitfish thrashing about on the surface.

Trolling around to the point of the reef just to the west of the bird island, where the northwestern point of the reef turns and starts running south again, I hooked about a thirty-five—to forty-pound rock tuna. These fish take awhile to pull in. I got it under the boat and off it took again. As I got it back under the boat, we were just a few feet from the reef, in calm water. A school of sharks came up and grabbed the fish. About ten of them were boiling around in a ball, tearing the fish apart, banging and bumping the bottom of the boat. They turned the water into a green cloud, not red, just below us. When the storm passed and we got back to Ponape, we found out that it had blown over many trees and dropped eighteen inches of rain in five hours.

The barrier reefs and the atolls in Ponape are very different from those in Hawaii. Outside the waves breaking on the reef, a coral wall drops hundreds of feet straight down in most places, until it reaches a pile of rubble that then drops sharply into a couple of thousand feet of water or more.

The most extreme case I've seen here is the western side of Pakin Atoll. Trolling one morning there during a low tide and calm seas, the reef was sticking out of the water about eighteen inches. With the boat running parallel with the reef and only five to ten feet away from it, I caught two forty-five-pound yellow fin tuna within about five minutes of each other. That illustrates how steep the reef drop-off is, sheer like a wall.

We weren't fishing all the time. We were spending maybe 150 hours or more a month building the new Kingdom Hall, along with doing some door-to-door ministry. I was also conducting two weekly Bible studies with people I had met that way. We were constantly on the go. I paid all our own expenses, airfare, food, whatever, only lodging was free. We would sleep on the floor of the small old Kingdom Hall. I could afford to do this from savings on previous jobs.

Still, three to five of us would take off in the afternoon at least twice a week to go diving. Either we'd go outside the western reef called Tauak, the pass by the main harbor entrance which was close by, or to the pass on the northeast corner of the barrier reef, Mant Pass. We called it "Pako Place," because we saw more sharks there than any of the other places. Pako means shark in the Ponapean language.

I never saw any sharks diving in Hawaii, but Ponape was totally different. Every time you dove there, you saw plenty, about twenty to fifty, depending on the place. Most were six-foot gray reef sharks, but occasionally, in the deep, dark passes, there was a tiger shark or a silvery shark that natives were afraid of.

I had brought a .357 magnum bang stick from Hawaii, thinking sharks were dangerous. I would quickly learn otherwise, that they're no problem when nature is in balance, as it is in Ponape. There's never been a recorded shark attack in its history. There have been plenty of attempted ones, especially by tiger sharks, as islanders tend to stuff speared fish in their pockets or pants.

A couple of the brothers were from Ngatik, an atoll ninety miles west of Ponape. Their favorite fish is shark. One of these brothers kept asking me to get him a shark. So like an idiot, I speared a six foot gray reef shark on a sandy bottom in twenty-five feet of water. I only had about eighteen feet of line from the spear to my spear gun. The shark stayed on the bottom, spinning around. As I grabbed the line, trying to pull him to the surface, the shark kept pulling me under. I couldn't get a breath. I held on, not wanting to lose my prized spear gun. He almost drowned me when the cable to the breakaway spearhead broke and off he swam, leaving me exhausted and with a circular spear. From then on, I only speared little wimpy three—or four-foot white tip reef sharks for food. But I kept my little sawed-off three-foot bang stick in the boat. I'd used it on sharks when out trolling, when they got hooked after devouring fish Amon or I were pulling in. But I hadn't used it when diving; it just lay in the front of the boat.

One afternoon at "Pako Place," three gray reefs were threatening to come in and take away a sea bass that I had just speared. I got the fish back to the boat and as I put it in, I heard Amon yell out, "Pako! Pako!" I'd never heard him excited like that, so I grabbed the bang stick and quickly swam over to him. One of the gray reef sharks was roiling around him, trying to get a fish he had just speared. I went right up to it and used the bang stick behind the gills. It spurted blood out and erratically took off down the reef walls toward the inside of the lagoon, through the pass. Watching to see if it would return, we saw two big tiger sharks rushing from the seaward side of the pass toward the area where the wounded shark had disappeared. I would estimate their length at about twelve feet. We continued to watch and after a minute or two, the two tiger sharks came swimming back by us headed back out to sea. To this day, they are the two most magnificent creatures I have ever seen, stripes and all.

In 1970, Kolonia was much more picturesque than it is today. Then, most buildings on the main street were wood and had an old western town appeal. The same went for the residential houses, even though most weren't much better than shanties. But to me, cheap wooden houses look better than the cheap concrete houses that started to be built in the mid 1970's. But the concrete houses at least hold up to the termites better than the wood ones. Termites are a major problem in a tropical jungle.

The roads were all unpaved then, just surfaced (at best) with dredged-up coral. When they were wet, cars threw the salty moisture and sand up on their undercarriages, dooming them to a life span of just a few years before corroding to unusability. Some owners never even bothered changing their engine oil because the life span of a car was so short. In 1970, there were very few cars and trucks, and maybe less than fifteen or twenty miles of drivable roads. The roads only extended a few miles each way out of town. When traveling to town, most everybody living around the island came by boat or walked on the old Japanese roads around the island. These roads were then too deteriorated or overgrown for vehicular traffic.

Chapter 18

Some Micronesian History

On March 3, 1971, my son Alex was born at the hospital in Ponape, which was then located next to the baseball field. Both were within the old Spanish Wall, the remains of the old Spanish Fort that was built by Spain sometime during the time it colonized Micronesia from 1875-1898.

In 1898, Spain sold its colonies in Micronesia to Germany, to raise money to fight the United States during the Spanish—American war. Germany then controlled Ponape with an iron fist, up until sometime during World War I. Then Japanese warships sailed into Kolonia's harbor, demanding its surrender. By the end of the war, any reserves Germany had were not in Ponape. They had to capitulate.

Before this, in 1911, German authorities had been conscripting Ponapeans for forced labor on public works projects. By this time, Ponape had five kings, so it was a collection of five kingdoms. The Germans required each king, on a rotating basis, to provide his subjects as the labor force.

One day in 1911, the German governor and other officials crossed a small bay by boat to the large island of Sokehs. It was about half a mile to the west of Kolonia. Going there to inspect a road project, pent-up resentment at a construction site caused the workers to snap and kill the governor and members of his party.

A couple of survivors made it back to Kolonia, where they, with others, prepared for a large attack. Many foreigners hunkered behind the Spanish Wall, waiting for reinforcements. This started the Sokehs Rebellion. The other four kingdoms did not join the rebellion, thus a large-scale attack on those behind the Spanish Wall never materialized.

It took several months for the German authorities to mobilize a sufficient force to attempt to crush the rebellion. That force arrived with several steel ships with modern cannons. But more terrifying to the rebels were the many black bushy-haired Papua New Guinea soldiers that the Germans brought with them. They all looked like cannibals to the Ponapeians, and some may still have been not too far removed from that practice.

The Sokehs people felt somewhat secure on the eight-hundred-foot-high mountain on Sokeh Island. These were in many ways similar to the mesas of the American Southwest, except heavily wooded. Its approaches could be easily defended with firearms that many of the rebels had acquired from island traders over the decades. They also felt safe from naval canon fire on those heights. But they were thinking in terms of the Spanish cannons of the former era.

The German forces blockaded Sokehs Island as best they could. Then they opened up with their naval guns, which were easily able to pepper the mountaintops. The Sokeh defenders sought to find shelter in caves and crevices. But they were so unnerved by the bombardment that at night they began sneaking men, women, and children down to and through the mangrove swamps and past the blockade, back to the main island of Ponape.

This started a campaign that lasted several months. The rebels and their families traveled the island seeking help, food, rest, support, and allies from the other kingdoms, but little to none was found that would sustain the rebellion, except sympathy. The German commander kept the pressure on by a continual pursuit with their Papuan soldiers, who were perfectly suited for the dense humid jungles. The Sokehs people were easily able to keep ahead of their pursuers.

It has been thirty-seven years since these accounts were related to me. I believe a couple of Papuan soldiers were killed in a failed assault on one of the rebel's temporary high rocky refuges as they sought to recuperate. Eventually, the rebels were worn down. Tired and hungry, they surrendered without ever putting up a major fight.

They obviously had never seriously considered the consequences of taking on a major power like Germany and the severity of their strict justice. Germany hung or shot somewhere between 17 and

28 of these rebels, depending on which source you rely on, and deported 460 of their remaining family members fifteen hundred miles to Palau, on the western edge of Micronesia. None of them were ever returned to Ponape, to my knowledge.

Only a few Ponapeans in Sokehs that took no part in the uprising were allowed to remain. The rebels in Sokehs lost everything. The Germans repopulated Sokehs with outer islanders from Pingelap and Mokil, who wanted to come to the big island of Ponape, which it was when compared to an atoll. Also, after a severe typhoon in the outer islands of Truk, five hundred miles to the west—in the Mortlocks to be precise—crops were ruined by saltwater invasion. Germany moved many of these Mortlockese into Sokehs as well.

One day I went with Carl and another of his coworkers, Elden Hellen, to an island in the lagoon. They were checking on a small water system for some remote houses that the sanitation department was involved with.

After inspecting this water project, we continued in the boat to the Nan Madol ruins on the southeast corner of the island. Ponape is the only island in the Pacific that has ancient large-scale city-like ruins, covering an area of well over one hundred acres. They are comprised of about ninety-two man-made islets interconnected by canals and waterways. Ponape is sometimes referred to as the Venice of the Pacific.

Some of the larger basalt rocks that were used weigh up to eighty tons, and it's another one of those ancient mysteries how the builders moved all those massive rocks, as no written records exist. Up until about ten years ago, the ruins were only accessible by boat. But now the road around the entire island has been recently paved, so it's relatively easy to get close enough to the ruins by car now. Then it's just a short hike to the largest structure there.

These are impressive, but my favorite parts of the ruins are better accessed by boat, at a medium or high tide, through the canals. I believe any tourist taking the trouble to come all the way to Ponape to see these ruins should see them the right way. I think that would be to go by vehicle and then board a small boat to tour the canals and see most of the impressive ruins.

From Nan Madol, the reef continues in a southwesterly direction, and three miles away, it reaches a historically significant harbor. It's called Lohd Harbor and it's the location of an event in 1865, that's very little is known. It's the site of the only naval action to occur in the Pacific Ocean between the North and South during the American Civil War.

The South near the end of the war, had sent out raider ships throughout the Atlantic, Indian, and Pacific Oceans, to attack and disrupt the North's maritime economy. The Confederate raider ship CSS *Shenandoah* arrived off the southern reefs of Ponape and caught three Yankee whaling ships at anchor in Lohd Harbor. After ordering the crews off and confiscating valuable cargo, the Shenandoah sunk the three whaling ships and departed Ponape, stranding the northern crews behind. Due to the lack of communications, it wouldn't be until later that they all learned that the Civil War had ended shortly before these ships were sunk.

Fortunately for the castaways, Ponape was a favorite reprovisioning stop for whaling ships, for obvious practical reasons. First, it has about fifteen major passes through the barrier reefs, so despite the direction of the weather, a sailing ship has several places to enter a safe harbor. And as one of the wettest spots on earth, water was easily available at any one of the numerous harbors or safe anchorages scattered around the island.

Remember that a whaling ship needs lots of wood to boil whale blubber down into oil before it is stored in barrels in the ship's hold. Also, Ponape at seven degrees north latitude, sat astride one of the richest whaling grounds in the world at the time, a place loosely called "the line" in whaling jargon.

"The line" is a narrow corridor, one north and the other south of the equator, where the swirling and changing equatorial ocean currents collide with the prevailing east-west currents in their respective hemisphere. The collision of these currents occur about four degrees north latitude in the Northern Hemisphere, stirring up rich nutrients of plankton, which support a whole food chain in this part of the world. This is where many whales migrate during the northern winters, and whaling ships sail down this "line" in search of their prey.

Excellent hardwoods to boil down the blubber were available right next to the anchorages in the mangrove swamps. Plus, the types of women the whalers were probably hoping to run into were readily available. I've heard that there's a book about Ponape's whaling days, titled *Wood, Water, and Women.*

Around the 1820s, Rohn Kitti harbor had more whaling ships provisioning there than even Lahaina, Maui, about 120 a year. That was not counting the other harbors on island that may have also been used. A pass on the southwestern area of the reef opens to Rohn Kitti Harbor. The largest river in Ponape empties here. Also, the biggest and certainly the best mangrove swamps on island, even to this day, are adjacent to this area.

Around the 1850s, the first Protestant missionaries arrived on island and became active in the Rohn Kitti area. They obviously had a lot of work cut out for them there. They were successful in getting the ball rolling toward all Ponapeans claiming to be Christians, but not in getting them to change their morals. Even today, these religions still have not had much success in this regard.

During these early whaling days, Ponape was also known as "Ascension Island," and in some literature, such as *Moby Dick*, it is referred to as such, so I've heard. There is an Ascension Island in the Atlantic Ocean, and Ponape was the Ascension Island in the Pacific Ocean. That's a fitting name because west of Hawaii, it is the highest island north of the equator in the huge tropical Western Pacific.

The captain of one of the ships sunk, the *Bar Harvest*, was John Eldridge. He returned to Ponape sometime later, married a Ponapean and raised a family. His descendants are quite numerous and own what I consider the most desirable property in Kolonia. It's on a high knoll next to the ocean, looking out over the bay toward Sokehs Rock and the open sea beyond. It's now the location of the South Park Hotel. I assume it was Captain Eldridge who acquired the property, because Micronesians usually aren't concerned about a view.

Many of these events were related to me by one of my Ponapean brothers who worked with me on the Kingdom Hall, Hiroshi Yamaguchi. He is also one of John Eldridge's descendents and of a WWII Japanese soldier as well, obviously. He's now in his late seventies and one of only two of my coworkers on the Kingdom Hall who is still alive.

Sometime around the middle to end of April 1971, my family and I returned to Hawaii and again rented a house on a short-term basis in Lanikai. My wife arranged to rent the house we had previously rented in Lanikai, the one three houses from the water, when it would be available again in a few weeks. We would end up staying there until late 1974.

In the meantime, I went back to working full time to support my growing family. Before looking for a job, I started building a small fifteen-foot plywood boat to try Micronesian-style trolling off the windward coast of Oahu.

As I was lofting the boat out on plywood, up drove Guy, the guy that Woody and I had previously been trying to convert into a piece working hawaiianized L.A. framer. It was a challenging project, but there he stood, looking as if he'd made progress while I was gone. Still a little bit nerdy though. Rather than wearing tourist shorts of the era, they were now something a surfer might wear. No more boots but tennis shoes, with white socks also. That was better than the multi—colored ones he'd worn before.

He wanted to know if I'd be available to team up with him to roll trusses, fascia board, and sheathing on a new condominium project just starting up in Kaneohe, close to the marine base. So off we went either that day or the next, in Guy's new Datsun truck that had a toolbox and lumber rack, to the job site. He was looking like the complete package. Since he'd lined the job up and had worked with Woody awhile when I was gone, I figured he was broken into piecework now.

So I told him to go ahead and negotiate the deal with the boss. I was horrified when he set up a by-the-hour deal for us, but I tried not to show it. Most everybody else on the job, except the pickup carpenters and us, were piece working. We could have made twice as much, probably more "piecing," but it was enough to live on.

Guy picked me up every day for the six months or so that the project lasted, and looking back I have this to say. I've worked closely with many witnesses and others over the last fifty years, and I have to admit that I enjoyed working with Guy more than I did any of the others. He was always cheerful, in a good mood, an unrelenting practical joker, and he had such a pathetic cornball sense of humor that he was actually funny. So money isn't everything.

Guy would go on to be a piecework carpenter, breaking in his oldest son to carpenter work. I would go on to break in a young eighteen-year-old fatherless boy in the congregation, Richard Ramsey, and he would stay my apprentice or coworker off and on for the next fifteen years. He would end up being more like a freeloading son many times.

Over the next several years, I would return to Ponape a number of times, for a couple of days, a month, six months, to visit with my new friends there. I'd fish and dive with Carl and Amon or another brother, Ohner Philipe, who had been in Yap when I first went to Ponape. Richard would go to Ponape with me in July 1972, for one month. At that time we went with some other witnesses to Kusie Island on the field trip ship. It's about three hundred miles southeast of Ponape and similar in some ways, a high island. It's about half its size, sixty square miles and mountains only about sixteen hundred feet tall.

Kusie, now known as Kosrae, has some interesting history and ancient ruins similar to Nan Madol, but much smaller in comparison. While there we went to a primitive theater and saw a James Garner movie in which he portrays a navy frogman who during WWII, is sent ashore from a US submarine to Kusie. On island, he rigs some diversionary explosions and while everyone is distracted, he sneaks into a temporarily vacated radio shack. There he photographs one of the secret Japanese military codes before returning to the sub undetected. It was based on a true story and was much more impressive seeing it on the island where it actually occurred—and also to talk to people who remembered those explosions and other interesting tales about WWII events that occurred in Kusie.

As we left Kusie, I let my trolling line out off the second deck of the small island cargo ship. Just as we cleared the reef outside Lela harbor, a fish struck my lure. Doing about seven knots, it took both Richard, me and another to pull the fish in, about a four-foot-plus wahoo. As it got near the back of the ship, islanders on the first deck assisted, pulling the fish over the railing and onto the lower deck. I immediately ran back to the stairs and down to the lower deck to claim my fish. It probably only took me about ten seconds to reach that rail, but I didn't see the fish anywhere. I thought perhaps it had gotten off the hook and slipped back into the water. Then one native turned around and handed me a six-inch chunk of the fish with a big smile on his face. I then noticed other smiling islanders walking away with chunks of my fish.

I would return to Kusie two more times in the mid-1970s to fish and dive. Both times I stayed with Freddy Edwin, the oldest of the brothers that worked with me on the Kingdom Hall in Ponape.

In Kusie, Freddy would talk with me about his experiences in WWII as a native forced labor employee of the Japanese military. He told me how when the Japanese troops arrived on Kusie, they were all crammed on the deck of a Japanese military ship, standing everywhere and sitting on all the gun barrels, saying there practically wasn't an empty space for another person on deck.

He related that one day he was walking on a mountain road leading down into the village of Malem, where the Japanese code had been stolen. A group of Japanese soldiers was training, double-timing it up the road as they came toward him. When they were about to pass him, going the opposite direction, one of the soldiers collapsed from exhaustion. His officer stopped everyone, went over to the fallen soldier and began to viciously berate him as a shameful, pathetic weakling, an embarrassment to the emperor. The exhausted soldier tried to get up as Freddy passed, but he collapsed again. His commander again cruelly berated him. Filled with shame, the soldier took out a hand grenade and hit it against his chest. The officer dove to his knees, trying to cover his head with his hands and elbows as the grenade went off. Freddy watched as the humiliated soldier was blown off the road, tumbling and crashing down the steep hillside through the vegetation. The officer though, died frozen on his knees and elbows, right where he tried to cover up.

On another occasion he was with his two Japanese supervisors just after sun rise on a Sunday morning, at the ship dock in Lela. In low out of the sun roared three American fighter planes making a strafing run. Taking refuge behind a well, these two Japanese were then killed on each side of him by the plane's machine guns.

Later, a new Japanese boss told him to get ready because they would board a ship for Ponape in the afternoon of the following day. He was told to prepare his food for the voyage. So the next morning, he was paddling his outrigger canoe through the mangrove swamp channels to get some local food in a place he had crops growing.

He then caught a glimpse of the ship already on its way out at sea. It had left early leaving him behind. Japanese ships had learned by then not to keep to any previously broadcast schedules, because of American submarines.

Late that afternoon, an American submarine torpedoed the ship. It surfaced and machine-gunned all survivors now swimming in the ocean. Four Micronesian men hiding under an overturned lifeboat survived the shootings. When the sub left, they righted the life boat and made it back to Ponape to report what had happened.

He related that because of the American submarine blockade, Japanese shipping to the island was cut off. Soldiers begin to starve. They would strip themselves down to their white underwear and headbands, sitting along the seashore in the sun all day long, slowly starving to death. When they eventually began dying in large numbers, a small island about fifty yards from Freddy's present house was used as the crematorium. His story was all the more powerful because I could see the island, a stone's throw away.

On these two trips in the mid-1970s, my second and third to Kusie, I again traveled there on the same small cargo ship called the *Kaselehlie* (Cas-se-lay-lea), which in Ponapean means both hello and good-bye, similar to the Hawaiian word "aloha."

The three-hundred-mile trip to Kusie usually took a little over two and a half days, with stops at Mokil Atoll, ninety miles east of Ponape, and Pingelap Atoll, about two hundred miles east of Ponape. On my second trip to Kusie in 1974, the ship developed problems with both engines in Kusie, leaving me stranded there for over two months while the ship waited for parts.

The island pretty much ran out of everything except canned mackerel and breadfruit, neither of which I cared for. Just to get back to Ponape and some real food, I caught a Nauru ship to Nauru, which stopped at the Lela harbor dock.

At that time, Nauru was the richest country per capita in the world, due to its recent independence and finally gaining control over its rich phosphate deposits, which were soon to be exhausted. They would squander their newly acquired wealth on a couple of small first-class jet airliners, a fleet of fancy cargo freighters, and other ill-advised expenditures.

I enjoyed the first-class meals, the British-style service with white tablecloths and a parade of servers dressed to the hilt, despite there being only five or six passengers on board. My ticket was only thirty-five dollars.

Nauru, four hundred miles to the southeast of Kusie, sat four degrees south of the equator. Kusie was four degrees north of it. The crossing was calm and the freighter big enough that I never got seasick on the voyage, something I always suffered with on the *Kaselehlie*. Nauru was only about fourteen square miles, and it seemed to take approximately twenty minutes to drive around it.

After spending about three days there in its only hotel, I caught the first available flight to Majuro, where I would connect to a Continental flight back to Ponape. When I purchased my ticket at the airport, the Nauru agent gave me the option of paying extra for a meal service during the flight. I accepted, wanting to put back on weight I'd lost in Kusie.

Boarding the plane, I was surprised to learn I was the only passenger. There were four flight attendants on the flight. They were so busy talking to one another that they never got me the meal I paid for, despite several of my reminders. This flight and my voyage on their ship gave me some insight into why the small nation of Nauru has now come to poverty, currently ranked among the earth's poorest.

About a year later in 1975, I took my third voyage to Kusie. The *Kaselehlie* was still in bad shape, reduced to now operating on just one engine instead of two. The outer islands were desperate for supplies and this was the only ship they had, despite now being able to make only three and a half or four knots. The voyage was agonizingly slow. But worst of all, the engine was belching black sooty smoke that enveloped everything and everybody the entire voyage.

Upon finally reaching Kusie, the *Kaselehlie* totally broke down and there I was, stranded again for another two or three months. The Trust Territory was eventually able to send Yap's outer island cargo ship. Its name was the *Yap Islander*, and it was the smallest of Micronesia's outer island supply ships, at eighty-some feet long.

When we left, the small ship was full to capacity, with people everywhere. We were supposed to voyage directly to Ponape. The only back covered deck was full of islanders camped out there, as staterooms were nonexistent on these outer island ships. I slept on the front cargo hatch cover with many others.

The ocean was rough, with steep swells that almost seemed to capsize the small vessel. Because it was top-heavy from all the people, I was concerned when the ship diverted to Pingelap to pick up a medical emergency for transport to the Ponape hospital. Two people were supposed to board, but sure enough, about fifty people got on. The same thing happened as we neared Mokil.

Now with an additional one hundred people on board, I kept my swim fins and mask within arm's reach. Maybe more than half of those on board were seasick, just lying around and throwing up all day. I was lying on a lounge chair-size mat I had brought to sleep on. The hatch cover was so crowded with people that I had parts of five other people's bodies on the mat with me. It was quite a balancing act to get up and slowly nudge my foot between bodies, trying not to directly step on anyone when attempting to walk to the restroom. All the while the hatch cover was pitching every which way. With no protection from the sun and rain, it was a thoroughly miserable voyage.

Carl Dannis, with whom I stayed for the first five years I came to Ponape, had the best stranded story. It was also due to the breakdown of an outer island cargo ship. In the 1960s as a sanitation department employee of the Trust Territory government, he and a coworker were sent to an isolated temporarily vacated island to eradicate an out-of-control rat infestation.

The island was Ujelang, over three hundred miles to the northeast of Ponape. It's actually part of the Marshall Islands and its western most island.

They were dropped off by the government's ship, which then left to service another atoll and was to return to pick them up in a few days. The ship broke down and there they were stranded with less than four days worth of supplies and no means of communication. Fortunately, Carl had brought his diving mask and simple local-style spear. The coworker was raised as a Kolonia Town city boy and surely would have starved to death had it not been for Carl. They spent four months alone there; eating fish and coconuts before another ship finally picked them up.

Of my three best Micronesian fishing buddies, Carl would be the first to die. Sometime in the mid-1980s, he and his son-in-law Wheat went out tuna fishing northeast of the island. It was a rough windy day on the ocean. Their motor broke down and they drifted helplessly for hours, back toward the most northern point of the barrier reef. Here, storm waves had broken off large chunks of the reef and these huge coral rocks had been tossed up along the reef's edge. Some stuck high above the water, even at the highest tides.

Just before dark, large waves crashed them onto the reef at high tide. Unable to touch bottom, and the water sweeping across the reef like a river, Carl yelled to Wheat to swim to the rocks. When Wheat made it and climbed onto one, he turned to check on Carl but never saw him again. Wheat was found the next day still clinging to a rock, but Carl's body was never recovered.

Ohner Phillipe was another of my favorite fishing companions. He was fearless out in the ocean. If he had to relieve himself, he would ask me to stop the boat and then jump into the water like someone might jump into a swimming pool, despite being miles out to sea. That made me so nervous; I'd put my mask on and watch for sharks. I stopped that once I got hit by one of his "floaters," figuring the sharks could have him.

If he was out tuna fishing and a school wasn't biting, he'd dive in and try to spear them. This stopped when one time down about twenty-five feet, a huge shadow cruised right above him, the biggest shark he'd ever seen.

When diving with me, he would take his pants off before getting into the water and there he was, in just his wife's baggy silky underwear. She was bigger than he was. Unable to stop myself, I teased him mercilessly.

Ohner never had his own boat, so he'd go with others, such as myself. Many times he would just walk out to the airport and spearfish off the west end of the runway, alone. Deep water starts immediately there, although there are some shallow areas to each side. On two occasions there, he had small fish tucked in his pants and was seriously challenged by tiger sharks trying to get the fish. Having to shoot these sharks, he twice lost his prized spear gun as they swam away with it. At least he saved his wife's undies. On a third occasion there, he speared a large green sea turtle in deep water. Unable to pull it up, it took him down fifty or sixty feet, causing him to let his spear gun go again or drown.

He worked for me occasionally and in late 1999, he would retire at sixty years of age right after we got a multiplex movie theater ready to open. Sometime around 2005, he again went spear fishing alone off the west side of the airport runway, but he didn't return in the evening. The next morning he was found dead in a foot of water there, tangled in the line to his spear. Autopsies are rarely performed here on island.

Only Amon Dannis, my longtime best friend in Micronesia would live into his seventies. In 2006, he would slowly die of cancer in a hospital bed.

Chapter 19

A New Life and Another Call to the FBI

During the early to mid-1970s in Hawaii, I had plenty of good work, mostly cutting and stacking roofs on houses and condominiums. I also designed and built four or five small boats as a hobby. I got certified as a scuba diver and did a lot of diving afterward with compressed air.

In late October 1974, my wife and I would divorce. I then went to Ponape and stayed until just before summer of 1975. Then I returned to Hawaii and California for some personal business. Before leaving Ponape I lined up a job building a new hotel, which was to be called the Village Hotel.

In Ponape again to start working on this hotel, I had previously built my own simple room onto Carl's house in Kolonia. To get to the hotel site, about five miles to the east of where I was staying, I had bought a motorcycle in California and shipped it to the island.

I arranged to have Richard Ramsey come to Ponape to help work on the project also. When we worked, not wearing socks with our tennis shoes; we usually had three to five pairs of tennis shoes. This was so some could be washed and have time to air-dry. I told Richard to travel light and bring just two pairs of his best tennis shoes.

My room had a covered porch with its own entrance. When Richard arrived on island he left his shoes on this porch. We were in the room for about fifteen minutes and when we left to go play tennis, we saw that there was only one left foot tennis shoe outside the door. A dog had run off with the right shoe and despite searching the neighborhood, we couldn't find it. At least he had another pair. As he unpacked his suitcase, he realized that when picking out his best tennis shoes to bring, he had selected two left shoes for the second pair. So here he was with three left feet now. That was typical Richard! I don't believe there were any kinds of tennis shoes for sale on the island in those years. He had to work and play in flip-flops.

Three years before when I first broke him into construction, he was just a big redheaded kid right out of high school. He had been a wrestler in high school and was very strong, able to toss me around like a rag doll whenever we'd horse around a little. He kept trying to bait me into wrestling him, but I knew better. I had learned long before from John Gormley, not to play around with bigger guys who were experienced wrestlers. Richard kept telling me though, "Anytime, anyplace, whenever you're ready."

He'd never been diving before when he started working with me. So I took him out spearfishing one day. He'd never used a mask, snorkel or fins until I taught him. For his first dive, we swam out from Lanikai to the reef and then to the Mokalua Island that has a beautiful little cove on the ocean side. On the way in, in about ten feet of water, I ripped his mask, snorkel and fins off and then practically drowned him. He was like a helpless baby. After he stopped spitting and coughing up water, while struggling to tread water, he spurted out, "Wha'd ya do that for?"

I answered, "You said anytime, anyplace . . . Well this was it!"

The Village Hotel was constructed local style with thatched roofs. When I started, the Ponapean men from Awak had already put the mangrove posts up and the roofs on. I just came in and out of the rain and in the shade joisted the floors and installed the 1X6 tongue and groove Philippine mahogany floors. I had Richard do the interior and exterior walls for the cottages. I did most everything on the restaurant and kitchen building, the floors, walls, handrails, bar, reception desk, kitchen, storage room, stairs, restrooms, and the gazebo.

The gazebo ended up being highly photographed on many tourist brochures and post cards about Micronesia. The main restaurant building has continued to be the largest thatch building in all of Micronesia. Later in 1988, when some US government agency started handing out ecotourism awards, the Village Hotel was the first hotel to win the award.

Bob and Patti Arthur are the ones that put the project together and they seemed to face serious problem every day, ones that could have ended the project at any time. They surmounted every obstacle and finally got it opened in 1976. They are still running it today and it's still the most popular tourist hotel in Ponape.

In 2006 after lunch at the Village, I talked to Patti and was surprised to learn that they had been supporters of the civil rights movement in the 1960s. Patty had even attended Martin Luther King's funeral.

While doing this job, I would get remarried. My new wife would have twin boys. They would be named Yoshitaka and Nobutaka. Their great-grandfather on their mother's side had been a Japanese soldier. He was the largest Japanese soldier in Ponape. Yoshie and Nobu, as we called them, would grow up to look like Japanese sumo wrestlers. Yoshie would grow to be about six-three and 370 pounds, and Nobu was not much smaller.

Back in Hawaii after the Village job, I was preparing a place for them to stay before their arrival from Ponape. I had been referred to an older lady in Lanikai, down near the south end. She wanted some rooms added on underneath her house, next to an existing bedroom and bathroom. Because of the hillside, there was room for a living room, kitchenette and another bedroom under the existing house.

This woman was in her late eighties and the widow of Colonel Bruckner, the Marine Corps commander of the battle of Okinawa. He was killed near the end of that engagement. He was the highest-ranking US officer killed in action in the Pacific during WWII.

We agreed that I'd do the labor after regular working hours and weekends, in exchange for six months of free rent. She expressed excitement over the prospect of having infants below, saying that their crying wouldn't bother her. She had never had any children though, so when they arrived she had a change of heart the first night she lost sleep. I certainly didn't want to stress her out, because she was old and fragile.

I contacted her nephew, a vice president for Bank of Hawaii. I had his number in case of emergencies involving Mrs. Bruckner. He was the one relative looking after her. He confirmed her delicate state and fading mental capabilities, plus that she didn't have the finances for the project's materials.

I then offered to take my family to my parents' in California. They were dying to get their hands on grandkids. We agreed that I could return and stay for two months in exchange for work completed, as I had a custom pole house for Pole Houses of Hawaii yet to complete.

It probably had the best view of any house I've ever built, looking out over Kaneohe Bay, with Chinaman's Hat and Kualoa Ranch area in the background. It was on a hill in Kahalu. So I took the family to El Segundo and returned to finish the pole house; then I went back to California to work for a few months.

While I was in California watching the news early one evening in mid to late 1976, the lead story was about the FBI doing a major investigation of James Earl Ray's family as possible co-conspirators in the assassination of Martin Luther King. It referred to the assassination as a Ray family conspiracy.

I had just turned the TV on and caught the segment midpoint, as one of James Earl Ray's brothers was being interviewed. As I realized what the news report was about and focused on the brother, I thought it could have been Jodi . . . but heavier now, with long graying hair. I only saw him for two or three seconds and didn't hear him speak, so I didn't have a chance to recognize his voice. I wasn't sure if it was Jodi. Maybe if I had seen it from the beginning and heard the brother speak, I would know one way or the other.

It had been almost nine years since I got out of Springfield. The gray hair was what threw me at first, but then I figured that being about five years older than I was, Jodi could be graying now. Even I was starting to gray and would start using Grecian Formula that year, 1976. I didn't see enough to be sure of the identity of the brother, to be sure in my own mind. I did hear enough of the story to realize that what they were investigating was what I already believed to be true. So again, despite Jodi being one of my all-time favorite people, I knew I had a higher obligation to do the right thing.

I got the phone book and again looked up the FBI phone number at the L.A. division headquarters. I thought this time should be different. They'd for sure be interested now! Well, they weren't. The man who answered the phone got rid of me in less than thirty seconds this time. I wasn't surprised though, knowing how the world has no real love of justice. Even though streets, buildings, schools, holidays, and other things were beginning to be named after Martin Luther King, it began to be more and more apparent to me that many people were just paying lip service to him.

Being out of the country for a while and then returning helped me notice the changes in race relations. They appeared more pronounced to me rather than gradual. Although society seemed to take several steps backward in many ways, at least the civil rights movement was beginning to open doors to start a movement toward equality of the races, from what I could see.

As time passed, I began to appreciate more and more the significance of Martin Luther King's contribution to improve this very real problem that had existed in the United States since even before its inception, slavery, and the continuing down troddening of a race of people. I especially appreciated his insistence on nonviolent response, even though those opposed to this movement continued to use violence and had done so going back hundreds of years.

Denny Gormley, whom I considered a second father to me, began to suffer mental deterioration. I was told that doctors weren't sure if it was Alzheimer's or related to his war injuries. Every few years, he had to be operated on, having built-up calcium deposits removed from his jaw because of the injury on Iwo Jima. He pretty much lived his life in pain, yet I never heard him complain.

From what I heard, his wife Ila knew there was something wrong when Denny would get up in the morning, see himself in the mirror and dive under the bed for his hunting rifle, thinking his reflection was a prowler in the house.

Before Ila knew how serious Denny's condition was, they had planned on taking a vacation to Puerto Rico. As they entered the terminal at LAX, Ila slipped on the wet floor at the entrance and broke her leg. A crowd gathered around as a policeman began to question her, writing down pertinent information. When the officer asked her age, she hesitated a bit. A woman in the crowd then piped up, "Good for you honey, and don't tell him your weight either!"

As Ila was still lying on the floor waiting for the ambulance, Denny said good-bye to her and caught the flight to Puerto Rico.

In early 1974, Ila brought Denny to stay with me for a month in Lanikai. She wanted to see if the mild Hawaii climate and salt water would be therapeutic for him. Denny still looked tall and strong; though not too tan when he arrived.

I had a new seventeen-foot Aquasport boat with a seventy-horsepower Evinrude then, which I took him out in several times. On one occasion just south of the Mokalua Islands, just off Lanikai, a mother whale and her calf were breaching time after time. I'm glad I got to see that with Denny. But with Richard and my son also in the boat, it was more like I had to keep my eye on three kids on this trip.

Ila would take Denny swimming a couple of times a day off the beach right of way, adjacent to where I lived. By the time they left, Denny was tan again and looked like his old self. Ila was raving how the trip did him a world of good. She claimed that for the first time in a couple of years, his physical and mental decline appeared to reverse, and in her estimation progress was made. The only downside to his month long visit was that after eating, while Denny was absentmindedly scraping the leftovers into the garbage, the silverware went in as well. So I had to buy new silverware after he left, but I didn't really mind.

The Aquasport was a great boat for Hawaii. One afternoon off Moka Manu, Peter Krainer, a Witness carpenter and I were able to catch ninety-six yellowfin and bonito tunas, each weighing six to eight pounds, in two hours. We could have caught a lot more but had to leave the schools to get ready for a meeting that evening.

On other occasions when the weather was calm and the ocean flat, we'd launch the boat after work and then speed directly from the Kailua boat ramp to the leper colony on Molokai, a seventy-mile run in two hours. We'd troll along the coast, some of the most beautiful coastline in the world. After a rain, some waterfalls fall directly into the ocean from the steep cliffs. We'd anchor overnight, night dive, troll in the early morning, then spearfish with scuba gear before resuming trolling and then heading back to Oahu. We'd always catch many fish there. What surprised me most about the place was that when trolling forty feet off the east coast of the old leper colony, we saw deformed lepers still living there, fishing off the rocks, and we could say hello to them in normal voices as we passed by.

Peter was born and raised in Tahiti, the son of the longtime Austrian Consul there. He spoke with an Austrian accent, just like Arnold.

By my visit back home to El Segundo in 1976, Denny had deteriorated to the point that he was confined to the VA hospital on the west side of the 405 Freeway, in what is considered either West Los Angeles or part of Santa Monica.

I went there with Pat Steffan, a young Witness carpenter that Denny had broken into construction and also studied the Bible with while I was in prison. He had grown up two blocks west of me, only about three or four houses away from Mr. Cummings's home.

At the VA hospital, I noted that Denny had aged quite a bit and had shrunk down to about my height, five feet nine. He could still recognize me, but his condition was pretty sad. A year or so later, in 1977 or 1978, I was again in Los Angeles for a short time. Pat and I again went to see Denny, this time in a state facility in the Gardena area. The VA hospital was denying that Denny's condition was related to his injuries on Iwo Jima and would no longer care for him.

Before we arrived, Pat told me what had happened a month or two earlier, when Denny's youngest son, Dan, came to visit him. He found his father black and blue, having been beaten up by an orderly. Dan made a few inquiries to determine what had happened. He then went and found the orderly, evening the score and then some. Dan had always been a bit of a rogue Witness.

I was to hear later that he had even tried his hand for a short while as a professional heavyweight boxer. Dan's son would become a professional heavyweight boxer as well. Pat would always affectionately refer to Dan and his wife as the Clydesdales. They were a big couple.

As we entered the section of the new facility where Denny was, he saw me coming from a distance and came up to me, smiling and happy, giving me a hug. But I couldn't believe how much he had wasted away in the last year. He now looked like he was in his eighties or nineties and was only about five feet tall, just a little guy now. I had tears in my eyes to see him that way, and he would die shortly afterward. He was only about fifty-two or fifty-three when he passed. I don't think it was Alzheimer's.

Chapter 20

German Business Partner and the Land

During the last few years of the 1970s, I traveled with my family back and forth between Ponape and the United States a couple of times. When I was in Ponape again in late 1979, a young German businessman was constructing several concrete rental houses. His name was Robert Etscheit, and he was from Dusseldorf, Germany. He was twenty-seven years old then.

We called him Robby. He had come to the island in 1971 after his uncle Leo Etscheit, a longtime businessman in Ponape, came to Germany to visit his brother. Robby was at his family's home in Dusseldorf for Leo's visit, as he was on break from a hotel and restaurant trade school he was attending somewhere in England. Since Leo had no children and was in his seventies, he recruited Robby to come to Ponape to be his heir, to inherit his business and land when he would pass.

When he first arrived on island in 1971, Robby lived with his uncle Leo and worked for room and board plus fifty cents a day for the first year or two. He worked his way up and by the mid-1970s; he began building a few rental houses. When working on the Village Hotel, Richard and I went over to examine them. Other than that, we'd only usually run into Robby at a restaurant or at the boat ramp where I kept my wood boat pulled up on shore. So I really didn't know him that well, or the history of the Etscheit family in Ponape.

By 1979, Robby had bought out a local construction company that had a number of Filipino contract workers. They had already built the first floor of Robby's retail store, Ace Commercial, and were now constructing some additional concrete rental houses for the future Federated States of Micronesia government, soon to take over the reins of government on Ponape and three other island groups.

The history of foreign rule in Ponape started in 1875, when Spain claimed it as a colony. Their highhanded tactics ignited religious wars between Protestants and Catholics on island. As mentioned before, Spain sold its Micronesian Colonies to Germany in 1898 to raise money to fight the United States in the Spanish-American War. Germany lost it to Japan sometime during WWI. Japan ruled it under mandate of the League of Nations but in reality treated it as a colony and private military base. The United States took it from Japan after almost two years of daily aerial bombing, occasional naval bombardment and submarine blockade during WWII. On September 11, 1944, after a surrender ultimatum by US Navy authorities, the Japanese commander on Ponape surrendered without a fight. This was extremely unusual.

This commander was educated in the United States and knew all Japanese would be well treated. At the time, there were about eight thousand Japanese soldiers and approximately eight thousand Japanese civilian colonists on Ponape. There were then only about six thousand Ponapeans at the time, many who had been pressed into forced labor during the war, beatings included if they slacked off.

The US Navy left eight American soldiers on island for the last year of the war to guard all these Japanese and they had no problems. The Japanese were allowed to police themselves. After the war, all Japanese were repatriated back to Japan, including my twin boys' great grandfather. Marriages between Ponapeans and Japanese were not honored. Families were split up, some having been together since the end of the First World War. Children who were half Japanese and half Ponapean were allowed to stay with their island mothers. Under Japanese rule, Japanese men could marry Ponapean women, but Ponapean men could not marry Japanese women.

During the twenty-plus years between the First World War and the second, Japan had actually developed the island quite extensively. They accomplished a lot more than the American Trust Territory government, which was to follow, ever would.

The Japanese would develop Kolonia into a picturesque town; roads had adequate proper drainage, not at all like the slum town it is today. They had several sawmills on island, successful truck farms and fisheries operations. Roads were constructed around the island and across the island. Also, a large sugar cane plantation in Madolenihmw, in the southeast portion of the island, had a sugar cane railroad crossing over the interior mountains toward Kolonia. Because of the war, this rail line would never be totally completed and in full operation.

The US Navy administered all of Micronesia until the 1950s, when the US Trust Territory of the Pacific Islands government was established. It then became an official US territory, which included the Marshall Islands, Ponape with all its adjacent atolls, Truk and its many atolls, the Yap group of islands, all of Palau and the Mariana Islands, which included Saipan, Tinian, Rota, and others. Guam is part of the Marianas but has a different political status as a permanent US territory. This had existed since the Spanish-American War, when it was taken from Spain, along with Puerto Rico.

The US Trust Territory of the Pacific Island's was created with approval of the United Nations, which mandated the United States to prepare Micronesia for self-government at some point in the future. So this was the political situation that existed when I first came to Ponape. As a US citizen, I could enter Micronesia without even a US passport; a driver's license from Hawaii was all I needed at the time.

In late 1979, looking for something to do for work, I approached Robby Etscheit and asked him if he had ever considered building wooden houses for his rental units. Like most others on island, he was concerned about the local termite problem. I explained that the southern United States and Hawaii had a similar problem, yet most all of their houses were wooden. I told him that these types of problems could be easily controlled with proper inspections, poisons, and maintenance at the appropriate times, saying that wooden houses were also more comfortable, especially in the tropics, and looked better. Robby told me to go ahead and prepare a small plan and proposal for him to consider.

By this point in time, the Micronesian people had pretty much decided their political futures and were into a transition process of establishing four separate new government entities out of the soon to be phased out United States Trust Territory of the Pacific Islands, headquartered out of Saipan. This transition process would gradually occur over a ten-year period . . . and even longer in Palau's case.

The Marshall Islands would choose to become its own separate island nation, independent of the rest of Micronesia. Palau would opt for a similar political set up eventually, but much later.

Saipan, Tinian, and Rota, would choose to become a commonwealth of the United States: the Commonwealth of the Northern Mariana Islands. I believe all its people are now US citizens. They have the US tax system and federal court system there now.

Ponape would opt to become part of a Federation of four other island states, called the Federated States of Micronesia. It's comprised of Kusai, three hundred miles to the southeast of Ponape, formerly considered an outer island of Ponape. Kusai changed its name to Kosrae. Also, Ponape would change its name to Pohnpei.

Truk and its outer islands are the third state of the FSM. It changed its name to Chuuk. Yap is the fourth state and the only one not to change its name after becoming independent.

The FSM retained a special relationship with the United States, called the Compact of Free Association. It allows it to retain many of the benefits of a US territory but still be its own sovereign nation.

Under this agreement, the US military is responsible for the military defense of the entire region. Funding from the United States for the FSM is provided over a thirty-five-year period in two phases, as agreed so far. Many US government programs are extended to the FSM.

FSM citizens can freely immigrate into the United States to live and work without a green card, and vice versa for US citizens.

Micronesians can also join the US military if they qualify. Many have. In fact as of a couple of years ago, Micronesians had the highest casualty rate among all ethnic groups per capita, of those serving in the US military in the Iraq war.

Now after almost twenty years into these new island nations' attempts at governing themselves, many feel that they've failed miserably to provide an atmosphere conducive to attracting foreign investors, which many feel is necessary to developing a strong economic private sector in order to create new jobs and have realistic, livable wages.

Others feel the Micronesians should have not fragmented but stayed one political entity. They point to the fact that with the Law of the Sea's "exclusive economic zone" of two hundred miles out to sea, Micronesia would have became the world's largest country, bigger than Russia, at least from the area of the globe that it would have covered and controlled. Of course, most of this area would have been ocean, as all of Micronesia is comprised of small islands with a total land area of not much more than two thousand square miles.

I'm sure much has been or could be written about the political situation in Micronesia. Like everywhere else in the world, it has many problems and is far from perfect. All human governments are plagued with multiple problems. The FSM has its share, but they're fortunately quite tame compared to most other places in the world.

My first ten years in Ponape were rather tame as well, except for a lot of exciting and memorable fishing and diving experiences. These were still continuing, although by now I'd only dive with scuba gear by the shear drop-off outside the reef. None of my buddies here had any scuba gear, so I'd go by myself. I wouldn't be alone though, there were usually six to twelve grey reef sharks tagging along twenty to thirty feet away. They'd get more of my speared fish than I would, darting in and even bumping into me occasionally, one even rushing between my legs once.

One time I wanted to see just how far down this drop-off went. It's not unusual to have 100' to 200' foot water visibility laterally here, but only be able to see 60' to 80' feet down, even at the best of times. That's because of a temperature inversion, so I've been told. I followed this shear coral wall down to 215' feet, where a coral rubble pile then tapered off at about a 45 degree angle, down into several thousand feet of water. It was like dusk here, but I could still see out about 200' feet, the water was that clear. When I looked up my boat was clearly visible, drifting above on its long anchor rope.

Coming up I stopped at 185' feet to decompress a bit. My nose had been bleeding in my mask and it was a dark dirty green color at this depth. Looking out I saw a ten foot tiger shark 150' feet away and a little deeper than I was. He was lazily swimming parallel to the reef, but when spotting me he turned and slowly made a bee line directly towards me. I had already been warned by two natives with firsthand experience, "don't piss-off a tiger shark!" They were sometimes known by some islanders to continue to fight with a diver if they were injured by him. I decided to just give him a gentle nudge in his nose with the end of my spear for starters. When he got within ten feet of me, he slowly turned again and continued on his way.

Unwittingly though, I was about to get embroiled in something far more risky than spear fishing among sharks. I was about to end up right at the center of one of the most serious problems in Micronesia, one that some government officials and others over time would warn could lead to bloodshed, a possible uprising in the island and even Ponape seceding from the union of FSM states. These wouldn't end up seeming to be just idle threats. I would get involved with this innocently enough, in a situation that I would view as a civil rights issue. Some would term it as a case that boiled down to reverse discrimination. It would grow to involve hundreds of people and have me again watching my back and eating with it to a wall for much of the next two decades.

All these situations to come get kicked off when I got back to Robby Etscheit, to see if he might be interested in having me build him one wooden rental house. He did. One house turned into two, then three, and so on.

Robby's uncle's store, Leo's Store, provided all the building material and I provided the labor. After the first house, Robby essentially started shutting down all concrete housing, and his Filipinos were put under my supervision. I'd have them do the plumbing, electrical, finish work and painting on the wood houses, although Robby paid them. Occasionally, I'd do the plumbing and electrical, if I felt like doing it. The Filipinos would also be relegated to maintenance on existing buildings, something I would be paid to oversee for the first several years. I had my own Micronesian employees and we always did the rough framing and concrete work, plus we put the roofs on, but had the Filipinos do most everything else.

Robby and I grew closer, becoming good friends. I had heard since first coming to Ponape that the Etscheit family owned a large piece of land. From Robby I would begin learning more about the history of their family and how they acquired this land, one of the largest private parcels in Micronesia, the second largest on Ponape.

I would also learn that they were the only white foreigners to still own land on island and that shortly Robby was to become the largest single landowner in all of Micronesia, certainly on Ponape.

Trouble had already surfaced many times over this land. A brief history would be as follows, as I was to learn. The previous owner before the Etscheits was a Polish botanist, Johanes Kubari, who apparently acquired it before the Spanish era, which started in 1875. Kubari associated with Protestants, from what I've read in court records on Ponape.

When Spain began ruling in 1875, the first Spanish governor was highly anti-Protestant. He did many things to enrage the Protestant community, which had first been established on island around the 1850s. He began to declare arbitrarily that all Catholics who owned land on Ponape had good title, but Protestants only had a leasehold interest—that the highest titled traditional leader in those areas still owned their land.

These and other actions of the Spanish governor led to a religious war breaking out between Protestants and Catholics. In some battles, twenty to forty people were killed. A number of Protestants whose lands were affected appealed and complained to the Spanish headquarters of the Pacific in Manila, Philippines. These superiors overruled the governor of Ponape and replaced him, restoring peace.

Time passed and Kubari committed suicide while owing several creditors. Germany bought much of Micronesia in 1898, including Ponape, from Spain. To satisfy Kubari's creditors, Germany puts his land up at public auction.

The bidding process took two or three years. Apparently approvals had to come from Europe, but Robby's grandfather, Dominic Etscheit, was the winner for fifteen thousand German gold marks.

In 1902 Dominic moved his wife Florentine, and second oldest son Carlos, to Ponape to become a copra planter. Their oldest son Leo, who was about five years old at the time, stayed in Germany with relatives to attend school.

The original German land register for Micronesia lists the land in hectares, which translates to about twenty-five hundred acres. I've seen it—it's in German—and I vaguely recall that it mentions other lands acquired by Dominic, either at the auction or later. It listed two entire small islands north of Kolonia in the lagoon, Dekehtik and Sapwutik. Two other lands were owned in Truk, a parcel on the main island in Truk Lagoon and a whole atoll or island, Olul, north of Truk Lagoon.

Later from Robby's father, Robert, I would learn that when Dominic first began to work in his new land on Ponape, he found it already inhabited by Ponapeans in an area called Kamar, which is one of the areas mentioned in the land register. These people threatened him with machetes, so he abandoned about half his land to them, concentrating his work in the uninhabited half.

Dominic and Florentine would have three more children in Ponape. They had a daughter Ella, and two more boys Millie and Robert, the youngest being Robby's father. When WWI broke out, Carlos traveled to Europe to join up. The family had dual citizenship, German and Belgium, which were on opposite sides of the conflict. But ironically Leo and Carlos were both on their way to enlist when they were captured by one side or the other. They then spent the duration as prisoners of war even though they hadn't joined either side yet.

This first worldwide turbulent period affected in one way or another over 93 percent of the earth's population. The Etscheit family in Ponape and the two boys in Europe lost all communication with each other.

Before the close of the Great War, the war to end all wars, as many politicians and religious leaders were calling WWI, Japan sailed into Kolonia Harbor and ousted Germany without a fight. It was rather a peaceful transition; they even passed out rice cakes to everyone. This was Japan's start of making Micronesia part of the Japanese Empire and a major part of its outer ring of defense of its empire.

As for the Etscheits and any other German or white foreigners, their lands and possessions were confiscated and they were all deported, only being allowed to take what they could carry in one suitcase. Arriving back in Germany after the war, the family was destitute and ragged, having lost practically everything. They had no idea if Leo and Carlos were even alive, fearing they may have perished during the war as so many others had.

The three younger children had never even met Leo because he had always stayed in Europe. The children had seen recent photos of him from just before the advent of hostilities in Europe, before all communications broke down. Leo may have seen pictures of his younger brothers and sister but they were now much older, obviously much changed.

One day the children are wandering some city streets in Germany looking like ragamuffin war orphans. All of a sudden they spot someone who looks to them like Leo walking down the street. They run up to him all excited. Leo wonders who these raggedly war orphans are, not at all recognizing them as his brothers and sister.

This chance encounter is how the Etscheit family was finally reunited in Germany. At the time Leo was working for the Belgium Embassy in Germany. Belgium had been an ally during the war with England, France, the United States, including Japan and other countries. Leo began to use his position and influence with the Belgium government to have it intercede on behalf of his family's Belgium citizenship, for Japan to return their land taken from allies. Belgium's efforts finally bore fruit. By 1926, Japan finally agreed to return the Etscheits' land.

Carlos was the first to return to Ponape that year and officially receive the family land back from the Japanese. Dominic was sick in Europe and died that year, 1926. Title devolved to Florentine and she would survive Dominic by fifty years more, eventually dying in Dusseldorf, Germany, in 1976.

In 1927 Leo went to Ponape for the first time. Travel then was by sailing ship. Florentine returned two years later, only bringing Millie backs to Ponape with her. Millie needed extra care, as he had been blinded as a child on island when some WWI munitions' he'd been playing with exploded. Ella and Robert remained in Germany.

Carlos developed a copra plantation in the southern area of the land, adjacent to the Lewi River. Florentine and Leo developed their plantations next to the Duanu River, which borders the northern area of the land. This river is the boundary between what was then the kingdom of Nett to the south and Kolonia Town to the north. Kolonia Town is mostly on a peninsula jutting out on the north of the island. The Etscheit land borders its southern boundary. It was a valuably situated two square miles of land.

During the mid-1930s the family would begin to feud among themselves over the use and distribution of this land. This would continue for the next sixty years. As World War II approached, Florentine and blind Millie took a trip back to Germany to visit relatives in 1939, especially Ella and Robert still in Germany.

As World War II broke out, it became impossible for Florentine and Millie to return. They were trapped in Germany. With the outbreak of the war in the Pacific, despite Japan now an ally of Germany and the Etscheits now playing up their German citizenship, the Japanese confiscated all their lands under duress for the second time. They imprisoned the remaining family, who were put under house arrest for the duration of the war. The Japanese built a high wooden fence around their houses, located near the bay in the northeast area of Kolonia.

When I first came to Ponape, this location was in the area of a Quonset hut and business called the American Club. It is now partially occupied by the present-day Micronesian Legal Services Corporation building. The Japanese never fed the Etscheits. They survived because Micronesians who were close to the family, threw food over the fence at night.

Leo had a milk cow inside this fence. After a while it went dry, or so he thought. He'd get up early but find it dry. According to him, after some time he found out that Carlos was getting up earlier to get milk for his three young daughters, Yvette, Monique, and Renee.

The American military bombed the island most every day for two years before the island commander surrendered. Kolonia was the only city in the Pacific, other than cities in Japan, that were firebombed by the US Air Force during the war. The inferno destroyed 90 percent of Kolonia. The Etscheit houses escaped damage because they were not directly hit. Also being close to the seashore on the windward side of Kolonia, these houses were in an excellent position away from the center of the inferno.

But that's not what the Japanese figured. They thought for sure that Leo and Carlos were American agents who had somehow signaled the bombers to avoid their houses. Some tense moments passed as the Japanese were threatening to kill them as they were screaming these accusations.

On the confiscated Etscheit land the Japanese established their primary military base, with barracks, hospital, tank depot and everything they needed. The copra plantations slowly had the coconut trees cut down to provide salad material from the top center portion of the palm. The Japanese then converted that land to a type of sweet potato cultivation.

Just up above the upper edges of the copra plantation, where the rain forest was still intact, the Japanese prepared a World War I-type trench warfare battlefield, ready to confront any Americans if they approached in the now wide-open former copra plantation. Throughout the jungle on the flank approaches to this trench system, were tank traps, slip trenches, and spider traps, all to ambush and slow down any Americans moving through the jungle if they tried a flank attack. Up through this now wide-open treeless copra plantation, slip trenches abounded. These lightly defended scattered positions appeared to be there to lure large numbers of American troops to the area before the main force would open up from just above the tree line from these camouflaged trenches. The Japanese fighter base was about three-quarters of a mile to the west of this prepared battlefield. Trenches abounded all throughout the area and all the way up to the top of the nearest high mountain, Tolokawp Mountain. I never imagined when first seeing this that I'd end up being the only American to ever fight on this battlefield.

Along the bay shore, near where the Liwi River empties into Kolonia Bay, the Japanese built four or five huge water tanks dug into the ground. One of them was not open-topped but had a concrete roof covered with dirt and vegetation, so it couldn't be detected from the air. This water system on the Etscheit land was important to the Japanese war effort, as it provided most of the water for the Japanese fleet stationed in the mighty Truk Lagoon, almost 500 miles to the west. Truk was the headquarters for Japan's Pacific fleet when away from Japan. Water would flow from these tanks to a rock earthen pier, where water barges would then load and transport it to Truk Lagoon.

About 150 to 200 yards from this earthen pier was the area where the military tanks were kept. By war's end for Ponape, this tank farm was the largest collection of undamaged operational Japanese military tanks found anywhere in the Pacific, other than Japan.

As mentioned before, Ponape was bombed most every day for two years. The military installations on the Etscheit land were a frequent target. It was also shelled by the USS *New Jersey*, sister ship to the *Missouri*, as the fleet passed by Ponape sometime in 1944. Right before the Japanese surrendered the island, the Etscheits were moved more toward the interior of the island, near a pointed mountain in an area now known as Erika. They feared they'd be killed.

Elements in the Japanese military actually prepared to kill all the locals, but the island's commander stopped them. Later, the Etschiets were thrilled to see one of the first early-American helicopters hovering overhead. After the surrender on September 11, 1944, American naval officers now on island were surprised to see two little blond European girls come running out of the jungle, Yvette and Monique Etscheit, Carlos's two oldest daughters.

Numerous air battles occurred in Ponapean skies during the war. I've seen wreckage of an American bomber out near the present-day FSM capital complex, which used to be the site of a second Japanese air base in Palikir. A Japanese bomber's wreckage lies across Kolonia Bay, near the seashore in Paliais, before Nett Point. Its engine lay under a house built by an American fisherman, Mark Tikell, who's now deceased.

A third crash site is of an American Corsair, apparently piloted by the son of some well-known US political figure of that era. This plane was reportedly damaged by antiaircraft ground fire.

Two Witness friends of mine here, both half Ponapean and half Japanese, were attending an elementary school in Rohn Kitti that was just for children with Japanese blood. Their names are Ampilina Norman and Hiroshi Yamaguchi; both are in their seventies now.

They, along with other children at school, saw the American plane smoking and sputtering as it was following the western reef south, at a thousand feet or so elevation. Turning eastward with the reef off Rohn Kitti, the plane continued turning inland. When over the school, it nosed into a dive and crashed not to far up river.

Many students ran to the crash site, but much of its wreckage had burrowed into the mud right next to the river. From reports, the pilot's body has apparently not been recovered even to this day. This I heard from one American who researched and visited this crash site about seven years ago. He showed me a small piece of sheet metal, light blue with part of a US white star still visible on it, which he had just taken from the site. This man stayed with Hiroshi when on that visit. The American man could likely get in trouble for removing artifacts, but I recently heard that he passed away in Clovis, California, not too many years ago.

Hiroshi told me that when he was a ten—or eleven-year-old, air raid sirens would frequently sound and he and other schoolmates would have to run for their lives to the air raid shelter some distance away. Afterward when returning to class, they'd sometimes pass schoolmates killed in the American bombing run.

Carl Dannis related an incident that occurred on Mokil Atoll, ninety miles to the east, during the period the United States bombed Ponape. As the American bombers returned to their Marshall Island bases, they would usually fly by in formation within eyesight of Mokil. Occasionally, these islanders would see or hear the bombers dropping leftover bombs in the ocean, as they preferred not to have any on board when landing back at their base in the Marshall Islands. There were no Japanese on Mokil at the time, nor had there been during the war in the Pacific.

One day as they were passing nearby, one lone bomber peeled out of formation and swung in over the atoll, dropping one leftover bomb. It killed a father and his young son.

In 1972, before Denny Gormley started becoming mentally ill, I related this Mokil bombing story to him. He surprised me by replying that they deserved it, that those native islanders were part of the Japanese Empire, because they worked for the Japanese military. As far as he was concerned, they were all "Japs." I countered that the only reason the islanders were then part of the Japanese Empire was because after WWI, the League of Nations mandated all of Micronesia to Japan's rule. The United States, as the driving force behind the "League," approved of it. Micronesians didn't ask to be ruled by Japan! I informed him that during the war, micronesian men were enslaved into forced labor, were never paid, and were severely beaten if they didn't comply. The Japanese didn't even feed them either, they had to stumble around in the dark after sundown, looking for their own food after they were let off work.

This was about as close to an argument as Denny and I ever had. My response didn't seem to make a dent in his viewpoint. He got hot under the collar over this issue. I could see he still had some hard feelings over the war, which he hadn't yet been able to get over.

I imagine that many people would find this understandable. After all, Denny had seen his best friend killed right in front of him as they stormed off the landing craft ramp on Tarawa Atoll. Plus he lived the rest of his life in pain every day from having his jaw blown off on Iwo Jima.

I just wished Denny could have had some of the experiences I would eventually have with my future German business partner. Through him, I'd come to know a number of German and Japanese veterans of WWII. These people were all perfectly normal and likeable people, the same as the many average Americans I'd grown up with.

I'll write about some of these Germans shortly. Mr. Nabishima though, was one of these Japanese veterans. He served in China. He would run a joint venture agricultural project with us on Robby's land. He grew vegetables, but mostly Ponape black pepper, considered one of the worlds finest. During an end-of-the-year dinner function for the project, several of our Japanese investors traveled to Ponape to attend.

I usually felt like a duck out of water at these types of events. We even had some people from our local United States Embassy attending. It was the smallest US Embassy in the world and was located only about sixty or seventy yards from my house that I would build in 1982 on the Etschiet estate. It was just across the Duanu River from my house, but in Kolonia Town and built later, in the mid-1980s.

At the dinner, I found I was most comfortable talking with one of the older Japanese visitors. We hit it off and spent most of the evening together, trying to avoid the bigwigs. After a while he asked some questions about Ponape's role in the Second World War. So I told him some of what I knew at the time.

I then asked if he had served during the war. "Yes," he answered. He went on to tell me he had been a "kaiten" pilot. I asked if that was a type of airplane. "No," he replied. He went on to explain that a kaiten was a one-man torpedo that is steered to its target by a single operator, which is launched from a submarine.

I asked if he'd ever almost been called to action. He said yes, explaining that on one occasion his sub commander was stalking an American ship, trying to jockey into position to attack. He was ordered to his station ready to be launched. Fortunately, he was eventually ordered to stand down when his sub couldn't get close enough to an advantageous firing position.

Much later watching a History Channel program on World War II, I learned interesting details about Japan's submarine fleet. They had essentially two types, conventional submarines that fired standard torpedoes of the era. They also had five or six huge submarines that were capable of carrying up to three airplanes and launching them at sea. These submarines were apparently also capable of launching the suicide one-man kaiten torpedo. So this friendly likeable older Japanese man was an extremely rare WWII survivor. It oftentimes saddens me to think about all the wonderful men on all sides of man's many conflicts, that didn't make it.

Back to the aerial battles in Ponapean skies, even my father-in-law witnessed part of one. As a four-year-old boy standing on the eastern bank of Kolonia Bay, he watched an American fighter plane flying by just above the water, with a Japanese Zero close behind. It was trying to get into position for a shot. They disappeared up the Kamar River Valley. A minute or so later, they both came flying back the other direction, this time with the American fighter on the Zero's tail.

I've heard that other American planes went missing in Ponape attacks, but their crash sites remain yet undiscovered, whether in the ocean or in the dense remote jungle areas of this island.

More planes were shot down in attacks against the Japanese installations and ships in Truk Lagoon. Many captured downed American flyers suffered a horrible fate there. They were executed and then eaten by some Japanese. After the war, American tribunals sentenced numerous Japanese soldiers to death, and the executions were carried out for cannibalism in Truk.

But before the Americans could take their revenge, some Micronesians struck first. This occurred on one or two lawless isolated outer islands in the Truk group. Some Japanese soldiers had been stationed there early in the war. Their cruel, high-handed tactics early on earned them the hatred of these islanders. As the war turned against Japan and shipping was cut off to many islands, especially to isolated units of soldiers, many began to weaken as starvation set in. These islanders could easily live off the land and sea as they always had; these soldiers couldn't. A few of the dominant islanders who were tired of fish began to take advantage of this situation and supplement their diet with fresh meat.

After the war, Leo and Carlos resumed operating stores again, something they had been doing since the late 1920s on island. In this early postwar period, Leo was able to acquire the original German land register from the early period of German colonial rule. Either the US Navy or early Trust Territory government appointed him as the first civilian "Distad," a position similar to Governor.

By the mid-1950s, hearings were held by the US Trust Territory government to gather testimony from those throughout Micronesia who had their land illegally taken under duress by the Japanese authorities, prior to and during World War II.

By 1956, the Trust Territory high commissioner officially returned the Etscheit land to its previous owner, Florentine Etscheit. She was still in Germany, staying with Robby's father in Dusseldorf. Never again would she return to Ponape. She continued to live in Germany until her death in 1976.

But within a week or two of reacquiring title to the land, after losing it twice to the Japanese, Florentine quitclaimed it to her five children, but in six equal shares, with two shares going to blind Millie because of his disability.

When returning this land, the Trust Territory did not want to return the two lands in Truk, including the whole island of Olul, for some reason. To this day, I've never seen any reasonable legal justification for this action.

I can only imagine the practical reason for this. The Trukese are notoriously violent and would most likely oppose white ownership being reestablished. The Ponapeans would eventually be bad enough. This antiwhite ownership mentality would develop only after WWII, when laws were passed that only Micronesian citizens could acquire any new title to land. Existing foreign ownership was allowed. But by 1979, laws were specifically passed to prohibit foreign owners from passing land to their noncitizen descendants. These laws were passed for the stated purpose, that eventually all land would revert to Micronesian ownership. These laws reveal the underlying resentment toward white or foreign ownership and were instrumental in fostering these attitudes among a new generation.

By the late 1960s, Florentine's children were in renewed disagreement over this land's use and division among themselves. In 1968, Carlos filed a "partition action," asking the Trust Territory High Court to partition its distribution.

Also around this time, the Trust Territory was having airports built in all the island district centers throughout Micronesia. These included, starting in the east, Majuro, Ponape, Truk, Yap, Palau, and then Saipan in the north. Kwajalein already had a military airfield, as well as Saipan possibly. Kosrae would get an airport about twenty years later, when it became a state of the FSM and changed its name from Kusai to Kosrae.

Majuro would get a new airport in the late 1970s or 1980s. The early one was quite unique that I experienced when traveling through on my way to or from Ponape. I think it was an old Japanese fighter base used during WWII. It was expanded for the Continental 727 jet route between Honolulu and Guam, with stops at all the islands. It was a coral paved airstrip, narrow, with coconut trees just outside the wing tips on each side. Plus it had a dogleg left runway, which followed the curve of the narrow atoll.

Between this old airfield and the new one to be built later is the overturned hull of the *Prince Hoiken*, the light German battleship or cruiser, which used to accompany the battleship *Bismarck* before it sunk off England during WWII. Prince Hoiken was captured and used by the US Navy in its atomic bomb tests of the 1950s in the Marshall Islands.

For Ponape, the Trust Territory decided that the best airport site was either the site where the FSM capital would later be built, an old Japanese airfield and government land in Palikir, about four miles west of Kolonia, or Dekehtik Island, a 460-acre island one mile north of Kolonia, inside the lagoon and owned by the Escheits. Before this, air service into Ponape was by seaplane out of Guam.

The Trust Territory government settled on Dekethik Island, considering it much more convenient because it was only a mile from town. The Etscheits didn't oppose this but instead gave the government, at their request, permission to start construction. They figured the Trust Territory would negotiate a fair lease rate for land needed, as it was doing with all the other landowners throughout Micronesia. So in the mid-1960s, the government started dredging a causeway across Kolonia Bay to Deketik Island.

This causeway to the new airport site would end up being a big environmental mistake for Kolonia Bay, for it cut off the bay's natural water circulation. The whole east side of the bay east of the causeway is now silted up and can only be navigated by small boats at high tide. Before, small ships could come all the way up to the shore on the east side of the Kolonia waterfront.

On the west side of Kolonia, where most visiting sailboats anchor, the water used to be blue and dolphins used to come right up to Sokehs Bridge. Giant clams used to thrive in these waters. Now they are all highly polluted, dark, and murky.

The causeway road to Dekehtik should have been built up on piers to avoid the siltation results. It wouldn't have helped the water pollution coming out of Kolonia, but the natural water flow may have helped carry some of the pollutants away, thus improving the bay water's appearance. Despite the negative environmental aftereffects of the airport being located on Dekehtik Island, it would end up being another major land disaster for the Etscheit family. This was because although the Trust Territory government was negotiating lease agreements with private landowners throughout Micronesia, they never even initiated serious lease negotiations with them. Instead, they moved directly to eminent domain condemnation proceedings.

When the airport was almost ready to open, which it did in 1969, the Etscheits were then informed of the Trust Territories' intention to take Dekehtik Island for a public purpose—not only for an airport and a new commercial dock, but also a tank farm. This tank farm was to be for the private business use of Mobil Oil Corporation. Taking land for a private corporation like Mobil Oil by eminent domain was illegal.

Eminent domain is only to be used for public purposes, only if no other sites are available and the owners refuse to sell or lease for fair market price. Numerous sites were available on Ponape, for

90 percent of it is government land and almost all of them would have caused far less environmental damage. Eminent domain also only allows for the taking of the exact amount of land that the project requires, no more. This airport, dock, and tank farm needed approximately 130 to 150 acres. The Trust Territory informed the Etscheits that they would be taking all 460 acres.

By the late 1960s, Leo and Carlos were not on amicable speaking terms, likely due to their disagreements over the partition case Carlos filed in 1968. Neither Carlos nor Leo knew much about the law and there were no lawyers in private practice on Ponape for them to consult with or hire. This ironic situation existed in Micronesia, despite that during the Trust Territory era, there were more lawyers in Micronesia per capita than anywhere else on Earth. But they all worked for the government, helping set up these new immerging island nations that would replace the US Trust Territory government.

But not wanting to appear to be railroading these white foreign landowners during the legal proceedings, the Trust Territory appointed a Saipan-based lawyer to represent the Etscheits. He arrived before trial to consult with his clients and prepare for the proceedings. But the trial was postponed. During the delay, the lawyer decided to take advantage of the opportunity to see some of the beautiful outer island atolls on one of the small cargo freighters. These deliver supplies to the atolls and bring back bags of copra to Ponape.

On the voyage, the Etscheits' new court-appointed lawyer got sick and died on the ship. He was then buried at sea with no autopsy, after radio consultations with Trust Territory authorities about what to do with his body.

Later back on Ponape, the trial continued without legal representation for the Etscheits. To make a long story short, by 1972, about three years after the airport had been in operation and jets had been landing and taking off, the Trust Territory High Court rendered a decision. It was of course, in favor of the Trust Territory, awarding all 460 acres to itself, despite only needing about 130 or so. But even more incredible was that it condemned the whole island for only $25 an acre, for a total of approximately $11,500.

The Etscheits were so outraged by this outcome, viewing the $11,500 as such an absurd insult, that for over twenty years this money had remained unclaimed by them at the courthouse. Also part of this Judgment" was that the Etscheits were to be allowed to keep 15 acres of filled land on Dekehtik. These 15 acres were never turned over to them; instead, the government began to use the area as a dump site, which it still is up to the present time, over forty years later.

Some might point out that Dekehtik is largely a mangrove swamp, large areas underwater at high tide. Land ownership laws are different in Micronesia, and many older large parcels of land going back to the Spanish and German era, confer ownership out to the seaward edge of the mangrove forests.

These mangrove forests are not the scruffy short little bushy mangroves I've seen pictures of in Florida. These are big and have five or six varieties of high-quality hardwood and softwood trees that could easily fetch $25 worth of lumber, even from many of the small trees. Some of the larger trees might net over $1,000 or more per tree for top-quality wood, especially if properly exported.

Later by early 1984, I would start operating a sawmill on the Etscheit estate, logging over 700 to 800 acres of the 1,246 acres of their parcel on the main island. We did selective cutting over a ten-year period, cutting trees from about eighteen inches to about four feet in diameter. We may have only cut down four to six trees per acre.

I was always proud that on leaving a logged area, we could look back and from a hundred yards away, the forest still looked almost 100 percent intact. We could have done the same thing with the mangrove forest on Dekehtik, had not excess condemnation occurred. Of the total acreage, 330 acres should have stayed with the Etscheit family, and 130 acres could have been allocated for the airport and dock only.

A sustainable selective cutting logging operation of, say, 200 acres of Dekehtik could easily take $100 to $200 in lumber yearly per acre without any visible impact. That's $20,000 to $40,000 per year. Whoever valued Dekehtik as only worth $25 an acre was either in the government's pocket or an idiot.

By the late 1980s, Robby and I would have lawyers look into this excess condemnation issue. We thought that racism must have played a role in the Trust Territories' actions. After all, extremely large sums of money had been paid out to Micronesian landowners throughout the other district centers for airport land leases. Only the white Etscheits had their land stripped from them for ridiculously low prices, along with the taking of three times more property than was actually needed for the project.

Bingo! Our lawyers found a smoking gun memo in the Trust Territory archive files in Saipan, Mariana Islands, which are located north of Guam. The memo was between Trust Territory officials who were involved in these airport/dock projects throughout Micronesia. In discussing the acquiring of needed land for the Ponape project, words to this effect were recorded in the written records: "In this case we don't need to lease. We can take the land by eminent domain, and take the whole island even though we don't need it all, because the owners are white Europeans and nobody in Micronesia will have any sympathy for them!"

This is blatant racism. This type of racism would get worse for the Etscheits and would continue right up to the present day. Additionally, for two decades I would find myself right at the center of it.

By 1972, Leo and Carlos had a trial on the partition case filed in 1968. With no lawyers available, each pled his own case. Leo also spoke on behalf of Millie, Ella, and Robert, who were living in Europe.

I've read much of the record and their written legal pleadings and communications to the judge. These highlight their total ignorance of the law, especially regarding jointly owned land, tenancy in common. They make numerous admissions against interest, in other words, saying things that hurt their case. No wonder they were railroaded by the Trust Territory and didn't know what to do during the Dekehtik proceedings, being without legal representation.

Two or three year passed and the Trust Territory judge hadn't yet rendered a decision in the partition case. The Etscheits made inquiries and the judge responded in writing that he'd render a decision shortly. So not knowing whose land was whose, or how the judge would divide it among the heirs, much of the large heavily wooded land on the main island of Ponape was left unworked by either side.

Being adjacent to Kolonia and with its boundaries somewhat unknown to the public, also overgrown and obscured by thick vegetation, squatters coming into the land had been an ongoing problem since the late 1940s. Back then these people were usually from Sokehs Municipality.

The elected chief magistrate of Nett was also the king of Nett. A couple of his former municipal policemen, a municipal judge, and a secretary told me that this king would send his policemen to inform these squatters of their error and ask them to leave. The Etscheits and the king enjoyed a good relationship.

The former five kingdoms of Ponape are now also municipalities with a chief magistrate, but each still has a king as well. In Nett during this period, the king and chief magistrate were one and the same, magistrate being an elected office.

In the traditional system there are two lines of ascension to power. One leads to being king, called the *nanmwarki*. The second leads to *nahnken*, a title second only to the king, supposedly just a little less powerful but not always. If a nahnken is aggressive and a current king docile, the nahnken can in some cases exercise more power than the king.

Also, a king's son can never become a king but can only become nahnken, and not at the same time as his father is king, usually afterward. A nahnken's son can become a king eventually, but not while his father is nahnken.

It's all confusing to me, but this is how I understand it. I apologize to any of these people if I somehow have things mixed up here. But one thing I do know for sure is that nahnken can be very powerful with the local people.

From the 1940s through the mid-1970s, this king of Nett continued to help the Etscheits by having people leave their land that had recently started homesteading by mistake. By the '70s, these were beginning to be people from Nett, some who had come onto the land because a new road had been built two miles across the upper area of the Etscheit estate in the mountains, making access easy for them now.

This road was built to provide a route for a sixteen-inch water line to bring water from a new small dam on the Nanpil River, then across the Mallarme land and on across the Etscheit land, then up to a water treatment plant. The water then flows down into Kolonia, a total distance of about four miles. We called this road the "Pipeline Road," as it crosses Etscheit land.

This king of Nett, whose name was Max Iriarte, was also the elected chief magistrate of Nett. He was the government official who, acting on behalf of the Trust Territory government, negotiated these easements for this pipeline road with the Etscheits to cross their property. From the dam to the water treatment plant, only two pieces of private property needing easements were crossed. Lucas Mallarme owned a couple of hundred acres in the mountains adjacent to the Etscheits, the Lewi River being their joint boundary. I believe his parcel made him the third largest landowner on Ponape who has good, unclouded title.

The Japanese also took Lucas's land under duress during WWII. The Trust Territory Hearings of 1956 returned it to him. The Japanese cut down large areas of his forest and stationed troops in that location, ready to confront an American invasion as well.

In 1976 or 1977, Max Iriarte died, and a new king was installed. Max's son Salvador Iriarte, became the nahnken of Nett sometime afterward. Prior to this on the Etscheits' land, a few people had been clandestinely planting a few crops here and there, unknown to the Etscheits. But now they were openly expanding their crops and claims, building houses, claiming permission from these new traditional leaders and adverse to the Etscheits. Other new homesteaders join them now. Leo couldn't get any cooperation from the new king or new chief magistrate as before. So in 1978, in Trust Territory High Court, he filed a lawsuit against these people for trespassing.

By 1978 the Etscheits still hadn't received their decision yet on the partition case. The judge had retired and may have already died by that time. So they didn't have their individual certificates of title yet, other than German and Japanese records, and the 1956 and 1971 Trust Territory proceedings.

During the '60s, '70s and beyond, the Trust Territory government was progressively reregistering all lands under a new "Trust Territory title system." In 1970 and 1971, the Etscheits had gone through this process with public notices, hearings, and new surveys. During this process no other claimant came forward to claim any part of their land. This was because there were no others then, thanks in large part to Max Iriarte, Netts Nanmwarki (king) and Chief Magistrate.

Leo and Carlos could have gotten a joint title to the land in 1971, along with their other brothers and sister. But with a resolution to the 1968 partition case looking as if it might be resolved in a year or two, they opted to delay title issuance. That way each could get title to his respective portion, yet to be determined by the partition decision. It seemed like a reasonable thing to do at the time. None of them ever imagined that a resolution to this partition case was still twenty-five years away, not concluding until late 1996.

Chapter 21

Moving from Small Trouble to Big

By early 1980 as I was building rental houses up alongside the Duanu River, which is the boundary between Nett and Kolonia Town, I began having some encounters with squatters recently emboldened to build or plant on Etcheit land.

In one instance, after clearing one location for a house with my crew by hand with machetes, an old man across the river began yelling at me in Ponapean and shaking his fist. I asked my guys, "What was that all about?" They responded that the guy was upset, claiming we removed some of his crops when we cleared the house site. In those years I couldn't tell the difference between crops and the jungle; it all looked the same to me. The next day when we returned to the lot to start construction, it was full of grass and vegetation debris, pushed onto the building site by Carlos's D4 bulldozer.

This was my personal initiation into the feud among the Etscheits over their jointly owned land, which their parents had passed down to them. This was obviously part of the land that was in dispute in the partition case, which was now about twelve years old.

We had to clear the lot again by hand, build the house and go through it all over again when doing the next house. All the while Carlos's bulldozer was clearing areas next to us, keeping us bottled up along a narrow corridor next to the Duanu River.

We would laugh at how Carlos's pathetic old bulldozer couldn't even push over a coconut tree. But they had us so compressed by fences they had just put up, that in some areas we only had enough room for a road with a house on one side, despite the land being almost half a mile wide on the other side.

The narrowest lot we built on was where I built the fourth house. It was only about ninety feet wide between Carlos's fence and the Duanu River. When it was almost finished, one of my workers who had just separated from his wife needed a place to sleep for a few days. He was young and being from Saipan, had no other family here, so he asked if he could sleep on the floor there. All the windows and doors were already installed, plus the outside security lights were in operation. Between the road and river, the buildable part of the lot sloped down about ten feet. The floor of this house on its riverside was about eight feet above the ground. To the north, it overlooked a beautiful forested park like area across the river. There was a picturesque waterfall that could be seen from this side of the house. It had a sluiceway and a working waterwheel as well. Because of the unique view, I designed the house with the living room, dining room, kitchen, and deck overlooking the river and all of this. When setting up the posts and beams to support the floor on this side of this house, I had driven a number of two-by-three wood stakes into the ground to attach braces to during the framing process. When this building was just about done, I removed the temporary braces and stakes, all except one. One stake was driven into the ground so well that I couldn't get it out. It stuck above the ground about six to eight inches, just outside the northwest end of the building and it was as solid as could be. I chose to wait until another time to get it out.

The very first night that the employee spent in this house, he was awakened late at night by a metallic tapping and clinking sound coming from the area of the deck. It was totally dark in the house. Only three exterior lights were on outside, one lighting up the covered deck that overlooked the river. As this employee peeked out the bedroom door, he was shocked and terrified to see two men with black hoods on their heads just outside the deck sliding glass door. They were well lit up by the light there. One was tall and skinny and bent down trying to jimmy open the sliding glass door with a screwdriver. The other was short and heavier. He was up on a box on his tiptoes straining to reach the light fixture on the ceiling, trying to get the glass cover off to unscrew the bulb. Their caper could have been better served if they would have just changed places. Both also had to constantly readjust their eyeholes on their hoods, as it appeared they were having trouble seeing whenever they moved a bit.

As these two continued to labor to break in, my employee was beside himself not knowing what to do. Finally an idea came to him and he immediately took action. He only had a machete, so he yelled at the top of his voice "Quick Steve, bring the gun!" He then slapped the side of the bedroom wall with the machete as hard as he could, making a big *bang*! At this gunshot-like sound, the two took off running.

Unfortunately, not being able to see very well with their hoods on, they ran right into each other and both fell down. The tall skinny guy was up first and leaped over the three-foot-high handrail to the ground, eleven feet below. The short heavier guy was a second behind in jumping over the railing, but he went over in the same location as his accomplice. With these two guys' performance up to that point and now with screams, groans, and cussing erupting from the ground below, many of my employee's fears evaporated. He was now emboldened to hurry over to the living rooms windows to watch the remaining action by moonlight. The short heavier guy on top of the pile was up first and began to run west, past the window and up into the jungle where we hadn't yet cleared for the next house. The taller thinner guy was much slower in getting up but began to pick up speed as he followed after his partner. As he reached the corner of the building in full stride, he kicked that two-by-three wood stake and came skidding to a stop on his face. Good thing he still had his hood on.

He immediately tried to get back up but collapsed down with screams of pain and nonstop cursing in Ponapean. Now he was really hurting. Realizing he couldn't move and needed help, he began crying out to his buddy to come back to help him. This other guy came trotting back and hoisted his partner up over his shoulder. As he struggled to hurry away, the injured guy was raising his head up and screaming back death threats, shaking his fist back at the house, amidst continuing outcries of pain and cursing. As they disappeared into the darkness of the forest, additional sounds seemed to indicate that they may have run into a tree. They should have taken their hoods off sooner.

Just prior to this, Leo Etschiet was sick with heart problems and had been in Hawaii for a couple of months for treatment. Now about eighty-four-years old, he was back on island and anxious to get back to work and busy again. I'd see him several times going past my house to the Speaker of the Legislature's house, which was three houses past mine in Kolonia. This man was acting as Leo's lawyer.

This Ponapean man had some legal experience as a local attorney, and Leo had hired him to represent him against the new squatters who had recently come onto their land. By now, all these people were claiming the right to be on this land because of permission from the new traditional leaders. They were now saying that the king and nahnken owned it. So this case evolved into a "quiet title" case, with the traditional leaders representing all these people. It was scheduled to go to trial by the last week of 1980.

I had already asked Robby if I could buy a piece of land from them. I wanted to get out of Kolonia. Overrun by noisy drunken troublemakers, especially at night, it was like living in a Wild West town.

I was already slipping as a Christian and had knocked a few down who had threatened me. I had never been drunk in my life and never around them. I was finding out that I had absolutely no patience for putting up with them, especially when they were making trouble with my neighbors, my family, or me.

One time my neighbor came home late at night drunk and began beating his thirty-five-year-old sister, who was older than he was. They woke everyone up as she was screaming, begging for him to stop or someone to come help her. That was enough of an invitation for me. I ran downstairs, jumped a three-foot fence in a single bound, kicked his door open and grabbed him with both hands by the neck. I shook his head back and forth, telling him, *Shut up! I don't want to hear another peep out of you!* That worked. He never made any more trouble the rest of the time I lived there. His name was Aaron and he would eventually work for me. We'd always laugh about that incident.

It seemed that when I turned thirty-six, I was in a fight every month in Kolonia. Part of the problem was that the store that sold the cheapest beer in Kolonia was right across the street. It had a pool table too. So there were always troublemakers around. I had to get out of Kolonia and that's why I approached Robby, and Leo through him, about a new house site.

One time a bunch of drunks threw rocks though my windows, just missing my kids and ran off. Putting my tennis shoes on, I gave chase through the dark of night. I ran through people's yards, then in the front doors and out the back of a couple of people's houses in hot pursuit. But they gave me the slip after a couple of blocks.

I knocked another drunk out with one punch after catching up with him as he was getting away with a water cooler he'd stolen out of my truck. I left him on the edge of the road and went to the police station to get a policeman. When I returned with an officer he was still unconscious. Loading him into my truck, we took him to the station and once inside, he regained consciousness. He had a lump the size of a tennis ball over his eye. I then recognized him. It was Kenally, who lived at Leo's houses maid quarters, he being related to his maid.

A big part of the problem was that the police were ineffective. They had about sixty to seventy employees. But at night, only two would be on duty and that was when the majority of the crimes and trouble occurred.

There was also trouble during the day. One afternoon from my second-story window I saw two drunks attack a guy and girl walking past my house. They had the guy on the ground, beating and kicking him, when one of the attackers pulled a knife and was angling for position to stab him in the ribs. I was already downstairs with a stick to break this up. When I saw the knife and his intentions, I yelled at the guy to get his attention and charged him to drive him away from the victim. He backed away, never letting me get within ten to fifteen feet of him. I backed him down to the next block before returning to the victim, who was still being beaten. This second attacker ran off when seeing me coming back, giving me a wide berth. We put the victim in my truck and took him to the hospital.

The next day the victim's grandfather, the patriarch of a large family, came from Awak, about five miles to the east. He sat under my house in the carport for most of the day, as a sign of gratitude and friendship.

The most outrageous event I was to see occurred on a late Sunday afternoon. I witnessed five guys gang beat a guy unconscious. Four of the guys were drunk, but the fifth guy was a uniformed police officer. This occurred in front of the store across the street from my house. The uniformed officer then hustled the other four into a waiting truck, getting them to hurry and drive off, leaving the victim lying unconscious outside the store. Fifteen to twenty seconds later, a police truck sped up with three or four officers inside. They roughly grabbed the unconscious guy, as if he were resisting arrest, and dumped him unceremoniously in the back of the police truck before speeding off.

This did it for me. I had already tried reporting some of the other events I'd seen or experienced and others not yet mentioned, to the police. Nothing . . . No follow-up investigation, no questions, not anything. I was already convinced that the police department needed a major overhaul, so I drove a quarter mile up the road to the highest hill in Kolonia, to the governor's house. I'm sure I messed up his Sunday afternoon, but he was kind enough to see me and he listened to what I had to say. He thanked me and said he'd look into the incident.

Early that evening I answered a knock at my door. It was the police chief, hat in hand, apologizing for the department. I'm sure I ruined his Sunday even more. He would get even eventually, plus some.

My following the advice given me by the Ponape attorney general at the time, an American lawyer named John Brackett, would facilitate this. I'd gone to see him to complain about all the drunks ruling Kolonia at night, telling him about the useless police department and asking what could be done about it. He then gave me the worst advice I'd ever be dumb enough to try. "Make a citizen's arrest. It's perfectly legal."

In the meantime I was working on one of the rental houses for Leo and Robby. Up drove Leo Etschiet in his Volkswagen Beetle. I'd known Leo since 1970, when I bought most of our material for the Kingdom Hall from him. He ran the oldest store on island, the most successful, even though it looked like a run-down eyesore that should be torn down. Leo was deceptively wealthy now, a multimillionaire, but you'd never know by looking at his business. He would sit at his desk next to the entrance to greet and talk to everyone, waiting on customers, smiling. Everybody liked Leo, except perhaps Carlos.

He had the amazing ability to look at even a lengthy invoice and glancing down the list for just a few seconds, he could add up everything in his head and calculate the total right to the penny. He'd do this far faster than Robby could using his calculator.

This day that he showed up at the houses under construction was the first time I'd spoken with him since his return from the hospital in Hawaii. Leo liked the rental houses and told me to keep building more. They were made from materials in stock at his store. They were spartan in many ways, but all were built on wood floors at least three feet off the ground and all had wood decks with handrails. They would be more comfortable than the average concrete houses here at the time. I designed every house differently; no two were alike.

Leo went on to tell me that Robby had talked to him about my request to buy a piece of land to build a house. He said that was just fine with him, that I could look around all the land and build my house wherever I wanted to.

He went on to lament that he'd never been able to work the land after WWII, because he was single, with no kid and busy running his store. He said that he was hoping Robby could do this, but he would need help and he thought I might be the right person for that. Leo was talking like a man who realized he didn't have much time left. He was eighty-four. I felt he was letting me know that he was passing the mantle to Robby and some to me if I wanted it. This surprised me. I thanked Leo and told him I needed to talk with Robby about this. Later I would discuss with Robby the land for a new house for me. But not the latter issue. I wanted to see if Robby would broach this subject himself.

A short time later on October 11, 1980, two events occurred. At exactly eleven o'clock at night I walked downstairs to lock my entrance door for the evening. Just before shutting it, I heard a fight break out at the store across the street. It usually closed about eleven.

I would find out later that two drunks had entered the store right before closing. The owner informed them that he was closing. They demanded to be able to play pool and refused to leave. That's when the fight broke out. They threatened the owner with common wide-blade kitchen knives.

I went out to the edge of my driveway next to the road and saw the storeowner chase them out of the store with a cue stick held backward. About fifty to sixty feet away from me, the owner knocked one down with the cue stick.

The drunk got up and started running away down the street, straight at me, standing just off the edge of the road. The whole road was open but as he quickly neared me, he began swinging both arms as if he was going to hit me with some kind of flailing windmill swing. I stepped back with my right foot, planted it and knocked the guy on his back. He immediately jumped up and ran back where he came from, past the store and around the corner.

I then felt a wet, funny sensation on my face. I felt it and my finger went into a big hole. The guy had stabbed me and I had never seen the knife in the dark. I then chased after him. He had passed out a block away in a taro patch. When I arrived, five or six angry relatives of the store owner were bringing him up out of the muddy taro patch. These people were clearly about to work him over themselves. I was about to hit him again also, when he looked into my eyes and shook his head no, begging with his eyes, "Don't hit me again," all without saying a word.

I felt sorry for him and told the crowd, "Let's take him to the police station." We walked him back to my house, put him in my truck and I drove him to the police station. I then told the police officer I'd be back after getting sewed up at the hospital, to file a complaint.

As I drove past Leo's house on the way, I noticed many people there—and the type of activity that told me a funeral was just getting started. At the hospital it was confirmed that Leo Etscheit had just died there. My wounds were almost fatal too; the knife had just missed my jugular vein by about one-fourth of an inch. The knife had gone into my jaw and out a couple of inches later, right out the chin by the jugular vein. It never hurt.

Robby would tell me later that Leo had been feeling weak and gone to the hospital as a precaution. They put him on an IV. The nurse had the drip rate too high and he died of circulatory overload. That was one of the few things Ponape was good at: killing patients because of hospital foul-ups. Leo was extremely popular, well liked, and well known. Many people attended his funeral.

I had heard that a book previously written about Micronesia discussed a sometimes comical running feud between Carlos and Leo that had started way back in the late 1920s. Robby had told me about the book, some of its contents and other episodes he had been told directly by Leo. It wasn't over with yet, and Robby and I would end up carrying on the tradition occasionally.

Shortly after Leo's death, a D60 Komatsu bulldozer and five-yard Isuzu dump truck arrived. Leo was apparently going to surprise us with the tools to outcompete Carlos's D4 bulldozer. It was no contest. This D6 bulldozer could do ten to twenty times more work than Carlos's worn-out D4. So even after his death, Leo had made provisions to one-up his brother.

By early December of 1980, Robby finally had a serious talk with me. He let me know that he'd had a heavy load dumped on him by Leo's death. He now had to start legal proceedings to probate Leo's estate. He also had to deal with the partition case, the division of the land among the family. He said that the case was still pending but would probably need to start all over again, as the previous judge never issued a decision and had since passed away. Most troubling of all was the pending trial against the traditional leaders and their subjects, scheduled for the end of December 1980. Some of these people were calling Robby now with death threats. He was quite concerned about these threats and unable to sleep at night, maybe only a couple of hours at the most.

He related that he felt all alone against all of this and that if ever attacked at Leo's store, his workers would probably scatter like cockroaches. He thought I might be the only one who would stand by him if things got rough. He said he'd like us to locate a nice location on the land and each build a new house so we could watch out for each other. He offered me half the development rights to all his share of his undeveloped land, as to be determined by the eventual resolution of the partition case. I was to manage and develop his land, deal with his lawyers, squatters, and whatever needed to be done. He agreed to pay for any lawyers needed for future litigation or to draft and formalize these business agreements.

We had previously discussed what we could feasibly do with this large land. At this time, we hadn't identified a practical project yet and I told him it might take awhile to do that. I was concerned about its proper use, because the Trust Territory government had sponsored numerous agricultural and other land use projects that all failed. Ponape is among the wettest places on Earth. Because it's so tropical, crops and projects that work or grow in the States, and even sometimes in Hawaii, aren't successful here in most cases.

I said, "What if all we can do to start with is lease land to people for houses, since Kolonia is overcrowded and I know there's a market for that right now?"

He replied, "We'll split that too. We'll share everything, all the land's income, fifty-fifty." He also told me he'd pass title of the land for my house to my Micronesian family once he got title after the partition case was resolved.

I had serious reservations, however. I had heard recently that these traditional leaders in Nett were now claiming every single square meter of the Etscheit estate, that they'd lined up some high-powered American lawyers out of Guam and were now representing more than a hundred people in Nett, who were claiming they'd been living on this land for more than twenty years.

I'd just started hearing these claims, plus Robby and I had never been more than a half mile up into this land from the bay front. From the bay front, this land extends perhaps more than two miles up to the base of steep mountains on parts of its upper boundary. We had no idea at the time if the trespassers' claims were true or not.

By now Carlos had hired his own lawyer, Matt Mix, a former Peace Corps volunteer. Matt was just a trainee, being mentored by a real American lawyer working for the government, Alan Burdick. They were brothers-in-law.

Matt told me it didn't look good, that he had gone with one of the claimants, a relative of his wife's to see their parcel. They parked about where the Seventh-day Adventist school is nowadays. Crossing the Duanu River into the Etscheit estate, they saw a couple of houses. They then walked about a half hour farther into these foothills, crossing some rivers, and shortly thereafter, they reached a house with coconut and breadfruit trees more than twenty years old.

After losing their land twice to Japanese government authorities and now Dekehtik to the American-run Trust Territory, the Etscheits had to be prepared for another racist attempt to take their land again.

So I responded to Robby's proposal that I would need some time to think about it—that if the Nett people's claims were true, they'd probably resort to big-time violence before they'd ever let the Etscheits evict them. I had already been involved in too much trouble and didn't need to exchange problems in Kolonia for problems in Nett. I told him, "Let me go to the upcoming quiet title action trial," a week or two away then, "and hear the evidence and see what I think."

The trial started just after Christmas and lasted three days. The courthouse was packed, standing room only all three days.

The traditional leaders' lawyers only called three witnesses. For the trial, a map of the land in dispute had been specifically made; trial sketch 166-1 was its designation. It was the same as the map made during the 1970-1971 land determination hearings, when after public notice, nobody from Nett or Sokehs made a claim.

Two of the three witnesses that would testify marked their locations as within the upper boundary of the Etscheit estate on this map. The third witness said he wasn't sure of his location, so the court allowed someone else to mark his location for him, also within the map. All three claimed they'd been living in houses there for twenty to thirty years. One, a Ponape policeman, claimed his house was a concrete house.

The Etscheits' lawyers, apparently never during discovery proceedings or any other way, verified these claims. At trial they didn't even cross-examine these witnesses or ask one question. They sat there like two bumps on a log. What I didn't know about at the time and wouldn't see until later, were the written trial briefs submitted by each party's lawyers. Alan Burdick had prepared the Etschiets' trial brief.

Later after the trial, I told Robby that it didn't look good, but that I wanted to go myself and see these areas marked on the map. General testimony indicated that the areas above the future Seventh-day Adventist school had been heavily settled in excess of twenty years. I knew enough by now about how Ponapeans work land, to know that they'd usually first plant coconut and breadfruit trees when acquiring any new land.

So just before the end of 1980, one or two days after the trial, I hiked all the way up along the Duanu River to the upper boundary. Then walking toward the interior, I searched for any evidence to support the trial's testimony. All I found were coconut and breadfruit trees no older than four to six months, along with some small seasonal crops like sweet potatoes and tapioca.

It was clear to me that the Etscheits were the victims of a racist community conspiracy by those now claiming under these new traditional leaders to take their land again, this time with deceptive testimony and outrageous lies.

As time had passed, I began to appreciate many more of the positive contributions by Martin Luther King to American society. I also began to feel increasingly haunted by my connection to his case.

I now viewed Robby's offer as an opportunity to help in this local case of racism, one that some might view as a case of reverse discrimination, brown-skinned people versus white. So after my hike that day, I informed Robby of my view of the situation and accepted his proposal.

At the time, Robby talked about his share of this land being worth about one million dollars, saying that he might be willing to sell it for that if he could find a qualified buyer. He was dreading all the legal problems that lay ahead of him. Little did we imagine at the time that in about five years, we would come to realize that his land was actually worth more than one hundred times his original estimate. Others would advise us that in all of Micronesia, it was probably the single most valuable asset owned by one person. Also, that when I accepted his proposal I had unknowingly become an instant multimillionaire, at least on paper.

The reasons for this would be obvious to any real estate person: "Location, location, location!" First, Ponape is the most beautiful island by far in all of Micronesia, with the most untapped potential for future development. The Nan Madol ruins alone have yet to be promoted and developed properly as a world-class attraction. Then there's Sokeh Rock, which many think is the most beautiful rock promontory next to the ocean, anywhere on Earth. There are also the numerous impressive waterfalls. It has magnificent rain forests, with still untapped potential for hiking trails all over the place. It has sixty square miles of mangrove forests, which are a kayaker's dream. Its historical involvement with the early whaling industry could be developed in numerous ways. It's also the site of the only naval battle in the Pacific Ocean during the American Civil War. It has many WW II artifacts and points of interest. Even the Etscheit estate still has that WW I-type trench warfare style battlefield. When I first saw it, it appeared it was only prepared five or ten years before. Ponape also has a one-of-a-kind island culture with five still-powerful kings. It has beautiful sandy-beached coconut-studded islets within the lagoon and a whole atoll of the like, just across a seven-mile channel to the west, Ant Atoll. Then it has its world glass reefs and fishing. It's also recently been discovered as a world-class winter surfing destination. Plus, Ponape is the closest full-on tropical island to Japan and Asia, which is as of yet undeveloped.

One of the biggest advantages we would have to be part of this future development would be the size and availability of private property for hotels, resorts, golf courses, and so forth. The majority of private property parcels on island are only a little over seven acres in size at the biggest. Most of the land in Ponape is government owned, 90 percent, and most of that is squatted on by Ponapeans who do not have certificate of title. There are only two large parcels of private property on this island that have good title. The largest is the Nanpei estate, about sixteen square miles of land on the island's remote southern side. The other is the Etscheit estate, with two square miles of land right next to Kolonia. Robby's projected share was to be 80 percent of it, at the very least. He had already acquired the shares of four of the five children of Dominic and Forentine Etscheit. He could potentially have enough land for five, six, or more full-scale resorts with golf courses.

The Nanpei estate appeared to be a legal nightmare in comparison. Its original owner left it to be jointly owned equally by all his current and future descendants. No provisions were made for any of them to be able to use or sell any of its land themselves. They were only to share in the profits from the agricultural businesses in existence as of the early twentieth century. These projects all failed by the 1930s. Now three, four and five generations down the road, with hundreds of descendants, plus untold numbers of informally adopted children of all these descendant also making claims, an amicable resolution to its legal problems seemed totally hopeless. Especially when all these heirs are without the financial resources needed to afford the massive legal process needed to sort out its legal mess. Even if they were able to, no two or three Ponapeans could usually ever come to an agreement nine times out of ten. The Etscheit estate's legal situation seemed easily solvable in comparison at the time.

The first thing Robby did when I accepted his proposal was to give me two legal size boxes of all Leo's legal papers concerning their land. Among these documents was the original German land register. Leo had acquired it from Japanese authorities just prior to their repatriation to Japan after the war. I would be in possession of these documents for about two years, before having the register passed to the proper authorities and giving the land papers to lawyers that we would eventually hire.

I would read all these documents several times. I knew enough about the law to know that I didn't know enough. But I did act as Robby's attorneys for two years in numerous ways, before things got complicated and real lawyers were needed.

I spent quite a bit of time over the next couple of years scouting out this land and interviewing former squatters, employees of Nett Municipal Government, or anyone else I was referred to. I prepared numerous affidavits and then took people to the courthouse to sign. For some I took the court clerk to their house to sign and notarize, as some were now old and invalid.

One of the first things I did was go to the land commission and examine aerial photographs taken of the whole island in 1974-1975. They were taken by a company called Asia Mapping. These photographs were to be used for accurate surveys and mapmaking.

Now most of this land up along the Duanu River was where Florentine and Leo had their copra plantations prior to WWII. These plantations' coconut trees were removed and eaten by Japanese soldiers. After the war Carlos would burn this land every dry season so that it remained mostly grassland, not allowing the jungle to grow back. They did this up until 1976, when the squatter houses began to appear about the time of King Max Iriarte's death.

The aerial survey photographs are each quite large, maybe about three feet in diameter and photograph an area between five hundred feet to a thousand feet each, if my recollection is correct. I haven't seen them in over twenty years. Not too far downriver from the area that the traditional leaders' case purported eight families had been living and working for over twenty years, is the island's high school. It's called Ponape Island Central School (PICS), and it is on the Kolonia side of the Duanu River. It's actually in part of Nett at this point, the boundary between Nett and Kolonia being the Duanu River just below the school, but not above.

When examining these photographs with the naked eye, many details can still be seen. In the photographs that show parts of PICS and the Etscheit estate across the river, something significant can be easily seen. Students were sneaking across the river into the Etscheits' land for various reasons like having lunch, smoking, drinking, being with their girlfriends, and so on. They were leaving trails through the grass that were easily visible on the photograph with the naked eye, leading in fifty to one hundred yards or so. This grass is usually about three foot tall, but not on these footpaths; it's beaten down.

Upriver in the photographs, in the area one man testified he'd been living for twenty years, plus the traditional leader's case purported seven other families had been living and working for over twenty years, there was nothing in the photograph. No houses, no visible crops, not even any walking trails through the grass. Nobody is even going there. If they were, there would be visible walking trails, easily seen in the photographs through this high grassland.

At that time, the land commission had the capability of making duplicate copies of these photographs. They made me copies of all the photographs of the upper portions of the Etscheit estate. I then took these to an older American man, Gorman Booth, who was living in Kolonia. He had worked for Asia Mapping and retired in Ponape after their project here was completed.

I arranged to have him examine these photographs with his magnifying scopes, searching for areas cleared and cultivated, or houses on this land. When he was done, he only found one house. It was about fifty feet inside the upper boundary of the land, just to the south of the old Japanese tank road that used to go up through the middle of the Etscheit land and continued to the Japanese fighter base in WWII, in Nan Pohlmahl.

In subsequent interviews with older Ponapean men who settled along this road on the government side of the boundary line in the late '40s and '50s, they told me the name of the man who built this house, Bermin Oliver. They told me when he first entered this land, "Just before the plane flew over." I had heard this expression before. It was used to describe Asia Mapping's plane that flew back and forth across the island in a grid pattern, to take all the photos necessary for this mapping project. They had to repeat it many times because of all the clouds in a place like Ponape, which was uniquely among Earth's wettest places.

A later look at this man's crops would verify their age as being from the early to mid-1970s. So these people would be the oldest current residents on the upper Etscheit land. Bermin Oliver was now deceased. His son Reed Oliver would be the easiest of these people for us to deal with. He had not testified in the traditional leaders' case.

Like Reed Oliver, most Ponapeans have many good qualities. They're a generous and hospitable people in many ways. As I talk about these escalating land problems on the Etscheit estate and the racism I encountered, I would like to clarify that it does not at all reflect the attitude of the majority of the Ponapean people.

As for the three men who had testified for the traditional leaders, I was to determine the following. The one who had someone else mark his location on the map at the trial was actually living less than one-fourth of a mile outside the upper boundary of the Etscheit estate, on government land alongside the tank road. The police officer who testified that he had a concrete house on this land, marking his location as within trial sketch 166-1, was also more than a quarter mile outside the boundary. His concrete house was actually near to the main road going through Nan Pohlmahl, which leads to the present-day electrical power plant for the island. Both these men later told me that others pressured and coerced them to testify falsely. All of the traditional leaders' subjects' testimony for their case was a lie.

But as I questioned men living along this tank road on government land and others, they all told me the same story. This area of the island during WWII was for the Japanese military. Islanders were not allowed to live in these areas, only soldiers and some Japanese colonists. So after the war, it was rather vacant over large areas because of all of the Japanese deportations.

About five or six men told me that before entering these areas in the late 1940s and 1950s to homestead and settle, they followed the custom for doing this. They all went to the king of Nett, Max Iriarte, to get his permission. The king gave it but told them that the Etscheit boundary was nearby and that they should go see Leo Etschiet, asking him to go with them to make sure they didn't cross over onto their property. A couple of these men told me that Leo did go with them.

Others didn't bother to see Leo and unknowingly entered the Etscheit property. Those who did were eventually informed by Nett policemen, sent by Max Iriarte, of their error and told to leave. I heard this from several people, and they were all old people from Sokehs. The Sokehs municipal boundary is nearby somewhere, crossing the tank road to the west of the Etscheit upper boundary.

I would have much of this also confirmed by two old former policemen from Nett, whom I interviewed with the aid of a translator. Long story short, there had been a long history of mistaken or intentional entry onto the Etscheits' land. The former king/chief magistrate, put a stop to this.

Chapter 22

The German Family

Robby had been telling me some of his family's history in Germany. I found it very interesting, almost unbelievable, as if a soap opera.

I would first meet Robby's mother in 1982, when she was already in her seventies. She was the best-looking seventy-some year old woman I'd ever seen. Early in World War II, she had been married to Germany's number one air ace, a fighter pilot. He was shot down early in the war and killed. In an elaborately staged state funeral, Adolf Hitler himself presented her with Germany's highest medal, posthumously for her husband.

She would later marry Robby's father, Robert. Robert, born in Ponape, would end up being some sort of pilot in the Luftwaffe also. He too was shot down and while recuperating in some field hospital not too badly injured, he responded to a call for any walking wounded to assist with the flood of casualties.

Robert ended up helping in the operating tent. Before long the exhausted doctors began to let Robert stitch up some of the wounded. He realized he had a knack for this. By war's end, he would pursue this discovered talent and eventually become one of two top plastic surgeons in Europe. I was always to call him Dr. Robert.

Robby's parents would have two boys, Robby and a younger son named Jost, before eventually divorcing. His mother would later marry another German veteran of WWII, Herbert Lose. Herbert was apparently set to represent Germany in the upcoming 1940 Olympics as a javelin thrower, but the games were canceled due to WWII breaking out in 1939.

Instead Herbert ended up in the Waffen-SS, walking and fighting his way through Russia and ending up in the battle of Stalingrad. In the very last of the battle, the German army had been surrounded and supply lines cut off, except for a few planes still able to land.

That's when Herbert lost one eye and was evacuated out, on either the last German plane to leave Stalingrad or the last day that the airfield was in operation. Ninety thousand German soldiers surrendered not too long afterward. By war's end, only four or five thousand of these soldiers would survive Russian prisoner of war camps and ever return home alive to Germany.

Back in Germany, Herbert had a glass eye put in. Then he was marched on foot again, all the way to Normandy this time, where he was captured on the fourth day of the battle. Being SS, he was interned in Canada and not released until 1947.

Jost, Robby's younger brother, would eventually take over his father's plastic surgery practice after Dr. Robert's retirement. Jost's wife, Betina Lucher, kept her maiden name. Robby told me she was a CNN news correspondent in Germany. I've seen her reports a couple of times on our CNN channel, dealing with German news. The last one was as US forces were transiting through Ramstein Air Base in Germany, on their way to Afghanistan shortly after the 9\11 attacks.

These people would all come to Ponape several times for visits, except Betina, who would stay in Hawaii with the kids while Jost came for short visits. Robby and I would most of the time meet these various relatives of his in Hawaii. I'd usually drive them around sightseeing, as Robby was not at all comfortable driving in Hawaii during the 1980s. Every meal was a major event in the evenings, costing one or two thousand dollars, sometimes a lot more in the finest restaurants. He'd pay for it all; I was just along to drive.

When it came time to pay, I'd try to slink out as Robby's tip limit didn't seem to exceed five dollars. I would always wonder if that was a European thing. Personally, I would have been content to go to Burger King, but I couldn't on these occasions. I was often suggesting new and different places, dreading going back to the same place twice, unless a couple of years had passed and the staff might have forgotten us by then.

In late February 1981, Dr. Robert and his housekeeper Gerta, returned with us from Hawaii. He was seventy-one years old then, recuperating from a heart attack and still weak. He stayed at Leo's house during that visit, and we met there with Carlos and two of his daughters, Yvette and Renee, with Matt Mix assisting them as counsel.

Negotiations between these relatives to settle out the partition case broke down again. They couldn't even reach an interim land use agreement regarding small areas, much less a division of the land as a whole.

The last place Carlos's family wanted us going was anywhere near the bay front. They had two houses in the area. It was the best housing location on the land, waterfront and private. The majority of this land was overgrown, undeveloped and possibly about fifteen hundred to two thousand feet long or more on the bay front. It was still jointly owned undeveloped land and they couldn't stop us, unless with an injunction and that was unlikely. Dr. Robert, Robby and I decided to use our new bulldozer to blitz them. Who better to help us do this than an old storm trooper! We prepared an eight-by-twelve shed next to an apartment house of Robby's, several hundred yards away from a choice bay front location.

Renee's house was within earshot of where the bulldozer would be clearing. So we waited for her to leave after lunch to return to Carlos's store. She'd be gone about four hours. We fired up the bulldozer. The shed had skids and it was towed down to the site after dozing in a road there. A large area was cleared shortly and a perimeter road dozed in encompassing perhaps four or five acres.

It was dry, so the area looked quite large and inviting. Canopy tin roofs were added around the shed to make it look larger. We hung some clothes on lines around and a cook fire, with a Micronesian family looking real settled in. Then we put up barbed wire fencing along the perimeter road, a trick we learned from Carlos, all before the end of the workday. By early evening Robby heard someone pounding on his door, crying and yelling at him. It was Renee. He was expecting her.

It all led to another land meeting at Leo's house the next day. Carlos's daughters then proposed a more realistic interim land use agreement, one that would be agreeable to both parties. They proposed that neither party would do any further development along the bay front or road front yet, pending future agreements of both parties—that they would concede a strip of land to us between the

Duanu River and what they called their long line road. As far as everything above the end of their cow fences, the forested mountain land, we could do whatever we liked there.

We agreed because there was an excellent site for our new housing area along the Duanu River, opposite the government's forestry station. It was also adjacent to some small dams and nifty waterfalls.

I then fenced in about twelve to fifteen acres and built three nice houses. Robby's was about sixty-five hundred square feet, mine approximately four thousand square feet under roof. The third house was for Masaro, Leo's former right-hand man at the store, now Robby's, at about eighteen hundred square feet.

I built a tennis court between my house and Robby's, which were maybe one hundred yards apart. Later I built a swimming pool next to Robby's house. This was all finished in 1982. Behind Ace Commercial, I built a new twenty-thousand-square-foot metal warehouse for Leo's store. Also during this period because of the threat of losing the land posed by the quiet title action case, we decide not to have all our eggs in one basket. We may need to leave Ponape one day, should the traditional leaders win the case. After what occurred over Dekehtik, we couldn't have any confidence in the Trust Territory High Court. So Robby bought three lots in Kailua Kona, Big Island of Hawaii. We begin to build some spec houses there; to have something to fall back to should things go bad in Ponape.

Richard Ramsey was living in Kona then, so I got him to do a lot of that work. I only designed the houses and spent five weeks there, getting them started. Then I left Richard to handle most everything else.

Chapter 23

Bad to Worse, Citizen's Arrest

As I was getting familiar with and investigating this land, I was finding new people still trying to enter the land, despite injunctions. We were getting threats also. I would go to the police station filing complaints, sometimes against a named person. I'd do this more than a hundred times over the next twenty years. In midsized notebooks, I kept a land log documenting details of each complaint and other relevant events on the land. As a construction guy who wasn't very studious, I'd go for years not writing them down in my log at times, switching back and forth doing this. But after two decades, I had pretty much filled up four notebooks.

The response was always consistent. There was no investigation, nobody ever got back to me, and absolutely no action was ever taken by the proper authorities at all over a twenty-year period. In the early to mid-1980s, several times I went to the Ponape attorney general or director of legal affairs to request action about threats from some of these people over the land. They would always say they couldn't get involved because this was "a matter of custom."

This would continue to be their excuse long after the Trust Territory High Court and other subsequent courts specifically ruled against this claim. There simply was no precedent to allow traditional leaders to arbitrarily declare someone's private property theirs. But ridiculous excuses like this would continue to prevail and be used by various government agencies. The most outrageous thing these men, who were the State's highest law enforcement officials, would have the nerve to tell me was "You'd better be careful. Blood is going to flow over this land. You should stop what you're doing!" They said it as if they were speaking for those making the threats.

The laws on terrorist threatening include those who even pass a threat along. Here were these officials, charged with protecting people from this type of crime, and instead of doing anything about it; they themselves were participating in it by passing the threat along to me again.

I would soon find that if I did anything at all the least controversial, I could find myself in custody in short order.

One day I went to see a person on their property. Before going to the location, I had prior permission from both co-owners of this property to go there to specifically talk to one of these owners. A third-party who also lived there didn't want me to talk to this co-owner and called the police, claiming I was trespassing.

Four police officers arrived in short order, despite being in a somewhat remote area, more isolated than most of the locations where I had filed complaints on our land. They asked me to go with them to talk down on the public road. It was a long walk to the road, about a quarter of a mile away. So I asked if I was under arrest. They said no. So I told them I hadn't come here to talk to them, but I would speak with them later if they'd like, when I was finished here. They arrested me right then, taking me to the police station, filing trespassing charges against me and even getting an upcoming court date.

I was surprised. Well not by the arrest, but by how fast and efficient they were responding to and processing a trespassing case, something they had been unable to do for me countless times. I guess I was just the wrong color. It would take me months to get these charges dropped.

Police officers and their relatives were among the many people I had tried to bring trespassing complaints against. Because the Ponape State system was failing us in so many ways, we would eventually have to sue them by civil action in the national FSM court system in the early 1990s.

Prior to these events, the state police would get me good on a couple of occasions. One occurred on New Year's Day 1982 and didn't involve trespassers, just regular troublemaking drunks. A week or two before, I had bought a brand-new 1982 Toyota four-door, four-wheel drive truck, the kind they only began making available in the United States around 2002 or 2003. (I can't imagine what took them so long to offer this model in the United States.)

After dark on New Year's Eve, I took the kids to the houses I was building on the Etscheit estate and shot off several marine flares for them. Next door was the last concrete rental house that Robby's Filipino crew had built. The first president of the Federated States of Micronesia, recently inaugurated, had just moved into it. I got a kick out of watching his rookie security detail fumble around like Keystone Cops, even bumping into each other, not knowing what to do, thinking they might be under attack. I even shot off a couple extra flares just to watch them run around some more. When done, I put the flare gun under the passenger seat until I could later put it away with my fishing gear. It was a model that could fire 12-gauge or all sizes of 25 mm flares, including large parachute flares. I had saved a few 12-gauge flares for my next fishing trip.

The next day my wife took the truck through town with a couple of her female cousins riding along. A group of drunks was walking in the middle of the main road, blocking it. As the truck slowly passed around them, my wife scolded the drunks. One of them kicked the door of the truck in response. They stopped and got out to confront this guy. He then pinned my wife up against the truck door, lifting her feet off the ground with his shoulder and then he began reaching behind his back with one hand for a knife he had stuck in his waistband.

One of the cousins coming around the back of the truck saw what he was reaching for. She was able to quickly grab his hand and keep him from grasping the knife. The drunk's drunken companions had more sense and pulled him away and on down the road they continued. I heard all about it when they returned, wanting me to now go with them to track these guys down. I told them, "No, we're going to do the right thing and file a complaint at the police department. It's their job!"

So off we went to the police department again. It was conveniently located only a couple hundred yards away. It was New Year's Day and only two policemen were on duty. One sympathetic officer thought he knew who the guys were and he took off looking for them. The other started writing out the complaint.

Fifteen minutes later we were finished and as we were heading out the driveway of the station, the other policeman was returning. Throwing his hands up he said, "I couldn't find them!" Well we knew what that meant, that this was probably the end of the matter as far as the police were concerned.

Going back more than a year before, I had been stabbed in the face. Following up with authorities afterward, I was told to wait, that I'd be notified before trial so I could testify. After my initial complaint, no one ever did a follow-up investigation with me, as if preparing for trial. Plenty of time passed and I heard nothing.

Finally I went to the state attorney general's office to inquire of this case's status. Another new attorney general, a local man, indignantly informed me that they had notified me of a hearing for the case and because I had failed to appear, he "had to drop the charges."

While I wasn't surprised, I was upset of course. I told him, "No, you didn't inform me. Show me the return of service!" They didn't have one. The attorney general was lying to me and trying to make it appear as if the dismissal were my fault.

I would find out later the real reason for these charges being dropped. A new policy regarding crimes gave the attorney general the discretion to dismiss a case if the defendant somehow formally apologized to his victim and the victim then forgave him. In this case, the guy who stabbed me apologized to the storeowner, who forgave him and the charges were dropped.

I knew nothing about any of this and was never a party to this apology process. I guess stabbing a white man wasn't a serious crime to these authorities, but interfering with a Micronesian trying to close his store on time was! With the aid of a sympathetic American lawyer, who acted as my ghost lawyer, I was able to file a writ of mandamus, trying to compel the attorney general to prosecute this case. But I'd be alone and on my own before the attorney general and judge in the courtroom, representing myself.

My 'writ' outlined what happened prior to my stabbing. That's the first time the attorney general knew some of the details, I believe, as the police had never conducted any type of an investigation.

The day of the trial the attorney general was at home and sent a subordinate. Right there in the courtroom, I was watching him look at the case for the first time and I saw when he spotted their defense: "Manzerrayous." That's the legal precedent-setting principle that gives prosecutors discretion to drop a case if a defendant had his mental abilities altered, such as by a blow to the head, before committing an act such as stabbing me. Thus he could be viewed as not being in his right mind. Therefore, by not possibly really knowing what he was doing, it was a legal defense.

During the proceedings I wished I'd had more experience before the court. I could have stressed that before the storeowner knocked the one down, both perpetrators had their knives out and were committing a felony. I should have requested that he produce all their investigative reports. I'm sure they contained no mention at all of the storeowner knocking my attacker down just before the stabbing. He had only spotted "Manzerrayous" when reading my complaint, which he admitted reading for the first time just before the judge entered the courtroom. I believe that Manzerrayous played no part in their previous decision to drop the charges.

Years later one of my employees, who was a relative of this attorney general who sent his subordinate, would inform me that his relative was so distraught over the "hearing" that he stayed home drinking that day and got drunk.

It ended up being a well-known victory for this attorney general though. The new FSM court would use it as one of their precedent-setting cases, using its legal principles as part of its bar examinations for new attorneys to pass before being allowed to practice law in the FSM, *Nix v. _____*. I won't mention his name, as I prefer not to name names of many of the people that I'm writing about.

Back to the events of January 1, 1982 . . .

As the policeman returned from his short search for the drunks, throwing his hands up and exclaiming that he couldn't find them, we knew that this was the end of the matter for them.

Thinking about this fiasco over the writ of mandamus and how good some government officials were at not doing their job, I remembered the advice of the former state attorney general, John Brackett. "Make a citizen's arrest, it's perfectly legal." Still highly upset, like an idiot I decided on this course of action. I had actually done it twice before but against only one perpetrator at a time.

Going by our house I picked up a pair of handcuffs, a can of mace and a replacement sledgehammer handle. We suspected these guys were from the east side of the island, so we went to that side of town first. Just outside the southeastern outskirts of Kolonia was Robby's Ace Commercial store, just across the Duanu River in Nett. Many people wait there for taxis or rides to the eastern municipalities of Ponape, such as U or Madolenihmw, as well as parts of Nett.

Benches across the storefront were loaded with people, including our drunk. I drive past the store and turn in on the road leading up to the houses I'd been building. I continued the turn until my truck was pointed north, parking on the south side of Ace Commercial. It seems everyone on the benches is intently watching me. The guy that had earlier tried to pull the knife was on the far side of this group.

As I approached them and they saw the sledgehammer handle, they all stood up and started moving toward me, about eight people. Now before this I remembered my wife using the term "group of drunks" and "bunch of drunks," but not eight in regard to them. The guy with the knife now had it pulled and was running toward me. The oldest guy of this group, in his mid to late thirties, came up on my right side with his hands up as if he wanted peace, but I know that he couldn't stop the others and they would take me out. One was almost on my left ready to throw a punch. So I mace the guy to my right and quickly took a baseball swing with the stick at the guy to my left, hitting him in the side of his head. He went down like a wet noodle.

The guy I mace weakly grabbed my right arm. I shook him off just as the guy with the knife was about to stab me. I quickly skipped a step back, planted my right foot and made an overhead swing at him with the stick. He immediately stopped and leaned back as the stick grazed down his forehead, face and chest, leaving a blood steak. Now surrounded, I was swinging in a circle doing damage I didn't even know about. The crowd backed off a bit. The unpaved road and parking lot provided plenty of material for these guys to then start throwing rocks at me. I realized I had better try something different or they'd take me out with a rock shortly.

I moved back to my truck, remembering the flare gun under the seat. As I loaded the single-shot 12-gauge flare pistol, it seemed those guys were still throwing rocks at me, but I believe they were missing, as I never felt any hit me. I fired the first flare into the ground hoping it would scare them back, but they were all so drunk they didn't care.

As I reloaded, I was still thinking these guys hadn't yet hit me with a rock. The guy with the knife was picking up a rock about as big as a bowling ball. I moved away from the truck, about twelve to fifteen feet from him and shot him in the head with a flare. It bounced off his jaw. I might as well have thrown a beanbag at him.

I was now cut off from my truck and had left my stick there. I was feeling weak and not up to taking these guys on with my fists. I figured I'd better run. So off I went around the south side of Ace Commercial to its west or back side. A long wooden Filipino construction barrack was back there. I ran to its north end and entered it, the drunk's right behind me. I had to knock one out of the doorway to close it. A piece of rebar was its barrel bolt that held it closed. It was no safe haven. It had one-fourth-inch Masonite walls nailed to two-by-three studs four feet on center. The guys after me had now picked up pipes and all kinds of handy items in this construction area and within about fifteen seconds, they had a hole in the wall almost big enough to come through.

So I ran down the middle hallway of the barrack and out a door near its south end, continuing back around to my truck again. I saw that someone had busted out its front window, so I had to jump into a seat full of glass. I reversed out of there just as the crowd reached my door. Reversing all the way to the top of the nearest hill, I waited by Jack Adams warehouse for the police to arrive.

Being called out of their New Year's holiday, they weren't too pleased, especially the police chief. This was his second day off I'd messed up. After dealing with the situation down at Ace Commercial, one of the police officers came up the hill to me and asked me to follow him to the police station for my own protection.

While at the station waiting, a big Micronesian I knew came into the room all upset, holding his injured arm. He was complaining to the police in Ponapean about his arm. Then he started doing it giving me dirty looks. That's when I figured he must be one of the guys I'd been fighting with and I was the one who had injured him. Then I realized that in the heat of the situation, I never even focused on the faces of most of those I fought, only remembering four faces.

I would become close with this man later. Ten years would pass and this man would then tell me that during the fight, I disheartened his group because I showed no fear, but fought them with a strangely normal look on my face.

When the police chief finally showed up, he was quite pleased to tell me that I was going to jail. I asked him why, stating that I was just making a citizen's arrest, something his policeman had been unable to do, that these drunks had resisted the arrest.

His response was that I used a firearm and going to jail was automatic. So off I went. I even got a private cell. There was a problem with it though. It was less than five by six feet in size. There was a toilet in the corner, but it was full to the brim and appeared to have never been cleaned or even flushed . . . ever. About half the cell floor was wet from its overflow. A window high up on the outside wall had heavy metal louvers but no screen. The walls had brown fecal skid stains everywhere, as high up as former "guests" could maneuver themselves for a wipe. A particularly handy spot seemed to be the corner protrusion of the doorjamb. I was amazed at how high some guys managed to get. I think it was really just a toilet room. It also had a solid steel door with a small site window, just like the doors on Springfield's solitary sections.

That door was the only similarity. At night, the mosquitoes were the worst I've ever experienced. I was probably only able to sleep less than an hour, hunched up in the cell corner. I preferred to lean up against a portion of wall that had a lot of dried fecal stains but where at least the floor was dry, rather than vice versa. If the United States had cells like these, there would be a lot less crime. I didn't think Steen could do time in this cell without crying for his mommy. Only one thing was better there than in the US federal prison system: their visitor system was very liberal. They'd let anybody visit you, no cumbersome approval process like in the US federal system.

An American on island whom I knew but never associated with much, J. D. Lowe, always came to visit me whenever I ended up in the Ponape jail. This wouldn't be the last time.

Late the next afternoon, some American public defender got me released. I was taken back to the police station, where the police grudgingly returned my mace, flare gun, handcuffs and stick to me, looking a little shot down.

I would learn that they had only questioned the drunks at the store and then arrested me, letting all of them continue on their way, a couple via the hospital. I was informed that I needed to go to a traditional apology ceremony, scheduled for the early evening out in Awak Pah, U, where most of these guys I fought with lived. It was to be at the house of the guy with the knife.

When I got home, the first thing I did was clean up. When I took my shirt off before showering, I couldn't believe what I saw in the mirror. My torso, front and back, was covered by large bruises from all the rocks those guys had thrown at me. I had never felt one of them hit me, only feeling weak before deciding to run. If I had gone down from a rock to the head, they probably would have finished me off.

As a people, Ponapeans have many admirable qualities. Among them that I admire most is how they can get together after serious problems and truly solve them, forgive and forget, by means of these traditional apology ceremonies that I was about to experience.

They can also sometimes blow up into violence. So my Micronesian relatives were apprehensive and explained to me the do's and don'ts. An important aspect of these proceedings is the drinking of *sakau*; it seals the deal so everyone will respect it.

But I had a problem with drinking sakau. Drinking it was closely associated with one of the major aspects of the old former pagan religious practices of the Ponapean people. Despite my questionable behavior, I still didn't want to imitate any of these. I was relieved to hear that I could take the cup, pass it on to a designated drinker, and he would drink it for me, thus satisfying everyone.

Back then and before 1982, sakau was usually only drunk during important customary occasions. Now almost thirty years later, its use has expanded to everyday usage by a large portion of the community. It's made by pounding the root of the sakau plant, then squeezing its juices out of it while encased in hibiscus bark. To me it looks like you're drinking watery mud that has a slimy mint taste. These people love it and most of them have to have it every day, as it's extremely addictive. Its modern day overuse has a number of negative consequences that are only recently beginning to be acknowledged locally. Probably others are yet to be realized.

Our peace ceremony nearly thirty years ago is still going strong. I would become close to three of these people afterwards. Unfortunately two have since passed away since then, one from a stroke and another was swept away in a rain swollen river. I also have to admit that I still don't know who four of those guys are yet, that I fought with that day.

Chapter 24

Police Start to Change

In early 1982, I got a tip that the police station had just received this year's shipment of license plates. Registration was now open. I raced right up there and only about three people were ahead of me in line.

Robby and I were always trying to outdo one another; among the rivalries was who could get the lowest license plate number. As I was waiting in line, a forty-some-year-old American woman who worked for the state court came in right after me. Her government-supplied house was right next door to the police station. She had previously been a justice of the peace somewhere in the United States.

Even though we just met, she immediately began complaining to me about how bad these police were. She related that the previous night, someone had broken into her house, threatening to rape her. She told me how she grabbed a kitchen knife, threatening her attacker until she backed him right out of the house. Shaken, she called the police, who just had to come from next door. Then as she related these events to the investigating officers, another one warned her that she was fortunate she didn't injure the assailant or she'd be in big trouble. She just couldn't believe that response.

A lieutenant then warned her that the rapist might try to return. He offered to stay awhile, suggesting she try to get some rest in her bedroom and that he'd stay in the living room as a precaution for her protection. She consented, still quite shaken.

About twenty to thirty minutes later, she claimed the police lieutenant entered her bedroom and started propositioning her, saying, "You know in Micronesia, when a man and woman are alone in a house together its customary for them to . . ." She had to chase him out of her house too, throwing some ashtrays in the process.

She was still livid as she related this story to me. I wasn't at all surprised. I was then called up to the counter to fill out my application and told to return to pick up my completed registration card and plate right after lunch.

On returning, I was again in a short line when into the station walked an American man in his mid-forties. I'd never seen him before and figured that maybe he was a tourist who had something stolen from him. So I told him, "If you're here to report a crime, you're wasting your time!" He looked at me somewhat strangely, and then he left the building. A few minutes later, I got my registration and license plate, number 004, which is the lowest I've ever gotten.

On leaving the station the new American was outside still. He came up to me and asked if he could speak to me confidentially. When I agreed, he led me to a secluded side of the police station and asked me why I said what I did shortly before.

I then told him some of the things I'd seen and experienced relating to the police, including what I'd heard that morning from the American woman who lived next door to the station. When I finished he thanked me and stated, "That's all going to end now! I'm the new police chief." He introduced himself as Wally Wattrick, just hired out of the Marshall Islands, where his contract as police chief had recently ended. Before this, he had worked in Los Angeles. He told me he had just arrived and that nobody at the station knew who he was yet. He conceded that the Ponape police department was bad and needed a lot of work, saying that he had been specifically hired to make changes and would do whatever it took to help the department improve. He wanted to remain incognito for another day or two so he could quietly assess the situation without any of his officers putting an act on for him. So he asked me to keep our conversation confidential for a couple of days more.

I was more than happy to cooperate with this man. Robby and I would go out of our way to assist Wally, hoping he could help the police department make the progress it needed, to be public servants to all.

The government house Wally was given needed a lot of work, as it was rather run-down. So when Wally asked our help with painting and tile work, to make his residence a decent home for his family, we sent some of our Filipino crew to do that work at below cost.

His superiors had assured Wally that they were glad they had him and that they hoped he would stay with them for years, expecting the police department's transition to take years. Therefore to get settled in for the long haul, Wally used his own savings to make the repairs to his government house for his family.

The police department needed a pistol range; we would donate a free property lease for this purpose. We had a couple of square miles of land to choose from. Wally wanted to take his son out fishing. So I took them out one day for about an hour and we caught three yellow fin tuna. Wally got seasick though, so he never wanted to go again.

One Sunday afternoon he wanted me to go with him to show him the land for the pistol range. He picked me up at my house. We then went by the police station to pick up some rifles, to shoot some target practice while there. He told me only two police officers were on duty that day.

At the station, one was out on patrol and the other was sound asleep with his head on the desk. We quietly walked past the sleeping officer, opened the gun locker right behind him and took out a Thompson submachine gun and an Uzi, plus ammunition, never waking the guy.

Up in the land, I got to fire the Thompson but not the Uzi. The Uzi had been confiscated from the luggage of some marijuana growers from the United States, busted at the Ponape airport. They were rumored to have been involved with a prominent local man. Wally would devote many of his efforts trying to build a case against this local person.

These were apparently low-budget United States marijuana growers. They had reloaded their own Uzi ammunition and didn't properly resize the shell casings, which caused the shells to jamb when firing. It jammed on Wally, so I didn't have the opportunity to fire it. On returning to the station we put everything away, again without wakening the officer. Wally said the guy would hear all about it tomorrow.

By mid-1982, my new house on the Etscheit estate was almost complete. I had gathered all the scrap wood one Saturday afternoon and was burning it. Wally drove up, coming to discuss a business proposal with me, to run by Robby. He explained to me how he had grown up on his father's cattle ranch in Elko, Nevada—that he knew the cattle business inside and out. He was suggesting we consider running a cattle operation on Robby's portion of the Etscheit estate.

Carlos had forty to fifty head of cattle already, but they were pets more than for business purposes. Wally outlined what they were doing wrong, what needed to be done differently, and said that he'd also be in a position to personally help us handle our trespassing problem in a proper and legal fashion in the future.

We still hadn't received the decision in the quiet title action case versus the traditional leaders. We'd also probably have to wait for an appeal process to run its course. So I told him I'd run this by Robby but that I couldn't imagine us committing to such an investment until the land's entire legal process was complete, reaffirming the Etscheit ownership of the land.

As we talked, a young Ponapean man came walking through our new housing area. It was now fenced in and posted with No Trespassing signs. I'd never seen him before but he walked right up to me and tried to sell me some marijuana. I thought, *Oh, this is going to be fun!* So I told him, "No thanks, but I think that guy over there will be interested in what you have!"

Wally was about twenty feet away, checking out the burn pile. The guy went over and offered it to Wally.

Wally asked him, "Do you know who I am?"

"No," the guy replied.

"I'm the police chief! Give me that! Get out of here!" Wally then threw the marijuana into the fire as the guy walked off. He was fortunate he wasn't arrested.

Wally would make catching the prominent Ponapean man, rumored to be involved in the local marijuana and drug scene, one of his top priorities. Lacking any subsequent prosecutions, much less convictions of this man, I don't believe it would be appropriate to reveal his name. Wally would confide to me many details of this investigation. Wally began to get the feeling that getting tough on all criminals, plus making all the changes necessary, even firing some, was meeting resistance as too politically unpopular here with state officials.

He decided that he would apply for the top law enforcement job for the FSM government, which was now open, feeling he could accomplish more there. The FSM said they couldn't accept his application. They felt they couldn't be seen as stealing Ponape State's top law enforcement official, especially after the state had already indicated to them that they fully intended to renew Wally's contract. That contract was to expire a day or so after the awarding of the FSM position.

An American named Joe Race was hired for the FSM position. Just afterward Ponape State informed Wally that his contract would not be renewed. Wally came to me very distraught. He told me he felt his zeal going after this one influential Ponapean had ruffled a number of political fathers and was the primary reason his employment hadn't been renewed. He also told me he was in a bad financial position because now in his second state government house, he had again spent all his savings fixing it up for his family. He apparently had truly believed that he would be here for a number of years.

He had been hired out of the Marshall Islands and Ponape State would only pay travel expenses for him and his family back to the Marshalls, which was only five hundred miles to the East. He was going to have to borrow airfare from his father to get back to Elko, Nevada, where he would have to work on the ranch until he could line up another law enforcement position. Only then would he be able to save enough to get his family back to the States. In the meantime, his wife and kids would have to stay in the Marshall Islands.

I felt sorry for him but there wasn't anything we could do. I was sorry to see him go and felt he could have made positive changes. But they were just too politically unpopular here at the time to make. Wally had stepped on too many toes of those who resist change. I would never hear from him again.

Chapter 25

A Traditional Wedding, Land, and Business Problems

I'd been getting too wrapped up in all these events. I knew that man could never successfully rule himself without some serious flaws in one area or another, usually many. I should have tried to stay neutral from all these negative events, like the drunks, trespassers, and the government's double standards in their protecting the civil rights of whites versus Micronesians. This is not to say that the local government wasn't also failing Micronesians in many ways as well.

This however, was now part of my job. It would also have a major negative impact on my spirituality. We had stopped going to the Kingdom Hall. I was feeling like a hypocrite, in part because of all the fighting. I didn't want to be seen there and have it reflect badly on the Witnesses. I felt I had betrayed my roots.

I was actually relieved when I was disfellowshipped as one of Jehovah's Witnesses. I didn't want to be wrapped up in all these events and others, and have it reflect badly on God's name somehow. My wife and I would divorce as well.

The last week of 1982, the trial decision in the land case came down in favor of the Etscheits. And by the last week of 1983, the appellate decision in this quiet title action case finally concluded this case, in favor of the Etscheits as well. But prior to this the traditional leaders were claiming victory and inviting many new people onto the land.

A dry El Niño season in 1983 would make it easy for many of these people to clear the jungle by lighting fires. A lot of damage was done to our forests that year. Of course arson complaints to the police were not even investigated.

Normally the dry season on Ponape only lasted two to four weeks, not even long enough to get the forest to burn. But the 1983 dry season lasted three to four months, even the Duanu River next to my house dried up to dust, not even a muddy spot anywhere.

In late 1983 after being single for over a year, I saw a beautiful young Ponapean girl at the post office. A month or so later my driver's license expired. To get a new license a picture of me was required. The only place to get that done here at the time was to go to the college in Kolonia and have the students in the photography class take it. As I was entering the college office to pay for the picture, out came this beautiful girl. I asked her name and she answered, "Casmira." That was about all that was said then.

My part-time housekeeper was a tomboy, one of the stars of the women's baseball league here and from Awak, U. Women's baseball was very popular on island and Elisophet was highly respected in the community. She would tell me where Casmira lived, that it was the last house before getting to the entrance of the Village Hotel in Awak.

A few weeks later I sent Elisophet across the river to the college which was only about three hundred yards from my house, to invite Casmira over for lunch. Because of Elisophet she agreed to come. While eating I played a movie on the VCR. It was the first time Casmira had ever seen TV.

She was the oldest girl of her parents' thirteen children. She had a good-girl reputation and had grown up poor, working like a dog, cooking, cleaning, and doing most of the raising of her eleven younger brothers and sisters. She only had one older brother.

She was beautiful in form and appearance but didn't know it. She had grown up having her mother telling her she was ugly, and so she believed it. That's because the majority of older Micronesians think fat and flat is beautiful. Casmira was the opposite of that.

It's quite comical to watch a group of Ponapean men sometimes. Around good-looking women they'll just ignore them, continuing to talk among themselves. But if a fat one passes by, they'll get quiet and all their heads will turn following her every move. The bigger the better, age doesn't seem to matter much—the whiter the better.

Overweight white American women, even old ones, are sometimes delightfully surprised at how popular they are here.

At this lunch the two girls ate together, I kept my distance. When Casmira got ready to leave, I asked her if I could go to her house on Saturday afternoon to meet her family. She didn't respond, so I took it as a yes. Later I would learn that she was so shocked by my request that she didn't know how to respond. But inside she wanted to say no. She just wasn't interested in guys yet. Those feelings hadn't awakened in her yet, as she was so consumed with her heavy workload at home up to that point in her life.

That next Saturday afternoon I went to Awak to her family's house. The grandfather's house was next to the road and he had a small local store there. When working on the Village Hotel seven or eight years before, I'd never stopped at that store. That was because at lunch I'd be looking for cold soda and they had no electrical power there, thus I assumed they'd have nothing cold. I would find out later that they did have cold soda in a kerosene refrigerator. But I do remember at the time seeing her mother and grandmother hanging around the little store, along with many little kids as I'd pass by on my motorcycle.

The parents' house was just below on a high bluff overlooking the ocean. It was pretty much a simple local house with a thatch roof, about as cheap as you could get here and still call it a house. There was no power, no running water, with a simple outhouse down the hill a short ways.

Some of her family welcomed me and had me sit down on the raised floor of the house. They told me to wait, telling me that Casmira was down by the ocean at the bottom of the hill at a spring, cleaning dishes and doing laundry. They said that she'd get cleaned up and be back to the house shortly.

So I waited and waited, some of her family looking embarrassed and going down the hill a couple of times to hurry her up. Finally after forty-five minutes of being pestered by her family, she showed up quite upset and said to me, "Can't you see I'm busy!" I got the message. I said good-bye to those who were there, left and forgot about Casmira.

Six days later on a Friday morning I heard a knock on my entrance door downstairs. It was Casmira. She told me that she'd

227

changed her mind and I could come to her house on Sunday at two o'clock in the afternoon to talk to her family if I'd like. Then off she went to the college.

That next Sunday I found myself sitting in a circle with about ten of her relatives questioning me. This went on for about ten or fifteen minutes. We were all sitting on the floor. There was absolutely no furniture in this house and not many walls either. When the questioning was done I'd somehow given the right answers. What they were I have no idea now. Casmira packed the only two dresses she had and off we went back to my house. That was one variation of a Ponapean traditional marriage ceremony. She was eighteen at the time and I was thirty-nine, two years older than even her mother.

As of this writing we're still together after over twenty-eight years. We've had four children, two beautiful girls, Ayla and Alye, ages twenty-one and eighteen. Also two good-looking boys, Bron and Kyle, twenty-five and twenty-three.

I've often said that marrying a Micronesian can be like playing Russian roulette. It's common for young Micronesian women to change completely, putting on a lot of weight after giving birth. Another pitfall is that a wife's family can treat their new white son-in-law as their own walking ATM machine. Further, some parents and even the girl's oldest brother can think that they are the girl's boss until the day they die, regardless of her age. Some older brothers will continue to beat up their younger sisters even if they're grandmothers and in their sixties. I've seen these things and experienced them personally.

But this isn't the case with Casmira and her family. They've been the best in-laws an American could hope to have in Micronesia. After twenty-eight years and four kids, Casmira looks better now in many ways than when we first met. In my opinion and based on what many others have said, she's still one of the best-looking women on this island and maybe even in all Micronesia. I've really sloped out. In about ten years she would begin developing another admirable quality, one more valuable than the others. I'll reveal more about that later.

With the final appellate decision in the quiet title action case reaffirming the Etscheit ownership, this still didn't stop the traditional leaders and trespassers from claiming victory and continuing to use this land. In the traditional leaders' trial brief, fifty two times they referred to all 1,246 acres of trial sketch 166-1 as Mpomp. After their loss, they began to now claim that Mpomp was now only a small area down by the bay. This was about two miles from where their three witnesses testified that they'd been living for twenty to thirty years. Two of them even testified that they were on Mpomp at those locations near the Etscheit upper boundary in the mountains.

Of course what was important was the land surveyed within trial sketch 166-1, not the defendants' revised definition of Mpomp after their loss. They couldn't fool us, nor would they later fool the court with this logic. But they would fool many of their subjects who wanted to believe this, so that they could get approximately seven and a half acres each of free choice land close to the outskirts of Kolonia.

Despite this, Robby and I began feeling sorry for these misled people. We began to discuss the need to search for ways to heal these problems in the community. To evict some of these families would leave them nowhere else to go. Plus, we also wanted to patch relations with these relatively new traditional leaders. The Etscheits had enjoyed excellent relations with all the people of Nett up until the death of Nanmwarki Max, and Robby wanted that restored.

Unfortunately, it was more and more looking as if the warnings from the attorney general and director of legal affairs that "blood is going to flow over this land," could come true. We were getting new death threats over the telephone. Others were arriving via the coconut telegraph. My neighbor across the Duanu River in Kolonia told me that he had seen armed men in the bushes near his house, watching mine. When he asked them what they were doing there, they openly responded that they were looking for a good place to get a shot off at my house. Others boasted that they had hid outside our electronically operated gate to our housing area, wanting to shoot Robby or me. But they decided not to try because we both had tinted windows on our vehicles. They didn't want to hit someone else by mistake and start a blood feud among Micronesians. Apparently, it was open season on Robby and me.

So there were business and safety issues that mandated an amicable resolution to these problems. We also wanted to find something we could do with this land to be using it ourselves on a large scale, to have a presence there to discourage anymore new people from coming in. I also received a couple of what I considered serious proposals to kill one of these traditional leaders, the nahnken, for large amounts of money. He had apparently made other enemies.

I told Robby that we could not get involved in any activities like this. I stressed that this could be the dumbest thing we could ever be part of. I believed instead that we could turn the king and nahnken into allies instead of enemies, to think along these lines and we should search for a way to work together with these two local leaders, to heal these wounds in the community. I felt that working with one or both of these men could be the key to solving the land problems.

I believed this was possible because when in federal prison, I had realized that even many of the worst criminals had a good side and you could make friends with most any of them. I was sure that if we tried, we could turn one or both, into a business partner in some area. I urged him to let me try it, telling him that it could be our best solution. Also, I wanted to know if he would be agreeable to letting go of some acreage that we could give to some of these hard-pressed squatters through the nahnken. That doing something like this would really make the concept attractive.

Robby agreed for me to look into this solution and see what was possible, adding that yes, land could be available, up to forty acres but it would have to be "conditional" to prevent a future repeat of these same problems. The opportunity for me to finally personally meet and talk with the nahnken would come about by unforeseen circumstances.

Robby had hired an American from Guam, Dan Sanders, to manage his Ace Commercial retail store. While in Robby's employ, Dan separated from his Ponapeian wife and had to move out of their apartment. Since I was single at the time, this being about two months before marrying Casmira, he asked if he could stay at my house until he could find another suitable rental. He stayed with me in one of my empty bedrooms for a little over a month.

While there one evening, he told me of a bad experience he'd had in Vietnam during the war. He had served on various types of gunboats that patrolled the rivers and swamps that were so numerous throughout that country. One day as their boat was slowly cruising next to the overgrown bank of a delta island, he saw a rocket coming from it that was about to hit their boat. He quickly yelled "ROCKET" while diving out of the boat and into some reeds along the island's edge. The rocket exploded and killed everyone in the boat. He was rescued by another gunboat in the area.

One day we both happened to be in Bank of Hawaii taking care of some business. When I finished, I left by a lesser-used exit next to the desk of the female assistant manager. I returned to my house for lunch. Dan showed up there a few minutes later and couldn't wait to tell me what had just happened after I left the bank. He related that as he was leaving by the same exit door twenty or thirty seconds after me, an annoying drunk was at the assistant manager's desk. He was hassling her for money and becoming enraged at her for turning down his request and asking him to leave. Dan stopped, tapped the guy on the shoulder to get him to turn around and then told him to get out of the bank also. The guy then started threatening Dan. Like me, Dan had no patience for these kinds of guys. He then knocked the drunk right across the desk and into the lap of the now screaming assistant manager.

Sometime later, Dan was walking from his new apartment to work at the store. As he was crossing the Duanu River Bridge, the nahnken came driving from the opposite direction. Dan alleged that the nahnken tried to run him over with his car. Dan jumped out of the way and pressed an assault with a motor vehicle charge against him.

The police actually processed this case and it was to go to court. At some point during these proceedings, Dan and the nahnken started talking. They bonded and Dan dropped the complaint against him. I told Robby, "See there! The nahnken's not so bad!" Later through Dan, I made an appointment to go see him one afternoon at his house near the Nanpihl River in Nett.

About two months before going to see the nahnken, Robby and I started a saw mill on the Etscheit estate, logging in the mountainous areas. This was where in 1981, Carlos's side of the family had conceded this land to us by saying we could do what we wanted, which was most of the forested land. The first several times that I had scouted out this land, I was so focused on looking for evidence of squatter activity that I hadn't even noticed all the big trees. Eventually I did and this is what we settled on doing at first, toward our efforts to use the land ourselves over a broad area.

The nahnken had a number of people that appeared to be part of his entourage. Others had characterized them as his bodyguards. Two of them were relatively new trespassers on the Etscheit estate. Others had warned us to watch out for these people, saying that it was from some of them that we were getting the threats.

A month before when discussing this group with Robby, I asked him which one of these guys he thought was the most dangerous. Which one did he think might come after him or me? What did he look like? I said that I needed to know whom I had to watch out for.

Without hesitating Robby said, "Semen Rodriquez." He told me that he was about my age, between five feet eleven to six feet tall, medium build and with a bad reputation on island. Among his stints in jail here, I was informed, was one for some sort of attempt to blow up the local courthouse with dynamite. He had apparently been processed through there so many times that he hated that building.

Sometime around mid-1984, I met with the nahnken for the first time at his house. While talking with him there were five guys standing behind me. Two of them were holding guns on me. Semen was among this group listening to what was being said.

At this meeting I talked to the nahnken about the things Robby and I had previously discussed, about the possibility of working with him to solve the land dispute, to heal this rift in the community. I mentioned Robby's willingness to eventually deed out land to some of the hard-pressed people who were truly there before Leo filed the lawsuit in 1978, and some of the conditions we would require. As for other newer people, we could assist them in moving to other vacant areas of Nett that the nahnken could make available, even building a road into these areas if need be. I said that perhaps we could look for a business venture that the nahnken could be part of—that we could look for ways to work together. I added that while most of our employees were not from Nett, we could go out of our way to provide more employment opportunities for nett residents in the future. Robby was already the biggest employer in the private sector on Ponape and we were looking to expand in new directions. I explained that I hoped this could be a start of this process for us and that if he would think about it and see as I do, that it is in both of our best interests and his people's as well.

I would eventually come to like the nahnken and even admire him for many of his good qualities. Among them, in many ways—some misguided I thought—he had his people's best interests at heart, putting theirs even ahead of his own sometimes. Also in future events, when some in Nett wanted to resort to violence, it was he who was the voice of reason, the one to keep the peace and cool his subjects down.

It would take us many meetings and about three years before we'd eventually arrive at a comprehensive agreement, one that we'd reduce to writing. But a week or so after this first visit with Iso Nahnken, "Iso" being another part of his traditional title, I got a visit from a Mortlockese woman. Her name was Nikes.

She was asking for a job for her husband. She claimed he had been at the meeting between the nahnken and me, saying that he was an experienced heavy equipment operator. I asked his name. She said it was Semen Cantero. I asked if he sometimes used the last name Rodriquez. She said yes, it was his mother's maiden name and all the Rodriquez clan in Nett were his uncles and cousins.

The Rodriquez's were notorious in Nett for being the biggest group of troublemakers and criminals in this municipality, possibly the island. A couple of Rodriquez's had been with Semen at my first meeting with Iso. Anyway, I told Nikes to check back with me in a few days, I needed to discuss this with Robby.

Robby and I were both concerned that Semen might be a spy for these squatters. We didn't know if we could trust him. However, I had gone out of my way to approach the nahnken and this was done at great personal risk. Some of those holding guns on me behind my back were the ones who had been threatening to kill us. We agreed though, that we should hope for the best and give him a chance.

Semen turned out to be the best and most valuable employee we ever hired. Without him we may not have been as successful as we were yet to be in getting control back over the Etscheit estate during the mid-1980s and early 1990s. Eventually I'd turn all logging over to him and by the mid-1980s, I'd stay out of the forest for the most part. This was because I didn't want to risk another violent confrontation with an angry squatter like the one that would occur in June 1985. It would be my last major fight here. But the aftermath was the biggest problem. This is what led up to it.

Semen fit right into our operation perfectly. Within a short time we bonded and his loyalty to me was unquestioned for a couple of reasons. First, Semen and my wife were close relatives. Casmira's grandfather in Awak, where she grew up, was Cornelio Cantero. He was Semen uncle, the brother of his father. His grandfather was Fredrico Rodriquez, who had been best friends with blind Millie Etscheit. Fredrico would also work for Leo on his copra plantation. After WWII, Semen and his mother lived with Carlos's housekeeper in Carlos's old house by the Lewi River. This was after Carlos Etschiet moved into his new one, the one his daughter Yvette and her family still live in today. So it was easy for Semen to want to be sympathetic toward the Etscheits' land ownership. He could see that this new challenge to their ownership only sprang up after Nanmwarki (King) Max's death.

Starting with Semen as I expanded the sawmill operations, I begin deliberately hiring people from Nett. Previously, most of my construction workers had been from Kitti or Sokehs municipalities.

As mentioned before, Semen had numerous problems himself with the police. One of his biggest involved his only sibling, a younger brother. In the early 1970s, this brother had been arrested for drunk and disorderly conduct out at the airport on Dekehtik Island. He died in custody, never surviving that night in jail. Being transported in a police jeep to the jail, he fell out on the bumpy road as the officers attempted to pass another vehicle and was knocked unconscious. Never truly regaining consciousness, he was driven past the hospital and thrown in jail. He was found dead there in the morning. Semen would always hold several officers personally responsible.

With Semen involved in our logging operation, I was now free to devote more time to construction projects. But I still enjoyed occasionally running our new John Deere 540B logging skidder, dragging logs out of the mountains as far as one to three miles to the mill. The skidder was like the ultimate four-wheel drive vehicle. It had huge wide tires like on a monster truck. It could go almost anywhere. The largest log I hauled out was four feet in diameter and over ninety feet long.

We milled and set up our construction and heavy equipment headquarters about one-quarter mile upriver from our housing compound. It was about three hundred yards downriver from PICS, the islands high school, which was on the other side of the Duanu River. We always referred to this area on Robby's land as the sawmill.

We made a good profit. Two or three times a year I'd be able to pay cash for a new bulldozer, backhoe/loader, dump truck, or whatever we needed at the time. We'd expand into being heavy equipment contractors, renting out heavy equipment, dredging coral with a draggling crane or excavator and building and repairing many secondary roads around the island. We even got the contract to do all the civil work on the FSM's new Community College of Micronesia. That's where a contractor prepares the building pads for construction, builds the roads, parking lots and drainage culverts. We'd buy new or used heavy equipment, mostly from the States. We would also scrounge up thrown-away government heavy equipment on island, rebuild them and get another decade or more of use out of them.

We'd eventually acquire over thirty pieces of major heavy equipment. I loved working with this equipment and would eventually let the sawmill and building construction languish for the most part, in favor of heavy equipment projects. Gradually as we phased over into heavy equipment projects I'd break my construction workers into dump truck driver, loader operators, whatever I needed them to be. Most of these guys would be with me fifteen or more years, just young Kolonia Town drunks or Nett troublemakers when they started with me. Some were so motley they even dressed as if they were right out of a Hollywood pirate movie.

They'd mature some, get married, raise families and learn a trade while working with me. One thing they never seemed to grow out of though, was that most of them were payday drunks. Some were so bad that I'd wait and give their checks to their wives; otherwise they'd blow the whole thing.

Some heavy equipment required highly skilled operators. I'd get the best ones on the island to run the bulldozers, building roads, dredging coral, running the backhoe and road grader. Still, converting these guys over to heavy equipment operations was a costly endeavor. Stupid mistakes would plague us. Fortunately our in-house trainees never had any serious mishaps, just a lot of small ones. I had to keep a full time Filipino mechanic and auto-body man on the payroll to deal with all this. They were always busy, never catching up with all the repairs. I would always worry every day though, dreading what the guys were going to do next.

Other Micronesian companies trying to get into the heavy equipment business with no experience were having employees killed right and left. One had four killed in separate accidents over a period of several years.

Another had at first gotten a bulldozer. For a year or two they would rent our lowboy trailer and Peter Built tractor truck to haul it to various jobs for them. Our thirty-ton Lowboy had a beaver tail but no ramps. We'd use a couple of blocks of wood set back just the right distance from the beaver tail, to safely load and unload a bulldozer under these conditions. Our experienced bulldozer operators would haul this company's machine, doing the loading and unloading for them.

One day the young man building up this new company had some surplus military tractor trucks and a small Cat D3 bulldozer arrive on the ship. He borrowed an old Lowboy that his father happened to have. But it had an even higher beaver tail than our trailer. With the rollover protective structure on the bulldozer removed for shipping and no experience of where to place the blocks of wood, his bulldozer climbed up the beaver tail, right up and over backward, crushing him.

I would take his death hard. He was one of Robby's cousin's sons, Carlos's grandson. I knew one day they would develop their portion of the Etscheit estate and have to deal with some of the threatening squatters, same as myself. I'd gotten protective of this cousin's three boys from afar. They were such unusually good kids and I had watched them grow up, first seeing them in 1970, before they'd even begun attending school.

On a couple of occasions, squatters on their portion of the Etscheit estate that we'd conceded to this cousin, made threatening comments to me about their boys. I then forcefully warned these people twice, that they'd better not go after these boys!

Remember Aaron, my drunken neighbor next door in Kolonia who had his head shaken like a bobblehead doll one night? He was a Pingelapese who had an eye disease that was common here but only among people from that atoll, no one else. When he finally came to work for me, his disease had progressed to the point that he had been declared legally blind. But he could still see just enough to walk around, so I gave him easy jobs like shoveling sawdust or moving and stacking lumber. He fit right in with my group of Kolonia Town drunks.

When looking at this group it was hard to imagine that one of them had actually been to the White House and met with the American president. It was Aaron and he had even shaken hands with President Lyndon Johnson. At about eleven years of age he'd been part of a group with this rare eye disease that was sent to Walter Reed Army Hospital for study and possible treatment.

As we were increasing our heavy equipment capabilities, an American engineer suggested we start doing waterline repairs for the government. A US company, E. E. Black, was currently doing this work on island.

They had originally been a Hawaii outfit that expanded to Guam and then throughout Micronesia. Mr. Black eventually retired and the company was sold and resold to a number of big name US construction companies.

This young engineer was passing through Micronesia as a backpacker tourist. He talked me into letting him stay in one of my empty employee houses at our sawmill. We had seven units. I was always taking in stray people who were passing through. This guy then approached the FSM Construction Division, saying that he could save them loads of money by having a local company do the waterline repairs, versus a high overhead US company such as E. E. Black, now Black Micro.

They hired him. He then approached me, asking what it would cost to dig a six-foot-by-six-foot hole, six feet deep with a backhoe. Then unbolt and remove a six-inch flanged waterline valve and bolt in a new one, which they'd provide. Finally backfill the hole with eight cubic yards of coral and pour a six-inch concrete cap back over the area. Broken down like this it sounded pretty simple, something that could be done in half a day it seemed. So he got me to agree to a bare-bones price.

When it came to doing the work, after dealing with paperwork worth more than the job itself, it was in the busiest intersection of Kolonia. I would then learn I had to have everyone stop ten or fifteen times during various stages of this work to wait for inspections, making the work take much longer. I also found out I had to provide barricades to childproof the hole and then go to Guam to buy blinker-warning lights for nighttime safety as well. Plus they demanded we provide a traffic director for all the nonstop parade of cars trying to squeeze by on the one remaining open lane.

I made a large Ping-Pong paddle-style sign, red with STOP on one side, green with GO on the other. Then I gave it to Aaron and turned him loose as my traffic director. My other workers told me that around noontime, the hospital director was slowly passing by. It appeared he was taking a visiting dignitary to lunch. He did a triple take at Aaron and excitedly said to his passenger while pointing at Aaron, "Hey, that guy directing traffic's legally blind!"

Well . . . I had to cut corners somewhere. I never took on another one of those repairs and I told the engineer to find another place to stay.

Another stray I took in a couple of times was Neil Goldman, from Evansville, Arkansas. He'd been married to a Ponapean and had his own house here but had separated from her while he was framing up some cheap small Farmers Home Administration houses we were building. He then relocated into one of our employee units. Neil was proud of his two kids from his first marriage to an American Indian woman, who had died in a car accident. His son Steve Goldman had become a successful country music video producer for Hank Williams Jr. and other recording artists.

He told me of an interesting encounter he had while framing houses on Kauai, Hawaii. He and a coworker were on their way to a store for a coffee or lunch break. As they were driving along, a woman came out of the bushes, obviously having walked up a hillside from a house and flagged them down. She asked for a lift into town. She was dressed plainly and wore no makeup. They made some small talk on the way and dropped the woman off where she requested.

Driving on, Neil's partner asked him, "Do you know who that was?" Having no idea, he said no, not having noticed anything special about the hitchhiker. "That was Elizabeth Taylor. She's probably on island visiting her brother," his companion responded.

Building FHA houses for us again, I had him framing one up three blocks west of the post office in Kolonia. On this one, the customers wanted the wood floor up on six-foot posts so they could use the underneath for something else. A mentally challenged man in his late twenties was living on the property, and he kept hanging around right under where Neil was working. As Neil began to stand up walls, I came by to check on the progress. I told him he'd better get this guy away from the building—that we didn't need anything to fall on him and he get hurt.

As I took off, Neil asked the two old women who looked after the guy to please get him away from the building. I went back to the sawmill. Neil showed up a few minutes later with his helper and all his tools, sort of shook up, not knowing what to do. He told me that as I was pulling away, the two old Micronesian women showed up with sticks and started whacking the guy, driving him away from the building like an animal. About ten feet away and with the old women still letting him have it, he dropped dead right on the spot.

Neil was concerned that he may have witnessed a murder. He asked whether he should report it to the police. I told him that it would probably be a waste of time, that even if the old women had shot him with a gun, the police probably still wouldn't jail them. Then learning that since other Micronesians had witnessed this, I suggested he should let them come forward, but that it was ultimately up to him. The poor guy was buried before sundown. I was concerned that they'd somehow find us culpable.

I had another some-what similar bad experience with them not too long before. I was driving down a hill toward the main intersection in Kolonia. It had recently rained, but you could see evaporation coming off the asphalt as the road was beginning to dry.

Just before reaching this intersection is an uphill driveway to the Bank of Hawaii and Bank of Guam parking lot and building, which accommodated them both. As I approached it, a car had entered and then stalled out at the top of the one-way entrance. It was now rolling backward, back down the driveway and into the road right in front of me. I slammed on the brakes, skidding down the wet hill and right into the car.

The woman driving had rolled about forty feet backward and didn't have the presence of mind to step on the brakes until after entering the road again. I came to find out this was her first time driving a stick shift and she didn't have a driver's license either. She had needed to go to the bank that day and had borrowed someone's car.

By the time the police arrived, the road has dried and my skid marks were plainly visible. Rather than focusing on the woman, they went after me. Measuring my skid marks, they tried to tell me I was doing forty-five to fifty miles per hour in a twenty-five mile-per-hour zone.

I told them I never speed, but if the skid marks were long, it was because I was going down a wet hill, that their skid chart was probably for a flat dry road. The woman's lack of a license and runaway loss of control mattered little it seemed, I was escorted to the police station. It would take our lawyer to get the police to back off.

Biased treatment like this seemed to be the rule rather than the exception many times, especially if you were a foreigner. Fortunately, as an American I wasn't always at the bottom of the rung of this unofficial caste system. Filipinos seemed to be. We'd see an example of this firsthand.

Before we got our Peter Built tractor truck, we'd haul our equipment on the lowboy trailer using our logging skidder. The skidder broke down for a while, so I asked Semen to use Robby's international tractor truck instead. It was a cab-over model, single rear axle with no power steering. He had never used it before and wasn't at all comfortable hauling a thirty-thousand-pound bulldozer through town with it. But I insisted, so off he went with the load.

Getting onto the public road by Ace Commercial, he crossed into Kolonia over the Duanu River Bridge and turned left at the first intersection. A Filipino going the opposite direction had to pull to a stop at the intersection and wait for Semen to complete his left turn right in front of him. Not being used to this cab-over model, Semen began his turn much too early. As the turn slowly progressed the lowboy was getting closer and closer to the Filipino's truck, finally colliding with it and damaging its left front fender.

The police arrived and of course gave the Filipino a ticket for Semen slow motion accident. The poor Filipino had done all he could to back up but was pinned to a stop by traffic behind. He was so upset, and rightly so, that he challenged all this in traffic court before a local state court judge. I let Semen handle this all by himself. I knew better than to show my face there; it might end up a Mexican standoff.

Semen was predictably victorious . . . and me vicariously through him. As we were chuckling over this absurd, illicit victory, I wasn't at all comfortable with this at the expense of another messed-over foreigner, even more so after questioning Semen. I got curious and asked to see his commercial driver's license for the first time. He did have one, but he looked twenty years younger in the photograph. That's because it had expired seventeen years before!

Imagine that? All through this process, no police officer or judge ever bothered to ask to see his driver's license, they were so focused on going after the Filipino. I would then wake up, checking all my employees' drivers' licenses. Most did not have valid commercial licenses. I immediately sent each one to get one. Even our insurance carrier hadn't yet asked for copies of driver's licenses, but they would shortly. I thought about offering the Filipino some money for his damages, but his vehicle was already such a piece of junk before the collision, that I couldn't see any point in that.

My favorite heavy equipment operation was dredging coral. I could never master the dragline crane, but I was okay on the excavator. But I just enjoyed spending several hours a day helping my operators and watching them dredge. Our dredge sites were mostly out on causeway roads dredged out on the reef flats, off between Kolonia and Dekehtik. The dredge site was about half a mile to the east of the causeway road leading to the airport on Dekehtik Island.

When out on these sites, it was peaceful and relaxing. I almost had the same feeling I had when fishing outside the reef in the open ocean. Every five minutes, we'd dredge up giant clamshells from the deep sediment. They'd probably died hundreds if not thousands of years earlier. Some were three to three and a half feet across. Every twenty or thirty minutes we would encounter a large coral rock that we needed to remove. Some might be almost as big as a small car.

Since we were making secondary roads, we were able to sell everything we could dredge. Making money with our dump trucks, loaders, bulldozers, compactor, and grader, dredging and road building was by far our most profitable operation.

Around this time in the late 1980s, the Federated States of Micronesia government took full political control as the Trust Territory was officially phased out. Ponape changed its name to Pohnpei.

Not too long afterward, the state government of Pohnpei would stop us from dredging. At first they would site environmental concerns as a reason. But the real reason was that the new governor of Pohnpei was playing politics with the chief magistrates of each municipality, who wanted to control and benefit from the dredging within each municipality's boundaries. In all fairness to this new governor, I don't feel he was properly informed and advised by those who should have done so. This man, I believe, had the highest standards of ethics of any politician I knew of in Micronesia. He would also be the only governor to try to help the Etscheits with their land problem during my time with them.

There were three companies dredging in Kolonia Bay in the late eighties and early nineties, including us. We had been invited by the State to dredge in these areas. They told us they had eight years left on an Army Corps of Engineers permit to dredge in Kolonia Bay. We were told that we could dredge there for them if we would each repair the main causeway leading to the airport, by filling thirty feet out from the road's asphalt edge as an erosion barrier with coral. In exchange we were offered dredging rights for ourselves as long as we completed the erosion barrier in our assigned area during the eight year time period.

The other two dredging companies were owned by powerful political figures. One was Bailey Olter, the current president of the Federated States of Micronesia at that time. The other was Peter Christian, a longtime Pohnpei state senator of the Federated States of Micronesia. Both were from Pohnpei.

So at least this stoppage wasn't racially motivated. They had stopped Micronesians as well. The good thing for me was that they were both popular political figures on Ponape.

Each of the four FSM states has one senator-at-large. Altogether there are fourteen senators from these four states. Two senators are chosen from Kosrae, four from Pohnpei, six from Chuuk, and two from Yap. The numbers are based on population.

These fourteen senators pick the president and vice president from among these four at-large senators, not by vote of the people. Presidents and vice presidents serve for four years, not to exceed eight years, as in the US system.

Having represented all of Pohnpei as an at-large senator, Bailey Olter opted not to sue over the dredge site. Plus he was the current president of this young nation and didn't want to be a party to a suit against one state. But Peter and I though, would agree to work together to sue the State for breach of the agreement.

At the time of this writing in 2011, Peter is the current senator-at-large for Pohnpei and will in all likelihood be the FSM President one day. But at the time almost 20 years ago, we got the best ethical lawyer on island in my opinion: Fred Ramp, an American attorney who was a longtime resident.

There have been many incompetent or sleazeball attorneys on island. To make our case easier, the State's new attorney general would process both of these qualities. He looked like a federal prison moonshiner to me. I'd seen plenty of them in Springfield.

He was according to rumor, hired right out of Hotel Street in Hawaii. Hotel Street is the downtown Honolulu red-light district, full of bars, prostitutes, and cheap hotels. I wish I could remember his name. If you ever have a lawsuit, this is the guy you want on the other side. This attorney was supposedly licensed to practice law in the State of Virginia. Another Virginia lawyer, Tom Beckman who worked for the state legislature, always played tennis with Robby and me. He would later find out that this new attorney general was currently disbarred from practicing law in Virginia, thus not licensed anywhere. Thank goodness no one would find this out until after our case was over.

Our deposition hearing was held one afternoon and it appeared to me then that the new state attorney general had a couple or one too many drinks for lunch. It was the first case he was handling for the State on his new job. At this deposition, he was touting his Virginia credentials as his qualifications to represent Pohnpei State, until he could satisfy the FSM bar requirements.

During discovery questioning of the state representative who negotiated the dredging deal with the three companies, which included ours, this man admitted to the following: there was "no deadline" for us to complete these repairs, other than before the Army Corp of Engineers' permit's expiration; we could dredge for ourselves for the entire eight years remaining on this Army Corps of Engineers permit; and that "very little of this permission was reduced to writing, but was verbal." As to the amount of repairs to the causeway our company had completed by the time we were stopped by the State, he stated that we were "almost done."

At trial six months later, the attorney general's recollection of his star witness's deposition testimony appeared to have long since been alcoholically erased. Obviously just before trial he came up with his last-minute brainstorm defense: that verbal agreements are not valid beyond one year if the causeway repairs were supposed to have been finished within a year and weren't—that thus they were justified in removing all of us from this project. This was now their reason we had been stopped, even though we had been working there for about two years before the stoppage. He also claimed the three companies needed to be removed, as we had collectively shown little progress in completing these repairs. This was the attorney general's stated goal, which he was now going to prove as he completed his opening statements to the court. It was the first we'd heard of this.

Fred presented our case first. When I testified, I related that the State's representative offered us an eight-year deal with no deadline for the repairs, other than before the eight years were up. Also, to think a company would agree to repair a half mile of the paved causeway roads erosion barrier in one year for free was absurd. I estimated the repairs to our half-mile section at $300,000, and both sides of the one-mile causeway road to the airport at $1,200,000.

I also testified that our company had completed more than 75 percent of the causeway repairs to our assigned section, saying that I had built a massive five—to six-foot-high seawall with the large coral rocks we had dredged up and pulled out with a chain. I explained that sometimes I'd have all three of our Cat loaders and a backhoe out there moving rocks, setting them and then backfilling, that it was no easy job because some of the rocks were as big as small cars.

When Fred was done questioning me, the state attorney general spent quite a bit of time trying to discredit my testimony. He was practically calling me a liar and trying hard to downplay the amount of work we'd already performed, including my estimate of its worth. He even claimed that I had exaggerated the size of coral rocks, that he would prove that coral heads or coral rocks never get bigger than about three feet in diameter. Well by then, I knew he knew nothing about what he was talking about. Court was done for the day, but it would continue the next.

The next morning at the sawmill I told the guys to take our twenty-ton hydraulic boom truck to one of our old dredge sites that was about a mile from the courthouse. Four years before, we had dredged much of the coral for the new FSM Capital complex then under construction in Palikir. At that dredge site, we had dredged up a rock so big we couldn't get it out of the water. But it was pulled high up on the side of the causeway enough to get chains around it, which could be lifted out with our boom truck. This one was easily as big as a small car.

I told the guys to put it on the lowboy and park it right across the street from the courthouse in Palikir, where it could be seen from the courtroom witness stand. Off I went to Court. The attorney general presented his case this day. The State's representative who negotiated the deal with us was his primary witness. He had him coached to testify in support of his new one-year idea that best suited the State's interests.

The attorney general had him testify that basically we were supposed to complete our repairs within a year and we had been told of that deadline. Also he didn't remember anything about an eight-year Army Corps of Engineering permit ever entering any discussions or verbal agreements. He said that he thought our company had completed few repairs in our assigned area, also saying that as an outer islander and diving all his life, he had never seen a coral rock or coral head larger than three feet in diameter. He added that he felt he could testify as an authority on this subject.

245

I kept waiting for my lowboy to show up. I was going to ask Fred to ask him on cross-examination if he could identify what was on the trailer out the window, across the street from the courthouse. The witness stand was directly facing it, so you couldn't miss it. If he needed to, I was going to ask Fred to ask the court if the witness could go over and take a closer look to make a positive identification. After all, he was an authority on the subject. And if so while he was at it, I just happened to have a tape measure with me that he could borrow, so he could tell us all exactly how big its dimensions were. If my memory is correct, it was about four feet high, five and a half feet wide and over eleven feet long. I've seen much bigger ones in Hawaii and huge ones tossed up on the reef by storms even here in Ponape.

I didn't have the opportunity to do this. Darn! Fred was now up to cross-examine this witness. The lowboy, due to a mechanical problem with a piece of equipment, wouldn't show up that day. But it wouldn't be needed.

As Fred cross-examined him under oath, he restated that the three companies were supposed to have completed this work within a year but hadn't, and that an Army Corps of Engineers' permit played no part in these verbal agreements. He further testified that they couldn't even find such a permit. Fred then walked back to our table and retrieved our copy of this man's deposition testimony taken under oath six months previously. He then showed the witness that six months before under oath, he had given entirely different answers to these very same questions. As Fred had the witness read these answers before everyone in the courtroom, he cracked. Now visibly nervous and flustered, caught in a lie, he immediately came clean and conceded to his deposition answers to these same questions as being the correct ones. This vindicated me and my testimony in this area, after the attorney general had spent so much time trying to discredit me.

Fred continued with additional questions. When he asked about the amount of repairs to the causeway that our company had completed, he again wavered, giving a lowball figure in line with what the attorney general had indicated the previous day. Again Fred had him read his deposition testimony, in which he stated under oath that we were "almost done!" He then became thoroughly deflated when caught in this second obvious lie.

Fred, Peter Christian and I were all surprised that any state attorney general could go into a trial with a last-minute strategy and not consider his primary witness's previous testimony. Not this attorney general though!

The State's star witness was now so totally broken, he conceded to our position in every aspect of our case. Even better, he testified that it appeared to him that our company was 100 percent done with the repairs in our assigned area. He also without being asked, revealed that the State had done a previous cost analyze of the project and the estimates had come out to $1,200,000 total, or $300,000 per quarter section. With this unsolicited admission, the attorney general just sat there with his head hanging.

Fred said that was the most fun he'd ever had in court. We would win the trial decision and the following appellate process. I couldn't believe the A.G. had the nerve to appeal.

But I still didn't quite feel vindicated enough; there was still the matter of the coral rock size left unresolved. I thought about dumping that coral rock in the drive-way where the states representative worked. But then I began to feel sorry for him, imagining how he must have been manipulated by his superiors to lie. Then I began to respect him for going out of his way to tell the truth when he was forced to realize he had been used improperly.

I never did see him again. I've wondered if his superiors may have had him transferred to one of the isolated outer atolls. He may have even quit in disgust and moved to the United States as so many other Micronesians were doing.

Chapter 26

Avoiding Peleiuk Peseng

Robby had hired a full-time American lawyer sometime in 1984, named Mike Berman. He had been working in Micronesia for a number of years, which included Yap and Ponape.

Robby moved him into the third house in our housing compound, the one I had built for Masaro, who had decided to stay where he was, by the Liwi River. He had many crops there that he didn't want to leave. Crops are important to many Micronesians, as I was about to have impressed on me shortly.

With the probate of Leo's estate, partition of the land, and squatters still left on the land, a full-time attorney could be kept quite busy. The probate of Leo's estate was top priority with Robby, so the other issues were put on the back burner for later. It would be left to me to deal with the squatters for years—actually, for more than a decade. Our strategy was to leave alone the few trespassers that were actually active on part of the Etscheit estate prior to the start of Leo's 1978 lawsuit. We would pursue a deal through the nahnken to solve this problem. I believed that would amount to no fewer than eight families, only two of which had actually been living on the land full time since the late 1970s.

Our sawmill and logging operation would use the entire land, though, to discourage new ones from entering or continuing to use these areas. We even used the land claimed in the 1980 trial by those represented by the traditional leaders, until such time when we could conclude a written agreement with the nahnken. We just wouldn't touch these people's crops.

Many new ones had entered prior to the appellate court decision during the El Niño dry season of 1983. For the first six months we logged in 1984, we only cut down large trees that these people had killed by land-clearing fires. With Semen wild man reputation spearheading our logging, most people never returned. We just never saw them or any evidence of their continuing activity. Since it was our land, I gave most of these former trespassers' crops to Semen or the worker that we had trained to be my lumberjack, Ohner Weital.

Ohner had been one of the few squatters that we almost had a violent confrontation with. He was staying in a new shack just off the pipeline road in our forests. His stepfather, whom he was staying with, claimed he was staying there with Leo Etscheit's permission. Thus not claiming to be adverse to the Etscheits' ownership, we left them alone and their crops. Later I would hire Ohner and have him trained to be our logger.

As for all the other new crops, I'd either rip them out so our forests could recover, or turn them over to Semen and Ohner. We even tore down some small houses recently built, after leaving notices there for months.

In early 1985, a man from Nett approached me in town. His name was Albert Rodriquez, and he asked me if I could accompany him to the land commission office to examine some maps. He explained to me that he heard we'd been removing crops on the Etscheit property, near its upper boundary, adjacent to the Liwi River.

He was concerned because he had some crops near there, but on government land he believed. He wanted us to look at the maps together to see what we could determine. The maps we looked at were survey-working maps of various sections of the island, apparently intended to assist Asia Mapping in correlating their aerial surveys with ground surveys to check accuracy. At least that's what I was later told at land commission as to their purpose.

Numerous areas on the map were sectioned up into mostly seven and a half acre parcels. I'd seen these types of maps eight or nine years before. The Ponapeans thought those seven—or eight-acre parcels were homestead parcels that the government was making available. People flooded into the land commission from all around the island, writing their names into blank sections of these maps to stake their claim to a free homestead parcel. They may have eventually been issued title in some public land areas based on these surveys, but never on someone else's private property.

Looking at the particular map now in question, Albert showed me his name on the map written in one parcel. We discussed the topographical features of the spot he was claiming. He told me that his spot is where the base of Tolakapw Mountain starts to go steeply up from the forest floor, which is relatively flat before that area.

With that information I was able to determine that he was just above the upper boundary of the Etscheit estate on government land, but everybody on the east side of him was on the Etscheit estate. He lamented that he had two brothers on that side next to him. As I checked the names on that side of the map, I commented that I only saw one spot with a last name of Rodriquez written in, besides his. He then pointed to the name Francisco Joseph, stating that this brother had changed his last name.

So I asked him why he changed his name. He said that when he became a policeman, he changed it because the last name Rodriquez in Nett was associated with the biggest group of troublemakers and criminals on the island—that he wanted to distance himself from them now that he was on the police force. He then warned me to watch out for this brother. While pointing to his name on this map, he said he was going to get me somehow because I had recently pulled out and removed his crops.

I asked him if these crops were on a spur ridge leading up to Tolokapw Mountain, about two hundred yards north of the Liwi River. He answered yes. I told him that these crops had just been planted. The young coconut trees hadn't even taken root yet. I admitted that I did personally remove those crops, even replanting three of the coconut trees in my own yard. I explained that his brother had obviously entered the land after the quiet title action case had already reaffirmed the Etscheit ownership—that if he claimed before, then he violated injunctions pending its outcome. Either way, his brother as a police officer, should know better than trespassing on the private property of others or violating court injunctions. I encouraged Albert to ask his brother to go to the courthouse and read the judgment for himself, to examine trial sketch 166-1, to see the land that was the subject matter of this trial. Then he would see that it's quite clear the land extends all the way up to the base of Tolokapw Mountain, on its upper Lewi River side.

Later I discussed this conversation and Albert's warning with Semen. He confirmed that Albert and his three brothers were all his first cousins, the children of one of his mother's younger brothers. He said that other Rodriquezes in Nett were descendants of the other younger brothers of his mother, all of them the children and grandchildren of Frederico Rodriquez. Before the Second World War, Frederico had been best friends with blind Millie Etscheit and a loyal employee of Leo Etscheit. But when discussing Francisco, his cousin who changed his last name, Semen became very somber. He told me then that Francisco was one of the police officers in whose custody his younger brother had died during suspicious circumstances in the early 1970s.

About four month later in early June 1985, I had four guys working in the mountains. Three were short-term temporary workers I had hired to replant eight thousand tree seedlings we had gotten from our local forestry station. It was located just across the river from my house. They had given us Philippine mahogany and Panamanian cedar tree seedlings about three feet tall each. Semen sixteen-year-old second oldest son, Steve, was one of these planters. I had them replanting areas burned during the 1983 dry season fires. This was in the areas adjacent to Ohner's house, which was just a shack. It was also in the area of the WWII prepared battlefield.

I had Ohner also working in this area, fixing a problem on the pipeline road at a narrow bridge crossing a small creek. The sixteen-inch waterline just off the edge of the bridge was exposed there with a blowout valve sticking out the top.

With our logging skidder, we'd drag one entire long tree to the mill each trip. Some had twists and turns in them, for the trees searched for sunlight in the dense forests as they grew. These wouldn't always drag straight behind the skidder, but off to one side or the other, off the road sometimes. One log had slid off this bridge and knocked the blowout valve off, leaving Kolonia without water for a couple of days until it was fixed. We were charged twelve hundred dollars for the damage. I tried to argue that the pipe in this location was outside the twenty-foot-wide road and pipeline easement and exposed on our land, which it was. The water authority was a State agency then, and they were always right. I got tired of arguing and just paid them; otherwise they'd mess me over in some other area.

251

I had Ohner cut a small hardwood tree about eight to ten inches in diameter and eight feet long. We dug a hole about four feet deep next to the bridge and stood the log in the hole to stop the log being skidded from sliding off the road again in this location. We would do the same in other similar locations, as a precaution. This eleven-thousand-foot-long pipeline road across the Etscheit estate crossed ten rivers and creeks. This is counting the Duanu and Lewi rivers, which are its boundaries on each side. This land was shaped somewhat like a pork chop, the small end being on the bay front and the big end up in the mountains.

When returning to the sawmill after lunch that day, I noticed a column of smoke rising from the vicinity of the pipeline road, about a mile farther up into the land from the sawmill. I took one of my longtime construction workers, Simai, and we drove up to see what was burning. On arriving, I found two of the temporary tree planters who had seen the smoke from the fire and were now in the process of beating it out with sticks. We joined them and soon had the fire out.

This was not the first time we had put out fires. I usually carried a stick behind the seat of my truck for just that purpose. The two temporary workers claimed that they hadn't seen who started it. They said they were some distance away and only responded when seeing the smoke. I then decided to drive south along the pipeline road to look for sixteen-year-old Steve or Ohner, to see if they saw anyone. I never ran across Steve, but about one-fourth mile south of the fire I found Ohner. He was right where he was supposed to be, digging the hole for the hard wood post. He claimed not to have seen anyone. As I was inspecting the hole he had dug, I heard a crackling, babbling sound that made me think it was the creek flowing. But as I looked at it I realized it was dry, not having rained much in the last week or two.

As I listened carefully to determine the source of the sound, I looked deeper into the forest and caught a glimpse of a flickering light. It was another fire just starting up. I said to Simai, "Grab your stick. There's another fire in there!" Not too far behind my truck I found a small trail leading into this area. Following this path led me right to the fire, a tire burning at the base of a Karara tree, lit to kill it. It was about 150 feet in from the road. Three or four yams had recently been planted around its base, the vines just beginning to sprout.

As yam vines grow they can climb a pole, rope, or even better, a dead tree to get more sunlight. I immediately pulled the yams out and tossed them. But then I realized that this fire had just been started several minutes before. The person had to be nearby. I followed the trail a little farther into the land, far enough that I couldn't see the road or my truck anymore because of the jungle. Simai stayed by the fire. As I walked in, a Ponapean man came walking toward me.

I recognized him as Ohner's uncle, his name was Martin Etnolt. I had seen him at Ohner's stepfather's house about six months before. I told him then that if anyone wanted to grow crops, we'd give them a free lease for that, but they couldn't remove or kill certain species of trees. If they were interested, they could come to our lawyer's office for all the details.

He actually showed up at the lawyer's with the head of one of the families that had been living full time on the land since the late 1970s, Masao Sultan. Masao Sultan's house was across the river from the present-day Seventh-day Adventist school. He was one of the trespassers who prompted Leo Etscheit to file the lawsuit in 1978.

They apparently didn't like our lawyer's offer, preferring to believe a lie instead. They never returned for a lease. Most people in Nett still didn't know or want to acknowledge that the traditional leaders lost that case. They preferred to believe those telling them that the Etscheits only won Mpomp, now claiming it's a small area down near the bay front. Oddly enough, it was Trust Territory laws that provided the catalyst for Masao Sultan, some of his immediate family and some others, that prompted them to move onto this vacant area of the Etscheit estate in the first place.

This was because for as long as most people could remember, landowners couldn't sell their land. They couldn't give it away, will it to their children, or dispose of it in any way. The only way it could pass was at their death, and then only by law, automatically going to the deceased's oldest son and no one else.

This law was finally changed in 1957, allowing an owner to dispose of his land by quitclaim or willing it to his children as he saw fit. But if he died without a will, which was the case with most

Micronesians, then it would still automatically go to his oldest son only. In later years, other changes to these laws would make allowances to pass land outside the immediate family. But not until late 1976 or 1979, would a law finally be passed that would allow an equal distribution of a man's property and estate among all his children, if he died without a will. Most families had many children.

Masao Sultan's father died before this law was changed. His oldest brother was an alcoholic and sold the family's property, where they had all grown up and were currently living, right out from under his siblings, small lots at a time to feed his alcohol addiction. So Masao was homeless and moved to the nearest vacant land that he thought was public land, something Ponapeans do all the time.

In 1976 I stayed with one of my wife's relatives who had just built his house on one of these lots. I was going to build my family a house and considered buying another one of these lots next door for eleven hundred dollars. This was in a community called Dolonier, located in the area to the west and north of PICS, close to the Etscheit land. I ended up building in Kolonia, where I had all the trouble with the drunks.

But most of these new trespassers were average Micronesians who already had a house and land, but were just trying their luck to score another choice property close to Kolonia for free.

Still Robby and I were hopeful that we could find a resolution to this problem. We were hoping it would involve the nahnken, without having to resort to eviction proceedings. The last thing we wanted was a violent confrontation. But we realized that if we didn't have a presence on this large land and use it ourselves, it would be quickly overrun by homesteaders who would want to believe others' versions of the quiet title action trial's outcome. The police and state officials wouldn't do anything to help us. They were actually a big part of the problem. A number of these government officials would use their positions in various ways to further these goals of taking Etscheit land for themselves, family, friends, even constituents. I was about to experience one of our worst fears firsthand.

This fire and encounter with Martin Etnolt on this day would kick it off. As Martin came toward me on the trail, I reminded him that he didn't have a lease, thus no right to be here, especially to be killing our crops, our trees. I told him that he needed to leave and not return unless he went to our lawyer and signed a lease. With his head drooping and a machete hanging down limply in his hand, he began to start walking dejectedly out on the trail. I was in his way, so I walked back ahead of him looking for a place to get off the trail so he could pass me with a safe distance between us.

Six months before when I first talked with Ohner's stepfather, who had since died, Martin walked up holding a machete in a threatening manner. He then stood off the road two feet higher than I was, very close, looking as if he was about to take my head off with his machete. So I wasn't about to let this man get close to me again, especially in this situation with a machete in his hand again.

Moving back down the trail well before reaching the burning tree, I found a place to move off the trail about eight feet or so. With a hill behind and thick brush on each side, there was no safe exit from this spot should Martin turn violent. I considered all this in an instant and resolved that if he made any overt threatening move toward me, I'd be forced to act quickly. This wouldn't include turning my back and trying to flee, because I was boxed in. I'd be forced to confront him.

The spot I had moved to tapered up about two feet higher than the trail. I put the bottom of my stick behind me on the ground and sat on its end, not wanting to appear threatening as Martin passed by. I just wanted him to leave so I could attend to putting the fire out.

As he reached the spot just opposite me, he stopped and angrily asked, "Did you pull my yams out!"

I replied, "What?"

Again enraged he asked, "Did you pull my yams out!" He could clearly see they were missing twenty five to thirty feet ahead. He'd been facing down the trail at the burning tree when he angrily asked me those questions. When I answered yes, he didn't turn toward me. Only his head turned with a look of rage, his machete came up threatenly and he took a side step toward me like a crab.

With that "overt action," I instantly decided the best defense is an offense. So I quickly skipped down the incline with my left foot forward and took a baseball swing at Martin's machete, which he was already swinging at me. In mid swing, Martin altered his swing to meet my stick rather than me. They clashed together. I was trying to knock the machete out of Martin's hand. I squared my feet toward him because I had to have an effective backswing to keep him from stabbing me. If I only made right-handed baseball swings, he could quickly thrust in a stab as I reset to swing.

A Micronesian with a machete can be fast. I'll be the first to admit that most any Micronesian is ten times better with one than I am. On my second forward swing though, my heavier stick went through Martin's machete swing, forcing it aside and striking him on his forearm. Unknown to me at the time, that blow broke his right arm, although he was still trying to hold and swing his machete with it.

The third fore swing caused him to stumble backward and fall. He then apparently hit the back of his head on a small rock. He still tried twice to lean forward and swing at my legs. Two times more I swung at his machete to knock it away, but he pulled it back at the last moment and blocked my blows twice with his left forearm. He did that so fast that I didn't have time to soften my blow much. I thought that I could have broken his left forearm with one of those swings.

As he tried to sit up a third time, I saw blood squirting from the back of his head. He didn't threaten to swing at my legs, so I held up my next swing as well. As he collapsed back down, I knew he was no longer an immediate threat. On the trail now, nothing was blocking my route of retreat, so I ran toward the road. Just before the road, I encountered Ohner coming in from it. As we passed I told him to go help his uncle.

I wanted to get my other workers and myself out of there, to avoid any further violence. I knew that right or wrong, 99 percent of the time Micronesians side with their family and relatives. Thus I had to be concerned how Ohner would react at first. He did have a semiautomatic .22-caliber rifle not too far away at his house, with the biggest drum clip I'd ever seen on one.

With Simai in the truck, I reversed about 150 to 200 yards backward to a turnaround. The two tree planters were there by then, so I had them get in. I didn't know where Semen's son Steve was, but I knew he'd be okay because they had no reason to go after him.

After returning to the sawmill, Simai and I left immediately to report this incident to the authorities. My first choice was to go to the director of law enforcement for the FSM, in Kolonia at the time. I had absolutely no confidence in the Ponape state police. When we arrived, his secretary told me he had just left for a late lunch.

I had asked Simai if he'd witnessed what had happened. He had answered yes. But in reality he had ran back to the road when he first heard Martin ask, "Did you pull my yams out!" By the tone of his voice he knew there was going to be trouble. I was only taking Simai with me because I thought he had witnessed some of these critical events. I didn't know he had run away before the fight started.

So at the time I thought I had a corroborating witness. But I still wasn't comfortable going to the local police. So on the way to the police station I stopped at our lawyer's office and asked him to go with us also. I didn't trust these police at all.

He begged off going with us, assuring me not to worry. I had a bad feeling about going to the police, with whom I'd already had so many negative experiences. They had never done one thing right concerning the Etscheits or me, and I thoroughly believed some of them were racist.

At the front desk a female officer had me wait, she was occupied helping others. After about ten minutes and still busy, she asked me to wait alone in an adjoining room until a detective could help me. The room had a coffee machine in it. Officers were coming and going, getting cups of coffee or proceeding to a room beyond. One officer who was briefly passing through asked what I was doing there. I gave him a brief ten-second reply to the effect that we had some serious trouble with someone we found committing arson on the Etscheit estate, saying I was here to report all of this and file a complaint. I was alone in this room for about thirty minutes until an officer told me to go two buildings over to where the detectives' offices were, saying they would take my complaint there. Simai was sent with me then.

We were told to sit on a couch and wait to see the chief detective. I could directly see him not too far away. Of all people, it was Francisco Joseph. He was the police officer who four months before, his brother had told me was going to get me somehow for removing his crops from the Etscheit land. He was already looking quite upset to see me waiting there. It seemed as if he kept us waiting for half an hour. After receiving one or more phone calls, he left the building and didn't return for over an hour.

I had by then been waiting for over two hours at the police station and still hadn't been able to tell anyone more than a few words. When Francisco did return, he looked even more upset. He finally came up to me, where we were still sitting on the couch. He then told me he had just returned from the hospital. He was short of breath and nervous, but with a quivering voice he was barely able to get it out that I was "under arrest!"

I had a couple of reactions to this. First, this was the weirdest arrest I'd ever experienced. I would have thought he'd be more proficient at it. It was obvious that this one was special for him; he could hardly contain his emotions. My second reaction was that I was fed up with the police department. I started scolding him. "What do you mean? You guys haven't even spoken with me yet. I've waited to file a complaint for more than two hours here now, and you just come up and arrest me!"

He started getting defensive, stating that he had spoken with Martin, who had a broken arm at the hospital. He said that Ohner's story corroborated Martin's, that he was my own employee and wouldn't say that unless it was true.

I told him that "anyone who knows Ponapeans knows that they'll usually always side with their relatives in the heat of a situation like this, whether right or wrong." I further stated that "Ohner didn't even see what happened or know a fight had occurred. If he had, I would never have been able to pass him on the trail after the fight without fighting him also, especially if what you want to think happened, he had actually seen!"

This was Francisco's big opportunity to get back at me for ripping his crops out and elevating his stature in Nett among those who supported the taking of Etscheit land, not to mention getting me convicted of assault with a deadly weapon for using my stick—and possibly deported as an undesirable alien. He finally had another officer take my statement of events. Then off I went to the Ponape jail again, the same disgusting cell, still not cleaned. Hunched in the corner, I was just mosquito bait. In the morning I was wondering if this was really happening to me again. Just then J. D. Lowe came to see me again, keeping up his visiting streak.

That night I was in jail was the night Gorman Booth, the Asia Mapping retiree, was murdered in Kolonia. He was the first white man murdered in Micronesia by a Micronesian in twenty years. They just missed out on having two killed that day.

Chapter 27

Another Trial

The following afternoon I was released on my own recognizance but charged with assault with a deadly weapon. With our lawyer Mike Bermin, we started preparing for a trial immediately. Mike felt bad about not having gone to the police station with me, feeling he could have taken charge of the situation somehow and prevented my arrest, or at least my spending the night in jail.

The night of or the next after my arrest, Casmira's housekeeper went out to drink sakau at a place in Dolonier. A number of Dolonier residents were among those trying to claim Etscheit land. Martin Etnolt was there with his arm in a sling. Our encounter was the big topic of conversation there that night. Sitting there, she heard Martin state in Ponapean that when he saw his yams pulled out, he "was going to *peleiuhk peseng* Steve, but he was too fast for me!" This statement of his was of course entirely in ponapean. *Peleiuhk peseng* means to chop you into little pieces. We would use this woman and this statement of Martin's in court to show Martin's intent when he made a move in my direction, initiating the altercation. So if I had not reacted so quickly and forcefully, he may have succeeded. His first machete swing was coming directly at me, until he altered it to instead meet my swing at his machete.

Ohner Weital would cool down pretty fast, returning to work in a few days. Martin would also, for a very good reason for Micronesians. Martin's wife and Casmira's father were first cousins. So in Micronesian custom, we were family. I found this out a few days later.

A couple of days later I was working on two houses I was building for an American lawyer, Jim Hagistrom. They were on the cliffs overlooking the ocean in Nan Pohlmahl, just above Dolonier. Martin and his wife walked by. I could see things were cool with them now, as far as their feelings toward me. I heard he had also tried to withdraw his complaint against me. Ohner also signed a sworn affidavit later as to the truth of his involvement that he simply didn't see what happened.

But the Ponape police and a new American Ponape state attorney general, who wanted to make a first good impression, simply wouldn't drop the charges. The chief detective, Francisco Joseph, was personally pushing this case against me and seeking deportation. He would have a muscle-bound bodybuilder detective, notorious for working suspects over, interview Ohner again. This detective was appropriately named Nero. He would threaten to beat up Ohner on this occasion and another before trial, which had Ohner quite concerned of course. But the truth was simple: Ohner wasn't an eyewitness to the fight.

We would learn that right after the fight the police gave Ohner a statement to sign as if he had seen the fight start. It also stated that he never saw his uncle threaten me. He signed it willingly because he was automatically on his uncle's side, right or wrong, right after the fight.

In a preliminary hearing presided over by an American judge, Judge King gave Owner and I strict instructions to not discuss this case among ourselves before trial. This was necessary because I hadn't fired Ohner. He continued working with me every day. In fact, first thing most every morning Ohner and I would go to our log landing, just he and I alone for fifteen to thirty minutes. He would hold the end of my tape measure while I marked out the length of each log from each tree skidded down from the mountains the previous day. I'd then leave and he'd chainsaw the logs to length before he and Semen would go to the mountains for the day.

This close contact most every day was driving these detectives crazy. They thought for sure I was tampering with or bribing him. The detectives were actually the ones tampering with the witness. I wasn't like them. Ohner and I never said one word to each other about this case before trial or during, nor did we discuss it through intermediaries. By then Ohner had given two different statements, but only the second one was under oath.

Jim Hagistrom, the lawyer I was building the two houses for, one for himself and one for his daughter, was following this case closely and wanted to help me. He offered at no charge to help my lawyer Mike with pretrial preparations.

Jim was a retired air force colonel who had become a lawyer during his military career, which was long. He had been a fighter pilot in the Pacific in WWII. He became a fighter ace in the Korean War. I've seen his picture in a book about fighter aces. He told me how for years he ran the air war in Vietnam as an air force colonel. He was the one who gave the hands-on orders directly to the flight crews for the secret bombing of Laos or Cambodia. Whenever the American president came out to the Pacific, he would be the one to meet with him as the air force's representative. He could go on and on about General Westmoreland. He just couldn't stand him, which I found quite comical. He had had a ferro-cement sailboat built in Santa Barbara, California, and he and his family had sailed it out to Ponape where he was now trying to retire.

Jim and I became somewhat close. We were both involved with trying to get badly needed development projects started on island, of the type needed to eventually kick-start a real economy here in the future. About all that existed at the time were local government jobs based on United States grant and compact money. Jim was working with one of the heads of the Nanpei Estate on experimental agricultural crops. Among them they had several acres of ginger under cultivation. At the time I was preparing to get my own ultra light two-seat airplane and had already built my own landing strip next to the sawmill. Jim had enthusiastically volunteered to be my flight instructor. Just before the incident with Martin, we had been making plans to visit all the local points of interests that we wanted to see close up from the air. I was looking forward to having someone of his stature teach me.

Besides him, I only knew two other notable air force retirees. One was Mr. Cummings and the other was the man who built our kitchen and bathroom cabinets in Kailua Kona, for the two spec houses we constructed there in the early 1980s. I forget his name. He told Richard and I that during WWII he had been shot down seven times as a bomber crewmember over Europe. Once or twice, he was the only survivor, and he ended the war as a POW in Germany.

Jim saw Ohner's two different statements and his possible different testimony at trial as a potentially dangerous loose cannon. He offered to help by taking a more extensive deposition of him, to more precisely lock his testimony down. Jim knew this was important with many Micronesians, as stories can change with each retelling. Ohner was also under intense pressure by the police. We might also need to impeach him as a witness, as he was set to be a State's witness. My lawyer Mike didn't seem to welcome Jim's offer. He would assure me not to worry about Ohner, that he could handle this case and didn't need any help.

This trial would be held in the FSM Supreme Court, presided over by Chief Justice King, an American. These proceedings are similar in many ways to trials in the United States but there is one significant difference: there is no jury. The single presiding judge determines guilt or innocence. Three other judges decide any appeals. The courtroom would be packed for this trial. All my employees and some of their family members would attend. Some squatters would as well, hoping I'd be deported, ending the Etscheits' use of this land through our logging efforts.

Jim Hagistrom would attend also, but just as an observer. Before the trial and during, I'd continue to feel that Ohner should have been subjected to a pretrial deposition as Jim had offered, as a precaution. This was my biggest concern, along with the fact that I didn't believe my lawyer, Mike, had any criminal law trial experience or very little at most.

The attorney general presented his case first with Martin testifying as his first witness. I could tell from Martin's testimony that he wasn't into this prosecution of me. He wouldn't admit though, to starting this fight by making the first move in my direction. I don't think "overt action" is a concept most Micronesians understand. Unless they actually strike someone, they usually think that threatening to kill someone or making threatening gestures with a machete or whatever doesn't matter, as long as they stop short. I've seen this many times, it's quite common here.

I believe Ohner was the next witness. When he testified he was obviously coming up with his third version of events as he was going along. Not only was he trying not to hurt either his uncle or me, but he was also trying to make the detectives happy, testifying as if he had been there and seen everything. It was quite a balancing act but not good enough for the detectives. Lunchtime was near so the judge called a recess, reminding Ohner that he'd continue his testimony in the afternoon after the noon lunch recess.

I had already heard enough. I told my lawyer there was no way Ohner had witnessed any of this fight. I suggested that maybe he should try to impeach him on cross-examination. He replied that he wasn't hurting us, so we should just leave him alone.

But a big help was about to come from one of the lug head detectives. As Ohner was filing out the courthouse door with everybody else, up came Nero. Right in the courtroom door, Nero for the third time threatened to beat up Ohner if he didn't change his testimony after lunch. One of my employees and two other spectators, both not connected to me, overheard Nero's threat. They all reported it.

When court resumed, Mike informed the judge of these events and complained about the police bringing their thuggish practices right into the courtroom. This was all taken "under advisement," and the court would deal with it later. Ohner resumed the stand and continued his testimony. I can't remember all the details, other than I thought he was making it up as he went along. He'd told so many falsehoods that he'd gotten himself painted into a verbal corner. Then the attorney general asked him such a troubling question that any answer might collapse and expose his verbal house of cards.

He was now at a loss for words, he didn't know what to say. The question was repeated two or three times but Ohner acted as if he couldn't understand the question, almost as if he couldn't understand English now. More than once they even repeated the question in Ponapean. He was doing all he could to play dumb in order to avoid the question because its answer could undermine his three-way balancing act, which the court appeared to be buying so far. The attorney general sensing his star witness may be in trouble, withdrew the question. The judge then took it up, as if he sensed the truth behind Ohner's performance. Also unable to get an answer despite several attempts, the judge moved on also. Whether he got the right take from all this, I wasn't sure at the time. Regardless, Ohner was let off the hook and saved from self-impeachment. My lawyer wouldn't act to impeach him, still claiming he wasn't hurting our case. I grudgingly conceded to my lawyer's experience, figuring he must know what he's doing.

At some point it was decided that the next morning the court would meet at the site of the fight. Ohner, Martin, and I were to give testimony there.

After Ohner's testimony this first day, the attorney general called Nero to the stand. He was apparently keeping to his witness list, despite the recent revelations concerning him. Nero looked understandably uncomfortable and embarrassed on the stand.

I don't remember much about his testimony, but I think it may have had to do with Ohner's first two different stories after the fight and his interviews with him. I was just disgusted to see his bully face up on the witness stand and from the look of the judge, it appeared he felt the same way. This new attorney general was still so new to Ponape that he apparently had no idea yet just how bad this police department was.

In the attorney general's defense, I will compliment him on three things. First he let us know that he would not be seeking deportation. Second, he obviously let the police know that this is Etscheit land, not what the traditional leaders or squatters want to think it is. This would be apparent by the actions of Francisco Joseph which I'll relate shortly. Third, that he would be bringing trespassing charges against Martin Etnolt and Masao Sultan, if they didn't sign a lease as previously offered by Robby's lawyer.

The next day court was held in the field on the Etscheit land, at the scene of the incident. Ohner was up first, showing the court the spot where the fight occurred and where he'd watched it from, close by, about fifteen feet away. The problem was that since he hadn't really been there, he had the location wrong. It was a little farther out the trail, away from the burning tree. When Martin and I testified, we would both show the correct spot of the incident. Martin would plainly state, "Ohner wasn't there." I'd testify that I didn't know where he was, only passing him after the fight near the road, as I was about to leave the trail and he was entering it. It was also quite clear from the site inspection that the fight could not have been visible by anybody on the road.

Testimony was limited in the field to issues that couldn't be dealt with in the courthouse. I don't recall spectators being allowed at the site either. Throughout the trial testimony of Martin and me, we would agree on most everything, except on what sparked the altercation.

Back in the courthouse the attorney general called one of the police detectives from the station to testify. He was the officer who had talked to me briefly when passing through the coffee room, before I was told to go to the detectives' building. We had only spoken for maybe ten seconds or less, but the man was now testifying as if he had conducted a formal interview with me in his capacity as a detective. He was stating that I showed up at the police station only wanting to file an arson complaint against Martin Etnolt, saying that I never even bothered to mention the fight at all, obviously trying to keep it quiet. Both he and the attorney general were highlighting this last part, painting a picture of me as a man who was trying to get away with beating Martin up deliberately, then attempting to burden him with an arson complaint, as extra punishment on top of the beating. I couldn't believe this. Logic like this could only come from people used to dealing with stupid drunks all the time. They must be contagious.

He had a lot to say for only a ten-second conversation in passing. I considered it deceptive perjury. My lawyer Mike, was able to work him over rather well in cross-examination. Did he regularly interview suspects in the break room? Where were his notes? Did he have a signed statement from me? Even the judge asked him some hard questions and seemed disgusted with him.

The next witness for the State was Chief Detective Francisco Joseph. We had tried to prepare for him to expose this prosecution as his revenge for my pulling out his crops and also show that he was a trespasser on the Etscheit estate.

In preparation I went back to the land commission to get a copy of that map with his and others' names, claiming areas of the Etscheit land. It had been wiped clean, even though the names had been in ink. It was on some kind of plastic/Mylar material. Impressions of names were still visible, but not on the spot where his name had been. His name's impression had been over impressed out on this material.

Later when locating his brother Albert, he didn't seem to remember his previous warning to me that his brother was going to get me for pulling his crops out. He even denied that Francisco had ever claimed any land up there, or even looking at a map with me at the land commission.

Francisco wouldn't stick his neck out so much as he had his underlings do on direct examination. But on cross-examination, Mike would get him also. He'd get him to deny ever trespassing on the Etscheits' land, having crops there, threatening to get me, or having his name removed from the land commission map recently. At least we knew he was a perjurer. The only issue we could nail him on was trespassing. Later when presenting our case, Semen and I would each testify that together we had run into him on one occasion in this area, trespassing without permission.

Most of the damage to himself would become evident by his own biased unprofessional conduct toward me, by allowing me to wait for over two hours without being properly interviewed. His personally ignoring me for over half an hour, yet running to the hospital to only interview Martin and Ohner. Then rushing back and immediately arresting me, having only bothered to speak to one side. Yet Simai and I had been conveniently waiting to see him right under his nose for hours!

The judge weighed in with his own set of hard questions and didn't look pleased at all with the responses. These state police were used to getting away with their questionable tactics. But most of their cases were against local drunks in state court, where the judges weren't even real lawyers. They had grown used to pretty much having their way there.

As for foreigners like myself, anything above a traffic ticket, had to be prosecuted in the FSM national court system. Here the courts were more sophisticated, with real lawyers for judges. A few Micronesian judges who were not law school graduates in the national system at least had full-time law graduates assisting them throughout the legal process. This system worked well down here. If I saw any major flaws with the national system, I'd be the first to complain, especially in this writing.

The state and municipal courts are another story that I could write quite a bit about, most of which would not be flattering. I've had experience in all three systems here with civil suits, as a witness, an expert witness, and now as a defendant, in seventy-five or eighty cases in all, maybe more.

When Mike presented our case I was on the stand quite a long time as I related events as I saw them, much as I've already stated. When it was the attorney general's time to cross-examine me, he asked the court if we could all go to the baseball field nearby for a demonstration. Judge King asked him what he intended to demonstrate. He wanted to hang a small metal trash can about head high and have me take a baseball swing at it with my stick. The judge didn't allow this, but he did have Martin and I stand together at the attorney general's request, to show the size difference. I was maybe thirty or more pounds heavier than Martin. I would guess I was maybe 180 pounds then and Martin was between 140 to 150 pounds.

The attorney general was trying to paint me as a big bully. I'd like to see him face someone with a knife or machete. I was just fortunate I had a stick with me to put out the fire. Otherwise I might have been *peleiuhk peseng* during Martin's initial anger over his yams, chopped into little pieces.

As the attorney general was bringing his cross-examination of me to a conclusion, he started getting excited and building his summation of this case up to a crescendo, just as Perry Mason used to do in that old TV series. I guess he was hoping I'd collapse on the stand and concede to his case. I just couldn't believe a real attorney would actually try this cornball tactic. As his voice got louder and picked up pace, I missed a couple of his words, so as he came to his climax, I thought *I'll fix him*! When it was my turn to give a one-word yes-or-no answer to this long, overdramatic question, I instead asked him a question. I asked him if he would please repeat his question, that I had missed a couple of his words.

He got quite upset with me and started whining to the judge that I was just messing with him, and to please instruct me to answer his question. I then spoke up to the court and basically said that my hearing had been somewhat ruined by twenty-four years of construction and heavy equipment noise and that I needed to be sure of every word of his, which was all true. The judge ruled in my favor. So he had to grudgingly repeat his question to me, but with nowhere near the same enthusiasm and luster as the first time around. When he was done, I quickly answered, "No!"

Simai, Casmira's housekeeper and Semens would all testify. I thought the housekeeper's testimony was crucial, but the court didn't seem to give it much credence.

On the third and last day of the trial, Friday, just before the two lawyers' final summation, the attorney general availed himself of his last opportunity to redirect questions to any of the witnesses. He called me back up to the witness stand. He intended to ask me some final questions and my lawyer wouldn't be able to respond by saying anything or question me to help qualify or clear up my answers. It was a legal trick to try to leave a final impression in the minds of a judge or jury, especially if he thought he had anything damaging against me.

He had a trap laid for me. He reviewed my testimony the previous day, when I'd testified that I had swung my stick at Martin five times trying to knock the machete out of his hand. Then he directed me to the statement I had given and signed after my arrest by Francisco Joseph. In it I had written that I had swung my stick ten or twelve times. The attorney general was now insinuating that in my court testimony, I tried to soften the beating I gave to Martin, which included blows to the head. He wanted to hear me get out of this, hoping he had me trapped in a lie.

I was stunned at first. I hadn't remembered writing down ten or twelve swings. Then it instantly came back to me. On the first statement I was counting my backswing as a separate swing. So now I went into more detail on this issue, which I hadn't previously.

I explained pretty much as follows," now two months after the fight, some of these events were much clearer in my mind. This was one. I had five forehand right swings at Martin's machete, thus also five defensive backswings, making a total of ten swings, not twelve. My backswings were to present a defensive wall until I could set to deliver a more powerful fore swing." I explained that "in trial testimony, I had only counted the more powerful fore swing as a swing—again, aimed at Martin's machete. They were the ones that did the damage. The backswings were to prevent Martin from having time to lung in and stab me, which he could have done if I'd just drawn it back as if resetting to swing a baseball bat. As for the injury to the back of Martin's head, I had never hit him in the head. I probably could have on any fore swing, but I was going for the machete, not his head. He probably hit the back of his head on a rock when he fell. Martin also never turned his back to me at any time, so that I could have hit him there. Martin fought me face-to-face, man-to-man, and never turned away. Even when he went down, he continued to sit up, attempting to continue the fight." I was paying Martin a big compliment here. I could find reasons to respect Martin in this whole affair. I couldn't find any reasons to do the same for the detectives. The attorney general may have been finished with me, but not with his redirect questions. Next he called Ohner Weital back to the stand.

Up to this point, ever since the detectives' conduct entered into the record, the judge appeared to be rather critical of the prosecution's case. Also my lawyer had never challenged that Ohner hadn't been present at or witnessed the fight or sought to impeach him for three conflicting statements, two under oath. This was despite the fact that Martin had testified that Ohner was not there, and I testified that I didn't see him or know where he was. I also testified that I only saw Ohner after the fight, as I was leaving the trail just before reaching the road and he was entering the trail from the road.

With Ohner on the stand again, the attorney general only asked him two yes-or-no questions. He showed him the statement he'd signed the day of the fight and asked him if was true, as he'd already testified a couple of days ago, that he saw this fight. Ohner answered yes without much hesitation. Then he asked him if it was true, as he stated in his signed statement, that he never saw Martin threaten me. With a bit of hesitation, Ohner answered affirmatively, appearing a bit troubled but answering in a way that was consistent with his first signed statement, which wasn't given under oath.

To me, this was the most damaging testimony of the trial, given that the court didn't seem to react to the housekeeper's testimony. Mike continued to downplay this problem, but I wasn't buying it now. It was too late anyhow. All that was left was final summation, which didn't take long. It was late Friday afternoon, sometime after 5 PM and the trial had lasted three days. I was exhausted.

Judge King stated that he'd pretty much made his decision, that he could render a verdict right then. But he said he wanted to think about it over the weekend and would issue his verdict on Monday morning. Over the weekend, I couldn't stop thinking about Ohner's last answer. By Sunday night I had myself convinced that if I were the judge and neither side had bothered to impeach Ohner and both lawyers conceded to Ohner's presence at the incident, Ohner's last "yes" was extremely crucial evidence.

I was then convinced that I was going to jail again. Not just any jail, but a truly lousy one. Plus, assault with a deadly weapon carries a maximum of ten years. Here they can make you do it all, no parole and no good time. I was already preparing myself for the worst that could happen.

The courtroom was packed on Monday for the verdict. Judge King stated that on Friday, after all the police misconduct; he was ready to find me innocent right then. But after thinking all weekend about Ohner's final statement, that he was present and never saw his uncle threaten me, I must've initiated the altercation. He then ruled that Martin hadn't made an initial threatening overt move in my direction as I'd testified. He found me guilty of assault with a deadly weapon and launched into a one—or two-minute condemnation and scolding of me. Then he launched into a five—to ten-minute scolding, quite severe, of the detectives' role in all of this, especially their multiple threats against Ohner, even right in the courtroom, their unprofessional conduct, and so forth . . . Having a front row seat to this and the officers' reactions was almost worth the conviction.

I wasn't surprised by this outcome. My federal prison experience had allowed me to observe, concerning others and myself, that justice many times doesn't prevail, but the more experienced attorney does. It's a system that wants to win, its participants just paying lip service to justice. This was long before the advent of DNA testing, which dramatically exposed many of the flaws with men's imperfect judicial systems and all the revelations that followed.

Mike should have taken Jim Hagistrom up on his offer and been prepared to impeach Ohner, relying on the truth to come out rather than trying to work with a lie. Better to have gone down with the truth. Judge King then allowed two weeks for a probation report to be prepared, after which a sentencing hearing was scheduled.

During this two-week period a lot happened. Mike felt so bad that for days he was holed up in his house, which was about sixty yards from my house. I didn't even notice him going to his office. But he wasn't idle. He was busy researching, preparing for an appeal. Also, he was so disgusted with events of this incident that he felt he couldn't practice law in Micronesia, and he began to make plans to return to the United States to practice law. He was right. Despite his rookie mistakes, it's difficult to practice law when you're dealing with de facto banana republic government agencies.

A day or two after being found guilty, Semen came to me saying his sixteen-year-old son Steve said to him, "Ohner really lied!" The day of the fight, Steve had been in that vicinity planting trees. We had never seen him that day, so afterward being so busy; no one had thought to question him. Ohner and Martin had not mentioned him, even though they had seen him. Steve had attended every day of my trial, quietly listening but not talking to anyone. After the trial when he finally said that Ohner lied, Semen asked him why he said that.

Steve then told him that he was standing in a thicket of dense trees and bush, just off the east side of the pipeline road, and watched as Simai and I drove by, stopping about fifty yards past him. He quietly watched as I got out and then talked to Ohner while inspecting the hole he had been digging. He then saw Simai and me return to the truck to get something and then hurry into the jungle off to the west side of the road, a short distance behind the truck. Ohner then walked to my truck and began eating a mango, casually looking around, oblivious to where Simai and I had gone. About a minute after going into the jungle, Steve saw Simai run out of it and back to the truck. Ohner then started to hurry toward the trail and into the jungle. A few seconds later, I ran out, obviously passing Ohner near the entrance of the trail, just as I had testified. Thus Steve told his father that there was no way Ohner could have been 150 feet down the trail to witness the fight. He was eating a mango by the truck when it occurred.

He then saw my truck reverse north past him, while he was still concealed among the trees and brush. Shortly, Martin and Ohner came out onto the road, walking toward him. He then came out onto the road and approached them. Ohner was upset, venting threats that he was going to get his gun and shoot me. As they were approaching Ohner's house, rather than going seventy-five feet west to it, they started going east toward the hospital. The three of them traveled together about a mile to the sawmill. Ohner and Martin then continued another mile further east to the hospital to get Martin's arm attended to.

Steve's comments about Ohner's threats verified the wisdom of my leaving the scene immediately, without rendering assistance; otherwise, I probably would have had to fight Ohner too. My being his boss would mean nothing when he saw his uncle's injuries and blood.

Oftentimes, if someone here accidentally hits someone with his car, for instance, near the home of the victim, the person might not dare stop to render assistance. This if for fear they'll be gang beaten by the irate family of the victim. Instead, they'll flee the scene, call the police, or proceed to the station to report it personally, primarily for their own safety.

When we reported Steve's story to Mike, he immediately saw it as new evidence and grounds for a new trial or appeal. Mike then informed me that the police tampering with the witness, as agents of the State, was grounds for a mistrial. Also, when you considered that Ohner told three variations of the events, the last under duress, Mike found it hard to believe that the court could have considered anything he said at all. Ohner had the location of the fight wrong, I'd said I didn't see him there, Martin had testified that he wasn't there! Only the attorney general and Mike by his silence, were akowledging that Ohner had been there, but neither of them was present either. This all seemed like a nightmare to now try to sort out. I couldn't believe how exhausting the first trial had been.

During this two-week period before sentencing, the thing that was the most awkward for me was dealing was the court's ombudsman, who was conducting the probation report. His name was Nikontro Johnny, and I had known him since 1970. He was the first Micronesian man that I had started a Bible study with when I was active in the ministry. With him now thinking I was guilty, I felt I was bringing reproach on God's name, even though I wasn't a Jehovah's Witness at this time. I still cared about God's name.

I was preparing for the worst, but I didn't want to do time in the Ponape State jail. It was right in the heart of Nett where I had made so many enemies, that I was concerned that someone would kill me in this jail. So Mike started making requests to the court to send me to Kosrae, three hundred miles to the southeast, if I was to do time.

I'd already decided what I was going to do there to kill time. I'd start writing this book. I felt that my connection to the assassination of Martin Luther King was a story that needed to be told one day. It would end up being postponed another twenty five years. Just as well, because other developments connected to the assassination were yet to develop. I will relate them shortly.

At the sentencing hearing Judge King scolded me some more, and then he sentenced me to one day in jail and eighteen months of probation. That was a big relief. Then he launched into another enjoyable condemnation of the detectives' conduct in this whole affair. *A fitting end to all of this,* I thought.

In some ways it had been a victory for our claims over the Etscheit estate, the FSM court reinforcing the quiet title action trial results. Even the state attorney general had told Martin and Masao Sultan to sign a lease or face prosecution for trespassing. This should have been a big wake-up call to the state police, who had for almost a decade been ignoring the Etscheits' property rights. That's what had led to all of this in the first place.

To seek a mistrial, new trial or appeal would mean continued legal attacks against Ohner and Martin. I wanted to patch things up with them. I decided that that was more important than clearing my name. Besides, one day in jail is a lot easier than going through another trial again. This would end up being the best choice, as far as my relationship with Ohner and Martin, my newest and bestest relative is concerned. Doing that would probably also save Ohner, and especially Steve, from another beating by the police. Steve already had a previous run-in with Francisco a year before when he was fifteen years old. When brought in for questioning in that unrelated incident, Francisco had beaten Steve to the point that he had to be admitted to the hospital. That probably accounted for his reluctance to speak up sooner.

I forget how long we had to appeal, but we'd keep our options open and let the detectives sweat it out as long as possible. They were already scrambling to deal with Steve's revelations. They were now accusing him of lying to save me, and that I was orchestrating it. They were also threatening to prosecute Ohner for his perjury, his multiple conflicting statements. They now wanted him to admit that I had put him up to it or else he'd go to jail. Apparently one day in jail wasn't enough for these detectives; they were still after me.

Mike saw this continuing conduct of the police as additional grounds for an appeal. After all, Ohner was the State's primary witness against me and even they thought he was a perjurer. To cover their tracks I heard they transferred Nero, their biggest liability, to some godforsaken outpost on one of the outer island atolls where he couldn't be subpoenaed easily. These places were usually alcoholically dry, a fitting punishment for him. The longer he stayed there, the better. I didn't see him for four or five years, until he came to the sawmill one day and asked to borrow $150. Wanting to restore relations with him too, I gave him the loan. He never paid it back. Years later I would even try to help Francisco, giving him a lot of free landfill material he was seeking, only charging him a modest trucking fee. It was probably the best deal I had ever offered to anyone here. I truly wanted to patch things up with all these people. I was pleased when I could see that my efforts toward Francisco had a visible softening effect on him toward me. By then he had been promoted to police chief. Unfortunately, this would not last long, as Francisco would pass away early.

I didn't wait too long to report to the jail; I wanted to get it over with. I went prepared this time, taking a futon mattress with a pillow and sheets, mosquito spray, ice cooler, drinks, and bags of goodies. By then I knew how to go to jail! I made some new friends there and saw some old ones. Uber Primo, the guy who tried to kill me with a knife on New Years Day 1982, welcomed me into his area. It was a room with about six beds off the floor, a much better place to sleep than my two previous stays. There was even decent entertainment. One guy was surprisingly good at singing and playing the guitar.

Another inmate there, Antonio, had been convicted of murder years before. He began pouring his heart out to me, saying that he'd been manipulated by these detectives into signing an inaccurate confession and had about fifteen to twenty-five years left to do, saying he just felt hopeless. He ended up crying like a baby to me, he was so distraught. I felt sorry for him, but there wasn't anything I could do, except commiserate with him about the detectives.

Eventually Antonio began studying the Bible with one of the Witness missionaries, Neal Maki. It was usually held once a week in the afternoon at the jail. One day at this time, one of the Witness traveling overseers was arriving, so Neal had to cancel the study to pick this man up at the airport that day.

At this particular time, a man we knew as one of the more potentially dangerous squatters on the Etscheit land entered the jail with a rifle. He began to call out several prisoners' names while keeping one or more unarmed correctional officers at bay. At one point he fired one or more shots at an officer but missed. Antonio then grabbed the rifle barrel and as they struggled, two shots went off killing him. Uber jumped in and wrestled the guy down until officers could react. The officers took all the credit.

A reliable source close to us with prior knowledge of parts of these events, led me to believe that this was the beginning of a coup attempt, prompted by the Etscheit land dispute. It also involved the 'prominent Ponapean man' whom I'd previously identified by those terms. This occurred about the time a lot of talk was circulating about Pohnpei seceding from the FSM. I'd always thought these guys might be stupid enough to try something like this. Yet I believed they'd muff it up somehow if they ever tried. Sure enough, it appears they did.

More than a dozen years before this killing, in late 1982, I had put this man on my list of future killers. This was after the recently hired head of the FSM police force, Joe Race, came speeding up to my house one day to warn me about this man. He informed me that he and some of his officers had just made a marijuana bust on the Etschiet land by the Lewi River, on a spot this man was claiming. As they stood by his small farmhouse and his officers removed the marijuana, this man spent the whole time venting threats against me. Joe said he also felt so personally threatened by this man's rants against me that he stayed at least ten away from this man, with his hand on his gun and the safety off. Two years later when I first talked to the nahnken at his house, this man was one of the two guys that held guns on me from behind.

Back to work at the sawmill, Semen didn't want me up in the mountains where I could be a target for another incident like the previous one. These types of injuries, micronesian on micronesian violence, occur most every week on Pohnpei and most times the police don't even do anything. They only made a big deal over my incident with Martin because I was white and Francisco had it in for me over the Etscheit land.

So I concentrated on construction projects and Semen handled all logging. I had to play it safe, as I'd be on probation for eighteen months and couldn't risk another incident. I would from then on try to always take one of my employees with me, one who could be a corroborating witness should I run into a troublemaker somewhere. Most of the time, it would be Casmira. We were inseparable much of each day, her accompanying me most places. We'd usually go out for lunch every day aswell.

A month or two later, I'd even hire Martin Etnolt. He would end up being one of my most versatile employees. He had previously been an experienced ship's crane operator, unloading cargo out at the docks.

He would eventually run one of our two sawmills, handling lumber sales if Casmira and I were gone. If we were off island traveling, he'd be totally in charge. Later when acquiring more heavy equipment, he would be one of my dump truck or Cat loader operators. He was my primary hydraulic boom truck and cement truck operator, plus he ran other equipment. He also acted as my go-between when we sought to settle the still ongoing land dispute with some of the older squatters. Martin would be with me for about fifteen years until his early death in 2001, from sugar diabetes. Living with another felony conviction, was worth the peace with Martin Etnolt.

Chapter 28

Hawaii Beach House, Tennessee Attorney General

Between 1986 and 1987, most trespassers had given up and left using the land and began homesteading land in other areas, some as far away as Kitti municipality. Only two families continued using the land, living in the former grassland areas across from the SDA School. These areas were beginning to have trees grow, now that Carlos was not burning the area every dry season. Through Martin, these people had been informed of our intentions to eventually work through Iso Nahnken to make provisions so they could stay. This would be conditional on several things, besides the nahnken's participation.

To start with, Robby getting his title once the partition case was settled between the Etscheit heirs. Also, these people could not be a party to inviting or assisting any new people in any way from entering this land. They also couldn't expand their claims or land use beyond three acres. All were already beyond that; they would have to cut back. They would also have to provide litigation support for us against any new ones who may enter. And they couldn't tell any lies whatsoever. Plus, the three acres might not be where they were claiming now, as we wanted to have no more than two contiguous groups of these parcels, not scattered about like postage stamps over eight hundred acres.

We already knew who might qualify, having recently deposed all of them. So they were pretty much locked into certain claims. Plus, we had the aerial surveys, which didn't lie. In addition, there were my investigations, as I'd interviewed more than a hundred people, one as far away as Chuuk Lagoon (Formerly Truk Lagoon).

Semen had done a great job. When he'd encounter a person, which was seldom, he would inform them that this was Etscheit property. I never heard of any arguments or confrontations. His oldest son Tio, who was not quiet eighteen yet, was working with us also. Semen by just being up there working most every day, convinced many people to give up and go work somewhere else off the Etscheit estate. But this cost him the hatred of many of these people and their other sympathizers in Nett and elsewhere.

In 1986, Tio and a sixteen-year-old companion were murdered one night in Kolonia, stabbed to death. The killer was none other than Uber Primo. Uber was the one who almost stabbed me with the same knife in that previous New Year's day, 1982 fight that I had with him and seven other of his relatives. Afterward, many in Nett would tell Semen that this was a revenge killing for his part in helping the Etscheits with their land problems.

Going forward twenty years to 2004, I'm living in a new house I'd built for Casmira on a choice parcel her mother gave her. It was just before the Village Hotel. We're sort of in the country here, the houses are far apart. Our nearest neighbors west of us are about two hundred yards away, a group of about four houses. That's where I had the peace ceremony with Uber in 1982. One of Casmira's sisters is married to Uber's brother, so he's another one of my relatives now. I sure have a lot of them; I have no idea who most of them are yet. Extended family is still very important to Micronesians.

Uber would do eighteen years in jail for those murders. Out by 2004 and back home, he's been trying to work and make changes in his life. As a reinstated Jehovah's Witness as of 1996, I occasionally conducted a Bible study with him. He's been to the Kingdom Hall a few times with my family. He wasn't immediately successful at turning his life around, but he was slowly trying.

In 2008 we would discuss those murders. Uber would claim that the incident involved Kolonia gang activity and was not related to the Etscheit land. He wouldn't convince me though, because he did have powerful reasons not to do so. I did see him just before those killings in a possible gang fight though, shortly after our incident on New Year's Day 1982.

It occurred as I was walking to a restaurant for dinner three blocks away from my house. As I came upon a crowd of people, I saw Uber and another man from U Municipality begin fighting with some Kolonia Town residents. Uber's companion was none other than the now former police officer that I had previously seen with a gang, beating a drunk in front of the store across the street from my house in Kolonia on a Sunday afternoon. This prompted me at the time, to report this incident directly to the governor at his residence. It may very well have been my report that resulted in this man now being a former police officer.

As these two fought against superior numbers, I watched from about twenty feet away as Uber picked up a rock and threw it as hard as he could, hitting one guy in the head and knocking him out cold. I thought to myself that Uber was certainly one of the most dangerous men on Ponape and that it was just a matter of time before he killed someone.

Through the years as Robby and I would file trespassing lawsuits that would affect hundreds of people, I would identify four other people, besides Uber, that I thought would resort to murder one day.

As time passed I would unfortunately be correct. Four of these five have now committed murder. Even Uber would agree with me that two of the other killings, other than his two, were over the Etchiet land. The police of course, never linked any of these four killings to our land problems. Only one of these killers did not have a link to the Etschiet Estate. It would involve a man I only came in close proximity to during our road-building activity.

The majorities of our road projects were in Sokehs Municipality and were FSM-sponsored projects. Occasionally we would do projects directly for Sokehs Municipal Government. They got their money from the Pohnpei state government, who got it from the FSM government, who got it from the US government. It took a lot longer to receive payment from them, and it necessitated numerous follow-up visits to that municipal office.

The municipal police chief was a small man who appeared to be full of pride, also openly frustrated and unable to control his visible emotions. He appeared jealous that I was there to collect large amounts of money, or that I was there with one of the most beautiful women on island, Casmira—probably both. I'd never had any dealings with this man or even spoken a word to him, but his total lack of control over his visible emotions gave me the creeps. I could see something dangerous in him and was prompted to put him on my mental list of potential killers. This man's greed and mean spirit would eventually get him removed from his position with Sokehs Municipality, for good cause. He would then move to the United States, along with many other Micronesians seeking better employment opportunities. He settled in Neosho, Missouri, among a group of about six hundred others from various islands through-out Micronesia. Some were his close relatives.

In August 2007, he would rape twice, a fourteen-year-old family friend while she cleaned his bedroom. His relatives, members of a small Micronesian church, castigated him for this. If he had done this in Ponape, nothing would have happened to him at all. But feeling humiliated by these men daring to reprimand him, two days later he entered their Sunday service and shots three of them to death, wounding four others and holding fifty hostages. In March 2009, Eiken was sentenced to three life sentences without parole, four thirty-year sentences for the assaults, and two seven-year sentences for the rapes, all to run consecutively. During a victim impact statement, one of the grieving widows that knew him stated before all in the court, "You are a greedy, jealous man!" Fifteen years earlier, I had recognized the danger of these traits in him, just by looking at him.

Sometime in mid-2008, Uber suffered a stroke that left him bedridden, unable to walk at all and unable to talk clearly either. A resurgent alcohol problem after his release from eighteen years in prison had led to his deteriorating health. Because of this problem, we hadn't studied for a while, but he sent word asking me to come see him. He wanted to resume his Bible studies. Because I could only understand about one out of every fifth word he spoke, I just read to him selected Bible stories directly from the scriptures. He enjoyed it so much that he begged me to come twice a week.

I'd read to him the story of Joseph, the books of Ruth and Ester, plus others. As I read, his face would light up like a child's, and he'd excitedly try to recap the story back to me, even though I could hardly understand a word of his. But it didn't matter, because I was just moved by the power of God's word, and how it could draw out this side of him, a man who had been one of Ponape's most prolific killers.

This went on for several months. As I finished reading Ester, I had a feeling that Uber didn't have much time left. I then read to him several scriptures about the resurrection hope, which is to occur during Christ's kingdom's reign, still yet to start in the near future. Two days later, Uber suffered a fatal stroke. Because of his notoriety and numerous relatives, about two thousand people attended his funeral. While there, I felt I had had a unique experience that few have seen, starting twenty-six years before. I had seen a killer at his very worst, coming within a fraction of a second from becoming his first victim. Then I saw him at his end, changed . . . and at his very best.

Previously, Iso Nahnken and I had reached a comprehensive written agreement. Both parties would honor this until late 1992. At that time Robby and the nahnken had a disagreement over an airplane ticket to Guam, and the whole thing unraveled. Shortly afterward, old and new squatters reinvaded the entire land again.

We sued over sixty family heads for trespassing. In depositions, they all claimed permission from the traditional leaders again. Because they were essentially making the same claim already adjudicated in the previous early 1980s case, it didn't even go to trial. We won a summary judgment motion against all these people for trespassing, prevailing in the following appellate process too. It took years though and cost a lot of money.

During this lengthy process, Robby bought a beach house on Kailua Bay in Kailua, Hawaii. I helped him pick it out and began planning to enlarge and remodel it. It was in such a nice area that later, at the end of 2008, President Obama would begin vacationing in a house nearby. There were maybe only four or five houses between the two. Robby wanted a big place where his European family could all meet and get together for visits away from the harsh German winters. They wanted to visit in a place with lots of shopping, restaurants, beautiful scenery, and beaches. That's Hawaii.

During the meantime, I'm busy not only with all these 'Trespassing' cases, but all the Civil Work on the Community College of Micronesia in Palikir, near the FSM capital. Working with our lawyer during the deposition/discovery process, I ask about 1/3 of the questions to these trespassers. Plus, I was the one who signed the legal complaint against each one. We also built some secondary roads and constructed an 18,000 square foot steel building for Robby and Tim McVey's True Value Hardware store in Kolonia.

In the evenings, I drew the plans for the Hawaii beach house renovation. Then I was referred to a Hawaiian draftsman/architect who took my plans, redrew them, and put in all the technical items to get it engineered and building permits issued in Hawaii. The permits were good for only six months. I had to start the project before the six months was up or go through the permit process all over again. So I took three of my construction workers to Hawaii to get it started in March 1994. We started working a day before the permit expired. My best Micronesian worker was left to finish the True Value Store. He'd join us later.

When he arrived, I then had four of them. This was their first trip anywhere on an airplane. They were all so excited that they couldn't wait to leave Ponape. Before long, most of them were so homesick that they were crying themselves to sleep at night.

The existing house was big, about fifty-five hundred square feet. We'd tear down half, live in the other half, and then vice versa. The house would end up having about eleven thousand square feet under roof, with seven bedrooms, seven bathrooms, two living rooms, two kitchens, and a large housekeeper quarters with a kitchenette.

The thing that was special about this house, though, was the standing seam copper roof we put on it. It's the only building I know of in Hawaii with an all copper roof, other than Bishop Museum on Oahu. We even bought a roll forming machine so we could make our own copper roofing and cut it to the exact length we needed.

In early 1995, while watching TV at night in Kailua, I saw a program about James Earl Ray. He was now claiming he didn't kill Martin Luther King, that he wasn't a racist and had never had any ill feelings toward Dr. King. It also claimed he hadn't ever made any threats against him or stalked him.

His spokesman was a lawyer, last name Pepper. The segment said this man was married to James Earl Ray's older or oldest sister. I was immediately wondering if this was the same sister who had visited Jodi Ray for his one and only visit while in Springfield. If she was, she was the likely source of relating the information to Jodi about James Earl Ray's intention of killing Dr. King. Given Springfield's strict mail censorship program, I could see no other way this information could have been related to him. Jodi had told me he hadn't had any contact with any of his family for years, except her.

As the TV program continued, Attorney Pepper was trying to cast blame toward other mysterious characters, painting James Earl as just a patsy. This was despite James Earl Ray's confession after his arrest, almost thirty years before. Now saddled with a life imprisonment sentence and a terminal disease, this appeared to be just an attempt to get James Earl released before his death. I also saw it as an attempt to draw attention away from family members and toward others, by presenting possible red herrings, not that there weren't other outsiders involved. But I do know that one family member knew about it, when he told me six and a half months before the assassination. And I personally believe other family members knew as well, from my understanding of the difficulties of information passing in federal prison, in that era over forty years ago.

This TV program went on to interview an assistant Tennessee State Attorney General, John Campbell. He was the one who spoke for that State's interest in opposing this release attempt, as the assassination had occurred in Memphis, Tennessee.

Despite this, I still felt I should call the FBI again. So I called the local Honolulu office, not the L.A. office. This time the receptionist at least connected me to an agent who listened to what I had to say for five or more minutes. He mentioned there might not be a response, but said he would pass the information on to his supervisor. That's the last I ever heard from them.

By mid-1995 with the house long since finished in Kailua, I was back on Ponape and it dawned on me one day: Why had I been calling the FBI? This was a Tennessee State murder case! I get the number for the Tennessee State Attorney General's office and called from my office at the sawmill. I informed the receptionist why I was calling and she connected me to John Campbell, the attorney general I saw interviewed on that TV program in Hawaii.

He was all ears, listened to everything I had to say and gave the call all the attention that I thought something involving Martin Luther King's case deserved. He had his investigator for this case interview me also. Due to James Earl Ray's attempt to seek release, the case was reopened and active. The investigator seemed skeptical at one point with my timeline, I don't know why, but in the end he asked if I'd be willing to be a witness should this current case go forward, which I agreed to.

The attorney general did tell me that they believed James Earl Ray did not act alone, that they were certain that there were still unidentified co-conspirators. He also told me that he wasn't aware that James Earl Ray had a much younger brother named Jodi, let alone one that had ever been in the Springfield Medical Center for Federal Prisoners. He said they'd look into it and get back to me.

Back in Pohnpei, the appeals of all those we sued for trespassing in 1992 and 1993 had been denied. During this lengthy legal process, the trespassers had violated numerous injunctions concerning inviting and assisting new ones onto this land and planting new crops, plus killing any of our trees, big or small. They pretty much ignored every single one of these injunctions and removed most of our forests, loading the land with their crops, including marijuana, rendering it useless for our ultimate purposes. This would have been ecotourism, which was to include walking and riding trails throughout our forests and on up to a magnificent waterfall, Liduduhniap, a quarter mile away from our upper boundary on the lewi river on public land. That's why we had only logged a few trees per acre. In the rain forest here, there might be two or three young trees sprouting in every square foot of land. So I would estimate the number of trees illegally killed by these people would be in the tens of millions.

The biggest problem now was these people just wouldn't leave. They didn't care what the court's Judgment said. The state police and state attorney general flatly refused to enforce the FSM court's judgment as well. Most of these new trespassers were young marijuana-growing toughs. They banded together and made blood oaths that they'd fight and die before ever leaving this land, while high on marijuana, sakau and alcohal. They openly let it be known that they would kill any police that tried to remove them. They even vowed to kill the nahnken, should he act to remove them. I heard this personally from two of these people on separate occasions. Local state politicians were getting involved too, threatening through the coconut telegraph that Pohnpei would secede from the union of FSM states and become independent, all because of this land, it appeared.

So much happened that I could write another book about it. There were numerous threats to attack us, some right in the courthouse. There were two unbelievably vicious attacks on our Japanese Pohnpei pepper plantation partners, an old retired Japanese couple. They were living on the plantation, surrounded by the worst of the worst of these people. In the first of these attacks, one of the more threatening and vicious of these new squatters knocked out cold our Japanese partner. Mr. Nabishima was in his mid to late seventies! The coward who did this was trespassing right next to Mr. Nabishima's house, when he started beating his two chained-up dogs for barking at him as he passed by and Mr. Nabashima protested. A complaint was filed and this man was eventually found guilty by a state court judge, but only given a suspended sentence and probation. This kind of watered-down justice was considered nothing by these Ponapeans, and it only emboldened them and others to continue their trespassing, threats, violence, and destruction of our property. A short time later, this man and another actually laid siege to Mr. Nabishima's house late one night while drunk. For about forty minutes, they terrorized Mr. and Mrs. Nabishima, screaming death threats and throwing rocks at their house, trying to break into it with them inside. Plus they slaughtered their two chained-up dogs with machetes this time. They would have probably done the same to the Nabishimas, had they been able to get into the house. Despite still being on probation for that first assault on Mr. Nabishima, and a trespassing judgment against him for even being on this land, a different judge again let him off with just a scolding, some toothless restrictions, and no jail time.

Many of these squatters around and among the pepper plantation had actually been Mr. Nabishimas's employees since the projects started in late 1989. Then in late 1992, the traditional leaders in Nett declared that the Etscheits' land was now theirs again. This time though, they included the statement that all the land in Nett belonged to them as well.

So one day Mr. Nabishimas's employees show up for work and declare that they now own the land the plantation is on—that the nahnken had given it to them. Some of them then built houses right amidst its crops. Mr. Nabishimas's attacker was not one of these employees but one of the many other new squatters who then reinvaded the Etscheit estate with the traditional leaders' permission. I first saw this man clearing land just to the north of the pepper plantation, about two month after this new invasion started.

I stopped my truck to inform him of his error. He approached me and considering the way he was carrying a three-foot piece of sharply pointed rebar, I was thinking this guy was going to try to run me through with it. I felt I could tell this just by looking at him. I seemed to have a gift for this ever since Springfield. I kept my truck in gear, foot on the clutch, waiting to see if he would actually try. When about five feet from me he spotted Semen in the passenger seat, then lowering his rebar he started talking to him. This incident prompted me to put him on my mental list of five future killers at the time. This man though, is the only one that hasn't killed yet, but it wouldn't be for a lack of trying when he attacked the Nabishimas' that night.

Except for Uber, all the other four were either cowardly back stabbers, gun down unarmed people, or only attack people in their seventies. I don't know how they can live with themselves.

For a long time I didn't send any of my workers up in our land, because I thought it was too dangerous. I didn't want to be responsible if one of them got hurt, because even some of them were being paid personal visits to be threatened by these people.

After first seeing this man who would eventually attack the Nabishimas's, killing our trees and clearing land, we had him and others in court in about two weeks. We were seeking a temporary injunction to put a stop to his and other trespassers' recent destructive activities. During the two-week period before having to appear in court, this man actually built a house right next to the pipeline road and now had his whole family moved in there. It was built on a lot that we had cleared a year before, which we used to stockpile our felled trees on when the weather was dry. We had eventually gotten to the point where we would only skid trees out of the forest when the land was dry, because we found that did significantly less damage to our forests. So in dry weather only, Semen would skid each tree out of the forest and park them on this cleared lot right next to the pipeline road. He could easily store twenty or more whole trees there if he needed to, or line them up single file along the side of the road in adjacent areas. Then when the rains started and everything was wet, he would skid them the final two miles down to our mill. This pipeline road was by far the best unpaved road on this island, made of heavy-duty hard-packed gravel. It never suffered any damage by our use over the years that we logged.

But at the temporary injunction hearing for this man, he testified that he and his family had been living in this house, on this location, for eleven years. Outrageous claims like this by even new trespassers, plus many others over the years, would consume a lot of Robby's money and my time. We had to respond and mount a legal defense to many of these types of claims.

Over my years with Robby, I would estimate that as much as one-third of my work time was spent as his private investigator for his land problems. This included working closely with his lawyer's throughout numerous meetings, hearings, depositions, and trials also.

One Saturday afternoon at our mill I talked to one husband and wife, whom we had a final judgment against, with their teenage son standing nearby. The son was off to my right about fifteen feet away. They were defiantly hanging around our construction area for no reason. As I talked to the parents, I kept track of their son out of the corner of my eye. A few years before when this teenager was only fourteen or fifteen, I had pegged him as one of the five people who I thought could murder one day.

Being alone this day, I reminded his parents that they were trespassing and should leave. Then I realized the son wasn't off to my right any longer. I quickly turned and caught him coming up ten feet behind me with an extremely sharp pointed hardwood stick in his hand.

Later in 2004 and now a young married man, this guy would stab to death from behind, one of Leo's store's oldest employees right in front of Ace Commercial store. This was after an incident in the parking lot, when he too reminded him that he shouldn't even be here, referring to the judgments against him and his family. I was fortunate that I knew better than to ever let this guy get behind me. This occurred on an Easter Sunday morning as this young man had been walking to church with his new wife. After the stabbing, they proceeded to a friend's house several hundred yards away, where he changed his bloody shirt. They then walked on to the Catholic Church a mile away in Kolonia, where he was arrested a short time later while attending Mass. Again, the State would not link this murder, the one at the jailbreak attempt and the two committed by Uber, to the Etscheit land problem.

This young man and his relatives and friends were originally from the Lewi River area just outside the southern boundary of the Etscheit estate. Some of the young people from this place were notorious for attacking others in gangs. One evening a group of them were drunk, making trouble in a bar near True Value Hardware store. When three police officers showed up expecting just another routine call, they were all jumped by these guys and ended up in the Pohnpei hospital. I remember the next morning as several carloads of state police sped through our sawmill area and up into our land, where these guys were also some of our squatters. This would be the only time the state police would remove any of our trespassers. But it was only until they made bail. Some things had changed at this time, making it more difficult for me to be involved in a potentially violent situation like this. For one, I was then over fifty and didn't feel as if I would survive another self-defense situation. Second, while in Hawaii doing the beach house, Casmira studied the Bible with the Witnesses and wanted to become one herself. So I returned afterward, getting reinstated as one again in late 1995.

So now I had to try to insulate myself from this impossible situation, leaving its resolution in the hands of the lawyers and avoiding any confrontational situations as best I could. From then on I didn't go up into the mountains except on two occasions, when the FSM court ordered FSM police to remove these people. The State refused to participate.

The national government brought FSM police in from the other island states, Yap, Chuuk, and Kosrae. I attended a meeting with one of our lawyers, the FSM attorney general, head of the FSM police, and a few others. The police were briefed and plans were made.

Every trespasser was to be removed, even if it took a couple of days, a lot of bold and tough talk by the authorities.

The next morning, seventy to eighty armed FSM police assembled at our sawmill. When they finally got to the first squatter house, some of our workers and I were hanging back by Ohner's house. He himself had been threatened and forced out of his home by these people. We were waiting to remove crops and each house as the people were taken into custody. This first house was right by where Martin Etnolt and I had fought more than ten years before, and which we had afterward leased to him. These people too had threatened Martin out also and he had to abandon his crops.

A few of my employees were with the police at the first squatter house and saw and heard everything. There were marijuana plants in plain view as the head of the FSM police started to execute the court order and instructions the previous day from his attorney general. This first trespasser started arguing his case. The guy spent fifteen or twenty minutes loudly presenting all the arguments that they had used in court, which already had been adjudicated in favor of the Etscheits in this present case and the previous one in the early 1980s.

This large police force was not sent here to hear these people's case; the judge had already done that. The plan was to move quickly along the road, making arrests, and get to the next house before warnings could be passed down the road and people become armed and prepared.

This plan was collapsing at the first house. The previously confident head of the FSM police now seemed to be realizing the potential for violence from these people, which I had tried to warn them about beforehand. Having now lost the element of surprise, he opted to play it safe and withdrew his forces. Similar later attempts to remove these people with a large force would fail as well. I was disappointed but also relieved, and I couldn't fault the FSM police for having reservations. This was a volatile situation and had only gotten worse, in my opinion, when our lawyer left the island the day before our permanent injunction hearing, due to a scheduling conflict with a Guam case. This was not Mike Berman who defended me in the Martin Etnolt case, but another lawyer who succeeded Mike. He had failed to properly brief a substitute attorney about the case and what needed to be done that day. Since we were seeking to change a temporary injunction to a permanent one, we had to do it that day or forfeit that right. That's what happened, and these people were allowed to stay during the lengthy legal process.

They were still subject to injunctions against planting any new crops or helping new people enter this land. These they violated every day. These injunctions were not enforced for several reasons, so these local farmers continued to invest their life's work in this land and were letting it be known they'd fight and die before ever leaving—that if we tried, they would kill us and any police sent to remove them. Some even again threatened to kill one of the Nett traditional leaders if he even ever tried to remove them.

These people were serious, especially as they were getting regularly tanked up on marijuana, sakau and alcolhol, plus whatever else they could get. Sympathetic local politicians were now getting involved, suggesting Pohnpei secede from the union of FSM States. This further empowered these people. They would additionally work themselves up while high or under the influence, making blood oaths to come to each other's aid and die together if need be. The situation was a powder keg now ready to go off.

Several times I had been to the US Embassy to brief them on many of these problems and see if there was anything they could do. They gave me a lot of sympathy, but that was about all. But just before two of these attempted surprise eviction raids by the FSM police, I made emergency appointments to see the US ambassador. I had to drive about a mile and a half around to get to this US Embassy, even though it was only about seventy yards from my house. I believe both times it was a women ambassador I spoke with on these occasions, although I've talked with so many there over the years that I really can't keep track of all my visits there. In one of these visits with a woman US ambassador, I could see my house out the window just behind her desk. I told her of our problems and said that I might be the target of a retaliatory attack starting as soon as the next night. I wanted to know if I would have the option to flee across the river at night with my family to the safety of the embassy.

She showed a lot of concern for our situation and let me know that predecessors had briefed her about this problem upon her arrival on island. But sadly, this embassy was so small that it was incapable of providing refuge, especially at night. They did have twenty-four-hour security, but they were unarmed and did not have the keys to the embassy, which was locked up after working hours. She informed me that most US embassies are guarded by armed US military personnel, but not here. Here they just use a local private security company and none of them are authorized to carry firearms. She said that I could find temporary refuge there during working hours in an emergency, but they had no facilities to house people.

I could easily see what she was talking about. Plus I knew it would be risky attempting to flee across a lot of open ground, cross a river, and then scramble up a steep twenty foot exposed embankment to the embassy, especially if under fire. Even if I made it, the Micronesian security guards there would probably scatter like cockroaches. I already knew that the best thing for me to do if under imminent threat would be to take my family to Awak, where they'd be safe, then return to stand by Robby's family. I couldn't abandon them.

Mr. Nabishima would be the first casualty of all this. He had gotten a one-million-dollar loan from a Japanese overseas development agency, JICA, to fund this pepper plantation. With his employees now robbing him blind, he couldn't make his loan payments within a short time. I would many times see these employees and other trespassers transporting or selling his pepper and vegetable crops in Kolonia, usually at restaurants where I was eating lunch. My complaints were ignored. Mr. Nabishimas's strict sense of Japanese honor had him returning to Japan to liquidate everything he had there, in a vain attempt to keep up with his loan payments. Pretty soon he was tapped out again and became ill from all this and had to return to Japan for medical attention, staying with his daughter. It wouldn't take too long before he would die there a broken man. His wife would continue to struggle for a long time to turn things around on the plantation. But she was facing an impossible situation and was eventually forced to return to stay with her daughter also.

Even now, over fifteen years since the start of this new invasion on the Etscheit estate, the squatter problem is still not resolved, and the land still overrun. In mid-1996 though, Robby was killed in a tragic accident with a forklift on his loading deck. His wife Agnes would inherit title to his land, the partition case being settled out of court shortly before his death. She would probably inherit more than any other woman in the history of Micronesia. Unfortunately, she would also inherit this land problem that was now seriously out of control.

Sometime earlier I had mentioned that there was an unofficial caste system here on island: Pohnpeians at the top, with outer islanders ranked below that, with Pingelapese at the bottom. Also that some Ponapeans are so jealous of others that they will actually go out of their way to bring people back down to their level or lower. I was told this in 1970, the first week after I first arrived on Ponape. Over the years I would witness many manifestations of this, although I will admit that it is improving as time goes by.

Agnes is a Pingelapese, and now as the largest single landowner on Pohnpei, her ownership would not be respected either. In fact, I was surprised by how many people made negative or resentful comments to me about it.

By the time Robby died, he and I had spent about seventeen years trying to finish what Leo had started, working through the government's legal systems. As for the FSM court, it performed as it should have, for the most part. But to begin with, this case was all about racism and jealousy at its core. These people just couldn't stand white people owning land in Ponape, especially so much, despite Robby being a naturalized Micronesian citizen as of 1978 or 1979. Now many couldn't stand an outer islander owning it for many of the same reasons.

This racism would also surface as many criticized and denigrated the judge, he being a Chuukese man. Now they couldn't stand that a Chuukese judge was deciding land ownership in Pohnpei. Long-standing animosity has existed between Chuukese and Pohnpeians. But this judge wasn't deciding land ownership. This was simply a bunch of trespassing cases. Ownership had already been reaffirmed by the Trust Territory High Court cases in the early 1980s. A big help to them at that time were all the legal documents, wherein the nahnkens's own father, the king of Nett at the time, Max Iriarte, negotiated the easements for the government to get the Etscheits' permission to put the pipeline and pipeline road across their land. That just spelled case over with for the present-day traditional leaders and all those claiming under them. It should also do the same for the State, claiming that this was a matter of custom and tradition. The 1980s case ruled against that claim as well. Do they think Max Iriarte violated the custom?

In addition, they had the 1971 land determination hearings, for which none of these present claimants even bothered to register a claim, despite public notices. They simply weren't there then.

Agnes seemed to have inherited an impossible situation. Robby and I had one or two legal moves left. Agnes would however, have her own ideas on how to solve this problem, now that she became the titleholder. Because of these still unresolved legal issues and other confidentiality concerns, it wouldn't be proper for me to comment on areas Agnes would like to remain confidential. She has her own ideas and a huge weight to bear, and I don't wish to interfere with her plans.

My final comments would be directed at Pohnpei State. It has the primary responsibility for protecting its citizen's private property through its police department and ever-changing attorney generals. The Pohnpei State Constitution espouses equality, all those noble-sounding ideals similar to the US constitution. Yet it has chosen to exclude the property rights of white citizens and their properly permitted foreign investors, despite the oaths of office they've taken to the contrary.

I'm the last to claim that I'm some sort of US patriot. But even I'm quite disgusted to see this state, which gets almost 100 percent of its operational funding from the US taxpayers, using that money to fund this outrageous example of racism. The State needs to wake up and stop using the lame excuse that it's a matter of "custom."

The United States, of course, doesn't have clean hands in regard to racism either, but they'll admit it. And we've all seen tremendous changes in this regard in the last forty years, thanks largely to Martin Luther King getting the ball rolling. Still, they haven't seemed to have made any progress in narrowing in on the co-conspirators involved with his assassination.

Going back to events in late 1996 or early 1997, this would become even more apparent to me about eight or nine months after first calling the assistant Tennessee attorney general. I hadn't heard anything from them, so I gave John Campbell a follow-up phone call from my office almost halfway around the world.

Mr. Campbell essentially told me the following, according to my recollection of the call. He said that upon calling the Medical Center for Federal Prisoners, they had been unable to verify that either I or a younger brother of James Earl Ray had ever done time there. He also said that they were unable to get any information at all from the US Federal Bureau of Prisons about either one of us. They thought that they knew all of James Earl Ray's brothers and that none of them had a name or nickname of Jodi, as far as they knew. Moreover, they didn't believe any of James Earl Ray's brothers had ever even been in Springfield Medical Center.

He did qualify his statement by saying that they could be wrong. He suggested the possibility that the Jodi I was speaking of could have possibly been a cousin or some other relative. Also, perhaps Jodi was not related at all but just happened to have the last name Ray and a few similar circumstances, which led me to believe that he was the youngest brother of James Earl Ray.

He questioned me if there was any other relevant information I could remember that I hadn't related to him during our first conversation or with his investigator. At that time I couldn't think of anything new or relevant. I thought I had been pretty thorough in my first conversation with the attorney general, I couldn't think of anything I'd left out.

Yet I was reeling from what he'd just told me. I was thinking, *How could I have been so sure for three decades? Could I have gotten this wrong?* After all, I was considering Mr. Campbell one of the world's foremost authorities on the assassination of Martin Luther King. He had to know a lot more about this case and James Earl Ray's family than I ever would. I was even feeling foolish, having called this man sounding so sure of myself.

I had to admit to myself that when Jodi first told me his oldest brother Jimmy was going to kill Martin Luther King, I had facetiously dismissed it in my own mind. I had said to myself, *Yeah, sure. He'd probably have to wait in a line with about ten thousand other racist southerners to be able to get a shot off!* I had believed, as many others did, that many racists from the south wanted Martin Luther King dead. That many would act if given the opportunity, and that it was entirely possible that a number of people with the last name Ray wanted Mr. King dead and would voice that desire. All these thoughts flashed through my head as I absorbed Mr. Campbell's words.

Mr. Campbell, though, would admit that there was a lot they didn't know, that they could be wrong. He encouraged me, saying that if I remembered anything else or learned anything new to please give him another call back. This second call occurred sometime in 1996. After the call, I couldn't stop thinking about the conversation and some of John Campbell's words. Could I have been mistaken for almost thirty years? Yet John had said they might be mistaken about a younger brother never being in Springfield. But I was wondering too, *How can they not find out this information and be sure? How can they not be able to get any information they want from the United States Federal Bureau of Prison, especially being a state attorney general, investigating in many people's opinions, the most high-profile civilian murder case in the history of the United States?* You would think they could get the highest cooperation imaginable, as fast as possible.

I knew from events a few months prior that I was in some kind of law enforcement database. I found this out when I went to Pennsylvania to pick up a concrete mixer truck, which I had specifically manufactured there. Since I was going to drive it across the country to the docks in Oakland, I was told I needed a commercial driver's license. So I thought I could just use my Pohnpei commercial license, which was also my regular license here, the one I also use when renting cars while on business trips back home in the United States.

In a previous renewal, the police department forgot to type in my commercial classifications. So just before the trip, I had the traffic division here correct this error and reissue it. Our licenses here are rather spartan, just heavy paper. For every new license lately, I'd just recycle my old picture, the one I had taken in 1983 at the college when I first met Casmira. Leaving that day for the trip, I hurriedly glued my old picture to the renewed license, which is what we normally did. I then had it sealed in plastic at a local hardware store. Some of the contact cement was oozing out under the side of the picture.

Then off Casmira and I went sometime in September 1995, looking forward to our first cross-country drive across the United

States. Arriving in Los Angeles, I used the license to rent an Alamo car and drove to Las Vegas, where I was buying some rock crusher equipment in nearby Boulder, Nevada. Then flying to Pittsburgh, we picked up the truck in nearby Indiana, Pennsylvania, and started our cross-country trip in a cement truck, after a tour of the factory.

This was a nice diversion to our usual routine on a small isolated island. I was however, having a problem figuring out the truck scales crossing state to state. Every one seemed different. There are none here on island. I had slopped out so far, until crossing Utah to Nevada, where I goofed up and got red-lighted. A speakerphone ordered me to park nearby and then cross over Highway 80 on a pedestrian bridge to their office, bringing all my paperwork.

When the officer saw my Pohnpei driver's license, he apparently was sure he'd caught a live one. He called in some off-duty reinforcements and the drug-sniffing dog. Casmira and I were detained for several hours while these authorities carefully examined everything. One off-duty officer that had been called in just to question me claimed that my driver's license looked like the worst forgery he had ever seen. Being older, he had apparently seen quite a few. I agreed with him that it looked bad, but that it was par for the course in Pohnpei and was a perfectly legitimate license.

He left me for a long time and when he returned, he told me he had just called the Pohnpei police department and had spoken with the police chief, Joe Roby, whose signature appears on the license.

Fortunately for me, Joe Roby was among the few Pohnpei state police officers that I've had consistently good relations with over the previous twenty years. As the new police chief then, he was unable to change the State's policy toward the Etscheit land. When Joe became the police chief, we had already initiated more than sixty-some civil actions in the FSM court and were in the midst of that process. Yet he would go out of his way to try to maintain the peace on our land during this lengthy process. I'm pleased to say that under his leadership, there have been many positive improvements with the state police right up to the present day.

So my interrogator acknowledged that Joe Roby had verified his recent signature on my license, and that I was a heavy equipment contractor on Pohnpei and would have all these commercial categories. But this officer would then tell me that an out-of—country commercial license is not valid in the United States when used for commercial purposes.

Then he went on to question me about my felony conviction. Even he had been able to get information on that, then almost thirty years later. He asked what it was for, so his information was limited. So later when John Campbell told me he couldn't get information, I was wondering if it was just that he couldn't get specific information.

I was let go on a technicality because the bill of sale was in my name—and so was the temporary registration. Thus not being in active commercial use, but for private transportation and sightseeing, they could accept my out-of-country license. We were allowed to continue our cement truck vacation.

So some information is out there. But I'm shocked that any state can't get information on any criminal, in any investigation, much less a high-profile case like seeking justice for Martin Luther King! As time passed, I couldn't get this issue out of my head. I needed to get more information, to resolve this mystery about Jodi Ray, so I could put it to rest for my own peace of mind.

I couldn't get information here on Pohnpei. I'd have to wait for a future lengthy trip to the States to try to see what I could find in a library. So that was about all I could figure to do, since I didn't have a computer and knew nothing about the Internet. I would wait almost four years for this opportunity.

Chapter 29

Researching the Rays

I was busy in Pohnpei setting up our own rock crusher and quarry operation, adjacent to our sawmill area. We were intending to make rock road base for our road-building operation. This became necessary because we couldn't get a coral dredging permit after we sued the State over that Army Corp of Engineers permit. Yet four or five other Micronesian-owned companies, all new ones, managed to get them. We were turned down for a permit three times. More racism again! Even Peter Cristians family's construction company was able to continue dredging. I was never even able to collect our monetary judgment from the State, on behalf of our company.

During this period is when I was reinstated as a Jehovah's Witness again. My biggest concern was that once active in the door-to-door ministry, I didn't want some squatter I sued attacking me and perhaps injuring some other innocent Witness that may be accompanying me that day. So I told our missionaries, who are the elders in our small congregation here, that I didn't want them sending me anywhere in Nett Municipality as a precaution. They agreed.

One of them, Neal Maki from Hawaii, took me with him on a Wednesday evening, my first return to the public ministry in more than fifteen years. There were a few in the group and the missionaries selected an area near town that they believed was part of Kolonia. But there were no clearly marked municipal or village boundaries on this island then. I however, knew where they were. They apparently didn't.

Neal took the group to Dolonier, thinking it was part of Kolonia. Dolonier had the biggest concentration of people we sued. On top of that, he parked the car we were in right next to the King of Nett's house. Well I didn't want to rain on their parade and cause a big disruption to the late afternoon's plan, so I kept my mouth shut. But I had already made up my mind; I would not be defending myself if threatened in the ministry. I'd been too successful at it and had caused too much damage in the past. I would die first. I might run, depending on the situation.

To start, Neal selected the house across the street from where we parked. Great! It was the house of two guys I'd sued and dragged through court, the Neor brothers. Previously when I had first seen them from a distance burning our land and approached, they had driven me away with gun fire. Now I was hoping they wouldn't recognize me dressed up, out of my usual shorts, tank top, tennis shoes, with short hair also. As we approached, three guys were in an outdoor open sided cooking shed that just had a beat-up corrugated tin roof. One of them was one of the Neor brothers, and I could see that my outfit wasn't fooling him. He was curious though, and politely offered us to sit down. They didn't have any chairs, just small chunks of firewood to sit on. So I sat on a small piece about six inches high. I was low and being over fifty then, there was no way I could spring up and move quickly if I had to from this position.

One of the guys was small, in his twenties, and looked as if he might possibly be mentally challenged. He was sort of serving or running errands for the other two and it seemed they'd been preparing to start the sakau process. The young guy was holding a machete next to me as the three of them listened as Neal started to talk.

Neal introduced himself and then me as Steve. The guy with the machete said excitedly, "What!" Neal repeated himself. The guy then quickly said, "You mean Robby's Steve!" He was now enraged and raised his machete to a position to take my head off, standing right above me. I had pitied this guy when I first saw him, knowing he'd never amount to anything in this society. As he was threatening me, part of me was instantly rooting for him—that if I was ever going to be sawn asunder by a Nett machete one day, let it be from him. At least he could be a hero in Nett and a "somebody" for a change here. This would probably be his only opportunity.

After a tense second or two the Neor brother interceded, barking at the guy to put his machete down, saying "Steve didn't come to make trouble but to talk about the word of God!" Neal was able to continue but when finished, he appeared a bit shaken as we walked away. I then told him that this is Nett, and that was the king of Nett's house right there, pointing to the house beyond our vehicle. Like many others, he just wasn't aware of some municipal boundaries.

After my first two phone conversations with John Cambell, I went on other trips to the States for business. But with Casmira accompanying me and business finished, we were in a hurry to get back home to our kids. I hadn't yet taken the time to do any research into the assassination of Martin Luther King and James Earl Ray's family.

In 1998, Agnes wanted me to build a multiplex movie theater. It was to be a joint venture between her and Wallace Movie Theater Corporation, a US-based theater chain. They had theaters throughout the mid to western United States and all the islands of Hawaii and other Pacific Islands. In a rush to get it opened before the end of the year for the holiday season, we'd open with a temporary jeri-rigged air-conditioning system and no toilets installed yet. If someone had to "go," they'd have the option to be sent off into the jungle next to the theater. Only in Pohnpei could we get away with this.

I got all the toilets installed in a few days, but it would take months for the permanent air conditioners to arrive. When I finally had them installed, I was free to take some time off. So in Mid-May of 1999, I took Casmira and our kids for our first family vacation back to the United States. My parents had retired to Morro Bay, California, and from there we were on the go in a rented Alamo Astro Van for five weeks. We even drove as far as Minnesota.

Spending five weeks in the States, I finally had time to visit a library. So one morning I went over to the San Luis Obispo Public Library to finally do some research. Everyone wanted to go with me, but Casmira and my younger daughter wanted to wait in the van, telling me to hurry up.

Rushed, I asked the librarian to help. She gave me three book numbers to find. When I located them all, I scanned the index for pages dealing with James Earl Ray's escape and his family members. These three books were written in the late sixties and early seventies.

Prior to this, I had only learned a few basic things about James Earl Ray or Martin Luther King's assassination from the news media. Most of what I thought I knew about Ray's family, I heard from Jodi Ray. But now after my conversation four years before with John Campbell, a Tennessee assistant state attorney general, I had serious doubts whether Jodi Ray's oldest brother Jimmy, was James Earl Ray. I was hoping that what I would read that day would convince me one way or the other, so I could put it to rest in my mind.

Here is what I read that day. First, James Earl Ray was from St. Louis, Missouri. Before escaping from the Missouri State Prison in early 1967, Ray had another previous escape of some sort. He had pulled off an in-house escape, successfully hiding in the prison itself, before reemerging a day or two later. In the meantime, I believe he had been listed as escaped. After his later successful escape from Missouri's State Prison, proud family members would boast to others that James had escaped from prison a couple of times. Prison is the term Jodi used with me, not Penitentiary. For guys like us and others, these two words are interchangeable. I can't remember if these books used the term Penitentiary.

Either after this successful escape or after the Martin Luther King assassination investigation began to focus on James Earl Ray, his family members did not want to cooperate with investigators. They'd claim that they had heard James Earl had died somewhere, which is what they claimed to believe. They couldn't, or wouldn't, provide any details beyond that. When questioned, family members would not even give the names of other brothers, sisters, or other relatives . . . and certainly not their whereabouts. They were uncooperative.

These authors related details about James Earl Ray's family as follows. His parents at first had five kids, three boys and two girls. But then it reported that the father was sent to prison for about ten or so years. Upon his release, James Earl's parents had four more kids, two boys and two girls. Thus there was a large age gap between the two batches of their offspring, due to the father's incarceration.

James Earl Ray's brothers were criminals also, except one of the younger boys, who drowned when he was twelve. And a younger eleven-year-old sister died in a house fire. In addition to St. Louis, the younger kids sometimes lived on their grandmother's farm in Indiana.

On the Indiana farm, the family was so destitute that they'd all sleep in one bed for warmth. The two younger brothers would hunt and trap anything for food, including things normally not eaten by others: raccoons, skunks, and so forth.

During my reading, the names of all James Earl Ray's siblings were mentioned at one time or another, all except one. I believe I came across all the girls' names, and I recall reading about the two older brothers from the older batch of kids; Jerry and John are their names.

I wasn't so concerned with the older brothers; I was looking for the names of the two youngest brothers. I came across a mention of one named Max, the one that drowned, I believe. But I never ran across a direct mention of the surviving youngest brother's name.

These I found by aid of the appendixes of these three books, by quickly reading pages I was referred to. Again, I found mentions of all siblings except one, the youngest surviving brother, the one who might be Jodi.

Being disappointed at not finding a direct reference to his name, I began widening out my scanning for names in other parts of the book, without using the appendix. I ran across some mentions of someone called Jack, but the context didn't clarify who Jack was. Perhaps Jack was the formal name for Jodi or the nickname of John or some unrelated person. I couldn't be sure from what I read. But the youngest surviving brother was the only one not directly mentioned by name.

I probably spent an hour and a half in the library, the first one I'd been in since Springfield's. It was the longest period I'd ever spent trying to read fast. So it took me a few days to truly digest and process in my mind everything I'd read. As I read, my belief that Jodi Ray was James Earl Ray's youngest brother was reaffirmed. But it would take me several days to digest and appreciate the totality of this information to support that conclusion.

This is what I read that day about James Earl Ray and his family, which coincided with what Jodi had told me almost thirty-two years previously, about his oldest brother Jimmy and his family:

Both families were from St. Louis, Missouri.

Both families were proud that Jimmy and James are career criminals.

Both families boasted that Jimmy and James had two escapes from prison.

Both families boasted that Jimmy and James had escaped from the Missouri State Prison in early 1967.

Both families were proud of other brothers who have also done prison time.

Both families' parents had initially had three boys and two girls, then no kids for about ten years, before producing more children, two boys and two girls.

Both families' reasons for this approximate ten-year lull in childbearing was that the father did about nine or ten years in prison.

One of both families' youngest two boys drowned when he was twelve years old.

One of both families' youngest two girls died in a house fire when she was about eleven.

These four younger children sometimes lived on their grandmother's farm in a nearby state, to the north or northeast of Missouri. I believe it may be Indiana. The two younger boys did a lot of hunting and trapping, eating whatever they caught, including things like raccoons and skunks.

Jodi had talked about these times on his grandmother's farm. In Springfield, I helped him check his traps outside the prison walls for groundhogs, and together we ran down jackrabbits, all of which he ate.

Jodi's older brother Jimmy escaping from the Missouri State Prison in early 1967 makes it obvious to me, that Jimmy is James Earl Ray. Unless of course, there was a second escape early in 1967 from the Missouri State Prison, by another man named Jimmy Ray, also from St. Louis, Missouri. But considering all these ten similarities made it overwhelmingly obvious to me, that there could only be one conclusion: James Earl Ray and Jimmy were one and the same person.

In addition to this, I would challenge anyone to look at mug shots of James Earl and Jodi from that era and not see the family resemblance.

They were obviously brothers. Now I was again 100 percent sure that Jodi was James Earl Ray's youngest brother. The books also gave me some insight as to why the Tennessee assistant state attorney general might not seem to know anything about this youngest brother, Jodi, or whatever his proper name is. I'm not even sure of his nicknames correct spelling, if it ends with an i or y. Remember that in Springfield, we were just numbers and any work passes we may have shared would only have our number on it. I have no recollection of ever seeing his first name written down. Even those books didn't mention his name, despite naming all the other siblings.

Also, one or more of the books commented that after Martin Luther King's assassination, the FBI conducted its largest investigation in the history of the bureau. Ray family members were not at all helpful. They wouldn't discuss other family members or reveal their whereabouts. That they didn't seem to know anything and were not at all forthcoming is also cause for suspicion. Likewise, considering Attorney Pepper's mid-1990s and later obsession to cast blame away from James Earl Ray, would all reinforce my personal belief in a Ray family conspiracy?

The fact that the youngest brother would manage to remain unknown to Tennessee authorities up to the present point in time, made me even more suspicious. I realized I needed to call John Campbell, the Tennessee assistant attorney general. During my last discussion with him about four years previously, he had asked me to call him again if I remembered or learned anything else or new.

Back in Pohnpei, I was preoccupied with work. There were problems as usual. These problems were different though, and I'm not at liberty to discuss them, so I won't. These problems would turn my life upside down and consume most of my time and energy, so that I wasn't even concerned with the James Earl Ray and Martin Luther King issue.

A fire consumed most of my business records at the mill, including many of my personal important papers, which I kept there as well. Among these were the phone numbers to the Tennessee attorney general's office, further putting obstacles in my way insofar as making the follow-up call.

Over the next ten years I would return to California and work for brief periods. In 2002, Casmira and I moved our family back to

California for good, or at least we thought so at the time, disposing of everything we had in Pohnpei. We bought a house in Yucca Valley, California, and I went back to working as a carpenter.

I enjoyed working hard again and felt healthier than I had in twenty years. I had had it easy for so long in Ponape that I'd gotten soft there. Sometimes having as many as forty employees, I'd seldom have to work hard physically, just driving around with Casmira, supervising various jobs, and going out for lunch every day.

Once in California, Casmira and the kids quickly tired of the barren desert landscape.

They were all homesick for Pohnpei, one of the wettest, lushest tropical spots on Earth, the total opposite of the desert. It was their home, where they were all born and raised and they also missed all their friends and relatives there.

So we moved back to Pohnpei in early 2003. Casmira's mother would give her a lot for us to build a new house on. This site was a diamond in the rough. It was just off to the ocean side of the road around the island, just before the Village Hotel, and it didn't appear to be anything special. That was because it was so loaded with breadfruit and coconut trees that you couldn't see the ocean from the road or house site.

I cut down over a hundred breadfruit trees but saved all the coconut trees. Then I built a simple island-style wood house with exterior covered decks, about eighty feet above the mangrove forest. It's high enough that we can look out over the lagoon, several islands, barrier reef, and open ocean beyond. It was like building on the cliffs at Carmel. The house was so close to the water that I could almost spit into the ocean from my deck.

I'm somewhat retired here now and have turned into a bit of a bird watcher. The adjacent forests and mangroves are homes to many seabirds, parrots, fruit bats, white and blue herons, and so forth. My favorite is a small black-and-red hummingbird-type nectar feeder. They can hover when checking under eaves for small spiders but land when feeding on nectar. Casmira loaded our deck with potted bougainvillea and hanging plants. Pairs of these birds have raised numerous sets of young in these deck plants, two eggs per nest. It's private and peaceful here.

Chapter 30

Finally Calling the Attorney General

As just mentioned, my life had been unsettled and stressful for almost ten years now. It all seemed to start with my reinstatement as a Witness and Robby's death not too long afterward, in 1996.

Casmira had taken to being a Jehovah's Witness like a duck to water. She was effective in the ministry, talking with Pohnpeians, sometimes engaging in the full-time ministry. Usually for every meeting at the Kingdom Hall, we were helping 10 or 20 new ones attend that she had been assisting. For a while between her, our children, and I, our family would conduct as many as thirty-five weekly Bible studies with interested new ones. During the annual Memorial of Christ's death, Casmira would usually bring 50 or 60 of these new interested ones. One year she brought 140.

This was one of the primary reasons we returned to Pohnpei, so we could continue to assist these people, despite having to put up with other multiple unusual problems that had caused us to leave in the first place.

The looming possibility of the Etschiet land exploding into violence was especially trying. There were other problems as well, which I'm just not at liberty to discuss here. But being a Jehovah's Witness again now, it really wasn't appropriate for me to continue to be a party to such a potentially violent, divisive issue. So when the opportunity presented itself to get out in 2001, I took it. It meant walking away from a potential fortune in the future and leaving the majority of assets I'd acquired over forty years in construction. I also had to consider my two teenage boys as well, who would shortly be coming of age here and could have been considered fair game for retaliatory attacks by some of the more violent trespassers. Plus

I'd avoid the need to take the next legal move I felt was necessary, which could have opened up a Pandora's Box. After 20 years of filing complaints and seeking the States help, I felt they were more than ripe for a Civil Rights lawsuit. But that would be extremely risky, given all the various threats. I was hoping to avoid doing this. I felt there was hope with Joe Robby as the new police chief who was currently making positive improvements with the department, that it could possibly be just a matter of time before he and some of the other good people in the State corrected this serious flaw. But that could take some time.

For me now though, I could justify walking away from all this with peanuts. This was when I considered Jesus' words in his Sermon on the Mount where he said, "If a person wants to go to court with you and get possession of your inner garment, let your outer garment also go to him; and if someone under authority impresses you into service for a mile, go with him two miles."

To make a long story short, doing that and going to California in 2002, was one way to get ourselves away from these problems for a while, releasing the pressures. Agnes Etscheit wouldn't miss me; she had four grown boys with her now, all of them bigger than I am. With them, her daughters, and lawyers, I wouldn't be needed anymore.

Finally starting to get back to normal on our return to Pohnpei in 2003, that's when I built our family the new house in Awak. Between 2004 and 2009, I traveled to the States five times and stayed on my younger sister's ranch in Templeton, California, helping after her husband's death. I was doing earthquake repairs and generally preparing the ranch to be put on the market to be sold. She was childless and it had become too much for her to maintain alone.

While there in the spring of 2005, I remembered that I still hadn't gotten back to the assistant attorney general of Tennessee, John Campbell, about what I'd read at the San Louis Obispo library in 1999.

I got the Tennessee attorney general's office number from the information operator. I had no idea if John Campbell was still with the attorney general's office; it had been almost ten years since I last spoke with him. Not being sure, I requested to speak with someone about the assassination of Martin Luther King. I was pleased when the receptionist patched me through to the right person and it was John Campbell who answered.

Mr. Campbell acknowledged that he did recall speaking with me, but that he might be a bit rusty on some of the details. So I briefly reviewed with him my recollection of my two phone calls about a decade before, much as I've detailed previously in chapter twenty eight. This included, in part, that after listening to everything I had to report, he told me he was not aware that James Earl Ray had a brother who had ever been in the Medical Center for Federal Prisoners in Springfield, Missouri, but that they would look into all this. Then in following up several months later, he informed me of the results of their attempt to investigate this information, that they couldn't get any cooperation from not only the Springfield Medical Center but also the United States Federal Bureau of Prisons. He couldn't even get them to verify that Jodi Ray (or a younger brother of James Earl Ray) or I had ever even been in that prison. He then suggested that the Jodi I spoke of could have possibly been a cousin, relative, or not related at all. Our call concluded with him again saying he could be wrong, and that if I remembered anything else or learned anything new, to please give him a call back.

I admitted to him that the last call between us had put doubts in my mind about Jodi not being related to James Earl Ray, that I realized I needed to find out more about Martin Luther King's assassination and the Ray family members. I told him this was difficult for me, given where I lived.

I then informed him that in 1999 while in the States on a family vacation, I was finally able to visit a nearby library to do some research into the subject. I told him that three books I scanned revealed numerous similarities between James Earl Ray, his family, and what Jodi had told me about his older brother Jimmy, and his family. I then related to him these similarities as detailed several pages earlier in the previous chapter.

When I was done, Mr. Campbell essentially told me that what I'd just said fit in with their theory of the case. They did believe that James Earl Ray did not act entirely alone, that he had help, that there were co-conspirators still yet unidentified. That in most cases involving multiple participants, eventually someone would always talk. That criminals would either brag to cell mates, friends, spill the beans when drunk, or reveal the information in exchange for a lesser sentence in another case, that criminals just cannot keep their mouths shut for long.

Mr. Campbel then said that the only way criminal conspiracies were usually kept confidential for long periods, was if loved ones, including wives, girl friends and family members were being protected. He mentioned that he now intended to get out the Martin Luther King file and look at it again in light of this. He said that he would need to locate this Jodi Ray after determining whether he was even still alive, access prison records and so on, and try again to get the information that he'd been unable to get about both of us in 1995. He told me it may take awhile. John then asked me about how old Jodi Ray would be now. I told him he was about five years older than I was, and I was almost sixty at the time, so he'd be in his mid-sixties. Remember that this conversation took place in the spring or summer of 2005.

I also told him of my suspicions that one of Jodi's older sisters, the one who had visited him a few months prior to his telling me about his older brother Jimmy, may well have been the one who told him about Jimmy's intention to kill Martin Luther King, and why. I said that she may also be the older sister who was married to Mr. Pepper, the lawyer. If so, I personally believed the 1990's movement to clear James Earl Ray in the assassination of Martin Luther King and cast suspicion toward others, could just be a red herring to draw attention away from a Ray family conspiracy.

Mr. Campbell seemed not to be aware that one of James Earl Ray's sisters was married to the lawyer, Mr. Pepper. I could be wrong about this, but I thought I heard they were married from that news program I saw in Hawaii in 1995. Yet my hearing has been flawed for a couple of decades now, due to construction and heavy equipment noise.

We concluded our conversation after I gave him my current contact numbers. I would hear afterward that Martin Luther King's children had apparently bought into Attorney Pepper's ideas of the case that he promoted. I heard he even went so far as to initiate a civil lawsuit that cast blame elsewhere, the details of which I'm not thoroughly familiar with. But I did partially see a TV news program about Mr. Pepper winning a civil case that found a cook, who worked in a diner in the building from which the fatal shot was fired, as the shooter. But that afterward, a key witness recanted her testimony. So I will reserve any further comments for now, until more information is available to me.

Chapter 31

The March

I can now appreciate the problems John Campbell had trying to get information from the United States Federal Bureau of Prisons, about Jodi Ray or myself. I started trying to get information myself in early 2007, after getting an address to the Federal Bureau of Prisons archives division. This was after being referred there by a helpful official during a phone call to the Medical Center for Federal Prisoners in Springfield, Missouri.

I was informed at that time that prisoner records are only kept at a federal prison for twenty-five years, and then they are transferred to a Washington, DC, archive division for storage. I then made a request for records for Jodi Ray and myself. About a month or two later, I got a response informing me that under the Freedom of Information Act, I could only request information about myself. To get information on another, I would need a signed form from them giving their permission. They even included the forms. I had no idea where Jodi was, plus he'd probably not give his permission. I haven't seen him since my last evening in the Springfield BOQ. But I mailed my completed form in with my information requests.

Back in Micronesia a month or two later, I got another letter from them at my Pohnpei address, acknowledging receipt of my request and informing me that they were processing it. The letter stated that it would take ten days or longer to process my information. I had requested whatever information they could release to me, including mug shots and so forth, but in particular any record pertaining to me from the warden's office from about September 20 to September 25 of 1967, concerning the reasons for my transfer to the bachelor officers' quarters. The information on this transfer would tell me the date, the exact day, that I was told that James Earl Ray was going to kill Martin Luther King. It also might mention Jodi's correct first name or prison number. I used to know it. If I were to hazard a guess, I'd say 9256. I'd have to wait and see what their response was, as it's been about five or six months now since they informed me that it would take ten days or longer.

I couldn't imagine the state of Tennessee being comfortable initiating conspiracy charges based on anything I'd said, being just one witness. It seemed a lot more would be needed before they would undertake that risk. After all, the authorities there have only one shot in court; there is double jeopardy to consider. Furthermore, I couldn't see the Ray family cracking easily under pressure either, because they have held it together for over forty years now.

I also feel rather uncomfortable talking about Jodi Ray. He is one of the few non-Witness men that I feel I've gotten close to in my life. As somewhat of a loner, I have only gotten close to a few non-Witnesses, all work related. I also believe Jodi saved my life in federal prison. I owe him a lot. But then again, I was only in federal prison as a matter of principle in the first place. Those same principles would never allow me to cover up or keep quiet about those involved in a murder, much less the assassination of one of the greatest civilian Americans ever, in many people's opinion. I certainly admire Martin Luther's nonviolent accomplishments in the face of such long-standing violent opposition.

My personal feelings about how Jodi might react should authorities ever bring charges against him in this regard are that he might relish the notoriety. I also believe he would probably plea bargain to protect his family if he had to. I can't think of anyone else I've ever known who seems to have been born to do "easy time" in prison, other than perhaps Captain John or Wolf.

I think though, that I could look Jodi right in the eye, smile and say "What's the matter with you? You should know better than telling *me* something like that!" Jodi is one of the last people I'd want to hurt or make trouble for. But I have obligations to a Higher Authority and his principles. I refuse to live my life by jailhouse rules either, so I don't care if some might label me a snitch. I've tried to report this several times over the last almost forty years now. I've lived to see a yearly holiday named in Martin Luther King's honor.

Roads, schools, and buildings have been named after him. His accomplishments were truly unique in this modern world, maybe only rivaled by Gandhi and surpassed by Christ Jesus throughout history.

Yet I've also seen how many have only paid lip service to him, the same as many do to Christ. I've personally seen on two occasions how the FBI promoted itself through the media as conducting investigations into this assassination, one of them billed as their largest in the agency's history. Yet on calling them the two days of those press releases with pertinent information about co-conspirators, they couldn't get me off the phone fast enough. They didn't really care about Martin Luther King! Why not? Just prior to his killing they had been actively engaged in a clandestine investigation to assassinate his character. They obviously didn't like him. This agency apparently, couldn't change its spots just like that!

In late 2007 I returned to California, staying until early February 2008, attempting to line up a literary agent for this writing. I also made follow-up phone calls to the archive division in Washington, DC, and John Campbell, who is now the district attorney in Memphis, Tennessee.

The archive division informed me that federal prison records are transferred to them once they are twenty-five years old. On reaching thirty years of age, they destroy them. Because my records were now over forty years old, they were unable to process my information request.

This helped me understand why John Campbell couldn't get to first base investigating what I had reported to him in 1995. I could also imagine the need for the federal government to destroy old paperwork. They generate so much of it that its storage is obviously a major problem. My experience in 1995 though, driving the cement truck cross country and over the truck scales into Nevada, showed me some information on felons is saved somewhere, but obviously not everything.

I informed John Campbell of this and he was already aware of it. He did inform me however, that the entire Martin Luther King case file had been sent to a congressional committee in Washington, DC, as they were looking into the assassination. He said that he had nothing left, no backup case files, that this committee requested absolutely everything in their file. So without these files, he could take no further action.

In Pohnpei my closest neighbors to the east are about a quarter mile away, Bob and Patty Arthur over at the Village Hotel. In 1968 Patty traveled to Georgia, attended Martin Luther King's funeral and participated in the march of both blacks and whites to the church where his services were held.

She related to me that it was an extremely hot day, or at least she thought so. Waiting around for a couple of hours in the sun and humidity, she and many others were thirsty. She then told me that while having a spirited conversation with one black militant before the march started, he fainted from thirst and collapsed right on her.

As they eventually started walking through town in the long procession toward the church, law enforcement officers lined the road on both sides of the route. They appeared to her to be lined up shoulder-to-shoulders in places, but no farther than three to five feet apart most of the route. From their various uniforms, it looked to her as if they were from numerous jurisdictions throughout the state. From their appearance, the one thing they all seemed to have in common was most were so over loaded with law enforcement paraphernalia, such as cuffs and chains; that they jingled whenever they moved a bit. Many also wore riot helmets, as if expecting to bust some heads that day.

Out of respect for Martin Luther King, nobody spoke as the march proceeded. But the police wore such looks of disgust and hate, that Patty was terrified that these officers could attack them at any moment. She was haunted by visions of dogs being unleashed on previous civil rights marchers and clubbings by police.

As the procession began to pass through a black neighborhood, residents came out with disposable cups of water for the many thirsty marchers. These cups were then passed through the crowd with blacks and whites drinking from the same cups. The police visibly found this thoroughly revolting and tensions were now escalated to even further heights. With everyone's nerves on edge, a kid dropped a soda can and it landed just right with a loud gunshot like "POP!" Many flinched and ducked, but Patty saw one officer who seemed to jump more than a foot at the sound. On landing he was visibly shaking, but pressing his arms and hands about his body trying to stop the jingling.

When finally reaching the church and mingling with the crowd outside, she bluntly asked a black militant group from the Boston area, if they came to make trouble? One immediately responded, "FOR GOD SAKES NO! We came to pay our respects, he was a man of peace!" But they went on to state that since Martin Luther King had been murdered, they felt it was a validation that his non-violent approach was wrong, and perhaps a violent approach should now be called for.

Fortunately it didn't come to that. The government initiated many of the changes that Martin Luther King hoped would come about one day. Whether any of his killer's co-conspirators will ever be brought to justice though, seems remote to me.

In January, 2011, Patty Arthur would help me learn additional things about Martin Luther King that I hadn't heard before. One was that he was insistent that should they ever be attacked, none of those in the civil rights movement should ever have on them, or readily at hand, any weapons. This was especially true for those close to him.

At Jesus's arrest, the apostle Peter had lashed out with a sword at hand. I was quick to use a flare gun on Uber during that New Year's Day 1982 brawl. Martin Luther King was among those who had known and we should all learn, that you can't show love for your enemies if you defend yourself with weapons at hand.

I had put this into practice during the years we had logged on the Etscheit estate. We never carried any weapons, despite the numerous threats. I don't count the sticks we sometimes carried to beat out fires. I was fortunate I had one during the incident with Martin Etnolt, or he may have chopped me into little pieces that day. Even then, I only used the bare minimum of force necessary to stop his rage, brought on when he saw his yams pulled out.

Afterward though, I would go out of my way with him and others to patch things up, to show love toward my enemies and not retaliate. This could usually bear fruit right away, but sometimes it was later, even decades later. Allow me to relate an example.

Many of our problems had been brought on by the actions of the nahnken of Nett, in the exercising of his "traditional rights" as he saw fit. In my opinion, this Nahnken, Salvador Iriarte, was the most powerful traditional leader on Ponape, more powerful than any of the other five kings on island. I could see this in numerous ways. For instance, he had been the spokesperson for all the traditional leaders for the last twenty years or so. He would many times be a speaker at numerous major governmental functions, on behalf of all the people. His power would also be evident to me by what he had been able to get away with over the years. He could be a rascal at times.

Something else that could be said about him which many of his people found endearing, was that "he didn't own a freezer." That referred to the practice of other traditional leaders storing away excess tribute in freezers for their personal use later. Instead, Salvador would only take what he needed for that day and divide the remainder up to be delivered to needy or deserving families in Nett. I had also seen other admirable qualities of his in the few years Robby and I had good relations with him, before our land problems escalated out of control again in 1992.

Going forward almost twenty years to December 2010, Casmira had been working for five years now for the Bank of the Federated States of Micronesia. She started as a part-time teller but is now the executive secretary for the CEO. One of her supervisors is Ruth Iriarte, the nahnken of Nett's wife. They became close, eating lunch together many times. One day she arrived home saying she had a message for me from the nahnken, which Ruth had relayed to her verbally. I had hardly seen him in twenty years, only at the Court House a few times and one brief chance encounter at the local EPA office, all in the 1990's.

In his relayed message, I was told that Agnes Etscheit had recently made a settlement proposal that would have him removing trespassers from her land. The nahnken wanted to let me know that he had declined to participate on the grounds that he wasn't happy that she had already removed the only two men that he had ever respected on the (Escheit) land. I was then informed that one was Masaro Olter, Leo and Robby's right-hand man at Leo's store. The other one was me. He then invited me to come visit him sometime, also telling me via our wives, that he loved me.

Given my background and all we had been through, plus the status of this former enemy, I take this as one of the biggest compliment I've ever received.